THIRD EDITION

Reading, Writing, and Critical Thinking

MARI VARGO

LAURIE BLASS

KRISTIN SHERMAN

Australia · Brazil · Canada · Mexico · Singapore · United Kingdom · United States

National Geographic Learning,
a Cengage Company

***Pathways: Reading, Writing, and Critical Thinking 4*, Third Edition**
Mari Vargo, Laurie Blass, and Kristin Sherman

Publisher: Andrew Robinson
Managing Editor: Derek Mackrell
Development Editor: Don Clyde Bhasy
Director of Global Marketing: Ian Martin
Heads of Regional Marketing:
Charlotte Ellis (Europe, Middle East and Africa)
Justin Kaley (Asia and Greater China)
Irina Pereyra (Latin America)
Joy MacFarland (US and Canada)
Product Marketing Manager: Tracy Bailie
Senior Production Controller: Tan Jin Hock
Media Researcher: Stephanie Eenigenburg
Senior Designer: Heather Marshall
Operations Support: Hayley Chwazik-Gee
Manufacturing Buyer: Terrence Isabella
Composition: MPS North America LLC

Student's Book with the Spark platform:
ISBN-13: 978-0-357-98010-1

Student's Book:
ISBN-13: 978-0-357-98011-8

National Geographic Learning
5191 Natorp Blvd, Mason, OH 45040, USA

Locate your local office at **international.cengage.com/region**

Visit National Geographic Learning online at **ELTNGL.com**
Visit our corporate website at **www.cengage.com**

Printed in China
Print Number: 01 Print Year: 2023

Contents

Scope and Sequence

Unit Title and Theme

Reading	Critical Thinking	Vocabulary	Writing
Reading Skill Understanding Cohesion Understand the Main Idea, Understand Main Ideas, Understand Details	**Critical Thinking Skill** Recognizing Claims and Counterclaims Predict, Infer Meaning, Reflect, Personalize	**Vocabulary Extension** *artificial* + Noun; *-ize* and *-ization*	**Language for Writing** Using Cohesive Devices **Writing Skill** Organizing an Essay **GOAL** Write an essay describing how an emerging technology will impact jobs in the future.
Reading Skill Understanding Appositives Understand Main Ideas, Understand Details	**Critical Thinking Skill** Understanding How Information is Organized Predict, Summarize, Compare, Infer Meaning, Reflect	**Vocabulary Extension** Nouns/Adjectives + *constrsaint*; Words with *counter-*	**Language for Writing** Using Appositives **Writing Skill** Structuring a Problem-Solution Essay **GOAL** Write a problem-solution essay about an urban challenge.
Reading Skill Using a Concept Map Understand Main Ideas, Understand Details	**Critical Thinking Skill** Applying Ideas Predict, Summarize, Infer Meaning, Reflect, Apply	**Vocabulary Extension** *ambi-*; *trigger* + Noun	**Language for Writing** Using Relative Clauses **Writing Skill** Supporting a Thesis **GOAL** Write an essay evaluating an example of visual art using aesthetic criteria.
Reading Skill Recognizing and Evaluating Different Viewpoints Understand Main Ideas, Understand Details	**Critical Thinking Skill** Understanding Multiword Phrases Predict, Infer Meaning, Evaluate, Reflect	**Vocabulary Extension** Business Words and Antonyms; *-ion* and *-ive*	**Language for Writing** Writing Sentences with Initial Phrases **Writing Skill** Organizing a Comparative Essay **GOAL** Write an essay comparing two companies in the same industry.
Reading Skill Understanding Complex Sentences Understand Main Ideas, Understand Purpose, Use a Concept Map	**Critical Thinking Skill** Evaluating Sources Predict, Infer Meaning, Analyze and Apply, Compare	**Vocabulary Extension** *co-*, *com-*, *col-*; *-ate* and *-ion*	**Language for Writing** Avoiding Plagiarism (I)—Paraphrasing **Writing Skill** Writing a Summary **GOAL** Write a summary of the reading passage, *The Smart Swarm*.

Scope and Sequence

Unit Title and Theme		
	6 **WHY LANGUAGE MATTERS** *page 123* Anthropology/Sociology	**Explore the Theme** Our Words Are Our Reality **Reading** Is Joy the Same in Every Language? **VIDEO** Discovering a Hidden Language
	**7** **RESOURCES AND DEVELOPMENT** *page 145* Economics	**Explore the Theme** 8 Billion People **Reading** The Shape of Africa **VIDEO** Honey and Pepper
	**8** **LIVING LONGER** *page 169* Health	**Explore the Theme** Life Expectancy in the Animal Kingdom **Reading** Beyond 100 **VIDEO** Longevity Village
	**9** **TRUTH AND DECEPTION** *page 193* Psychology	**Explore the Theme** The Best Policy? **Reading** Why We Lie **VIDEO** Learning to Lie
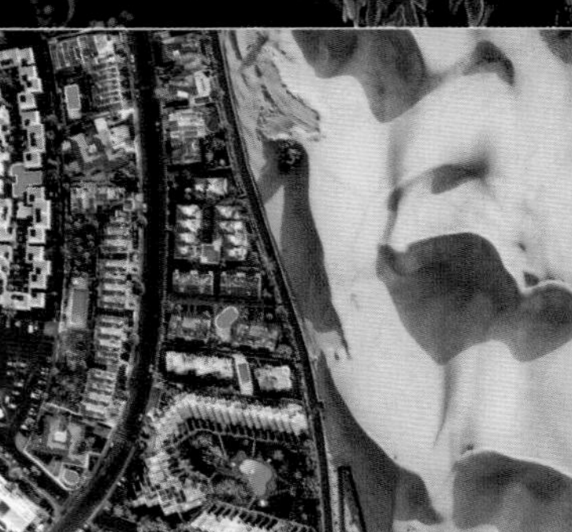	**10** **CHANGING THE PLANET** *page 217* Environmental Studies	**Explore the Theme** The Human Impact **Reading** The Human Age **VIDEO** Trees of Life

Reading	Critical Thinking	Vocabulary	Writing
Reading Skill Understanding Figurative Language Scan, Understand Main Ideas, Understand Details	**Critical Thinking Skill** Understanding Loaded Words Synthesize, Infer Meaning, Interpret and Analyze, Reflect	**Vocabulary Extension** Words for looking at things; Expressions with *horizon*	**Language for Writing** Adding Information with Verbal Phrases **Writing Skill** Writing Introductions and Conclusions **GOAL** Write an essay about the best way to learn a new language outside of school.
Reading Skill Annotating a Text Understand Main Ideas, Understand Details	**Critical Thinking Skill** Analyzing Point of View Predict, Understand Chronology, Infer Meaning, Evaluate, Infer	**Vocabulary Extension** Adjective + *economy*; *distinct* + Noun	**Language for Writing** Avoiding Plagiarism (II)—Referring to Sources **Writing Skill** Doing Research Online **GOAL** Write an opinion essay about how a country or region has been affected by its geography and history.
Reading Skill Asking Questions as You Read Skim, Understand Main Ideas, Understand Details, Understand Supporting Examples	**Critical Thinking Skill** Interpreting Visual Data Predict, Infer Meaning, Reflect, Synthesize, Evaluate	**Vocabulary Extension** Words and phrases with *life*; *out-*	**Language for Writing** Explaining the Significance of Evidence **Writing Skill** Planning an Argumentative Research Paper **GOAL** Write an essay about whether governments should invest in helping people live beyond 100 years.
Reading Skill Understanding a Research Summary Understand Main Ideas, Understand Details	**Critical Thinking Skill** Evaluating Research Predict, Infer Meaning, Interpret, Interpret Visual Data, Apply	**Vocabulary Extension** *-ence* and *-ance*; *deceit* and *deception*	**Language for Writing** Introducing Results and Describing Data **Writing Skill** Summarizing a Research Study **GOAL** Write an essay summarizing a famous research study.
Reading Skill Understanding Rhetorical Purpose Understand the Main Idea, Understand Main Ideas	**Critical Thinking Skill** Synthesizing Information Predict, Brainstorm, Summarize, Interpret Visual Data, Infer Meaning, Reflect	**Vocabulary Extension** *-logy*; *dramatic* + Noun	**Language for Writing** Using a Variety of Sentence Types **Writing Skill** Reviewing Essay Writing **GOAL** Write an essay about how the activities of a charity are having a positive impact on the environment.

NEW AND UPDATED IN THE THIRD EDITION

Compelling photography and infographics in **Explore the Theme** draw students into the unit, develop their visual and information literacy skills, and get them speaking.

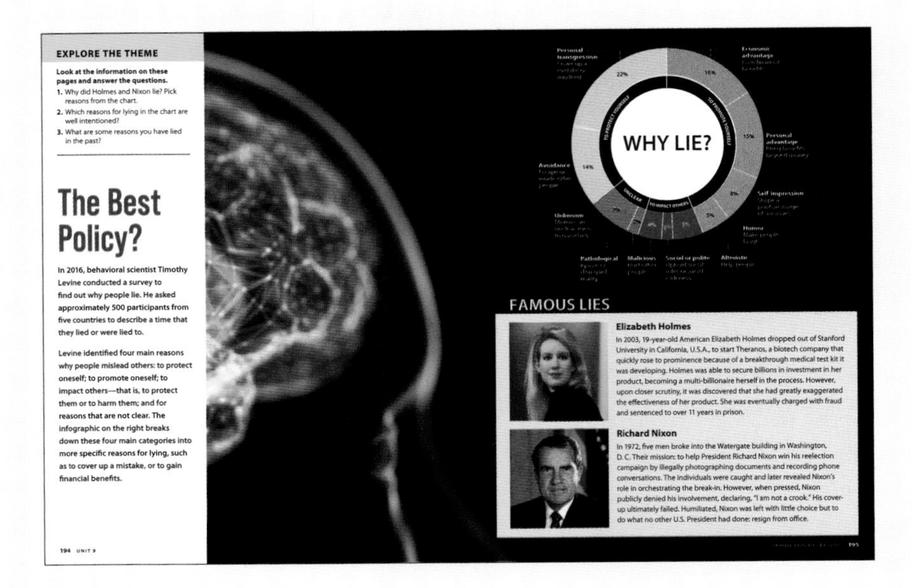

EXPLORE THE THEME

Look at the information on these pages and answer the questions.

1. Why did Holmes and Nixon lie? Pick reasons from the chart.
2. Which reasons for lying in the chart are well intentioned?
3. What are some reasons you have lied in the past?

The Best Policy?

In 2016, behavioral scientist Timothy Levine conducted a survey to find out why people lie. He asked approximately 500 participants from five countries to describe a time that they lied or were lied to.

Levine identified four main reasons why people mislead others: to protect oneself; to promote oneself; to impact others—that is, to protect them or to harm them; and for reasons that are not clear. The infographic on the right breaks down these four main categories into more specific reasons for lying, such as to cover up a mistake, or to gain financial benefits.

FAMOUS LIES

Elizabeth Holmes

In 2003, 19-year-old American Elizabeth Holmes dropped out of Stanford University in California, U.S.A., to start Theranos, a biotech company that quickly rose to prominence because of a breakthrough medical test kit it was developing. Holmes was able to secure billions in investment in her product, becoming a multi-billionaire herself in the process. However, upon closer scrutiny, it was discovered that she had greatly exaggerated the effectiveness of her product. She was eventually charged with fraud and sentenced to over 11 years in prison.

Richard Nixon

In 1972, five men broke into the Watergate building in Washington, D.C. Their mission: to help President Richard Nixon win his reelection campaign by illegally photographing documents and recording phone conversations. The individuals were caught and later revealed Nixon's role in orchestrating the break-in. However, when pressed, Nixon publicly denied his involvement, declaring, "I am not a crook." His cover-up ultimately failed. Humiliated, Nixon was left with little choice but to do what no other U.S. President had done: resign from office.

194 UNIT 9

195

New videos and readings provide academic content with close connections to students' lives beyond the classroom.

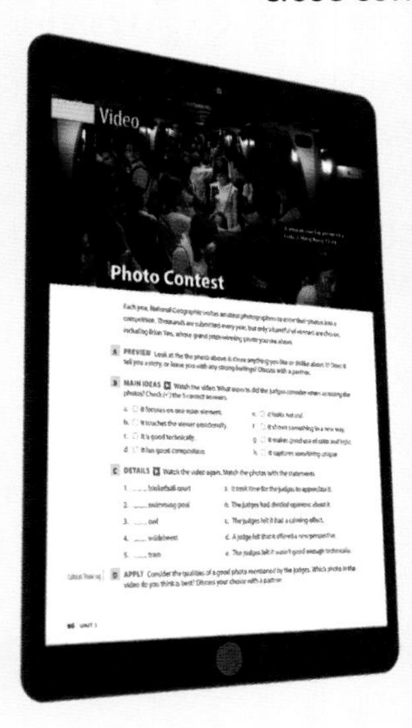

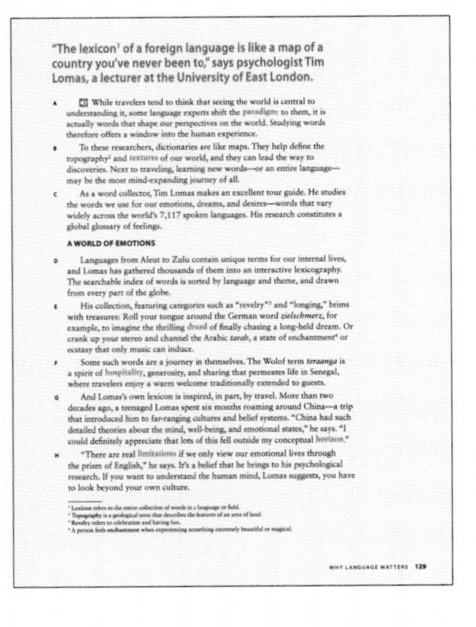

"The lexicon[1] of a foreign language is like a map of a country you've never been to," says psychologist Tim Lomas, a lecturer at the University of East London.

A While travelers tend to think that seeing the world is central to understanding it, some language experts shift the paradigm: to them, it is actually words that shape our perspectives on the world. Studying words therefore offers a window into the human experience.

B To these researchers, dictionaries are like maps. They help define the topography[2] and textures of our world, and they can lead the way to discoveries. Next to traveling, learning new words—or an entire language—may be the most mind-expanding journey of all.

C As a word collector, Tim Lomas makes an excellent tour guide. He studies the words we use for our emotions, dreams, and desires—words that vary widely across the world's 7,117 spoken languages. His research constitutes a global glossary of feelings.

A WORLD OF EMOTIONS

D Languages from Aleut to Zulu contain unique terms for our internal lives, and Lomas has gathered thousands of them into an interactive lexicography. The searchable index of words is sorted by language and theme, and drawn from every part of the globe.

E His collection, featuring categories such as "revelry"[3] and "longing," brims with treasures: Roll your tongue around the German word *zielschmerz*, for example, to imagine the thrilling dread of finally chasing a long-held dream. Or crank up your stereo and channel the Arabic *tarab*, a state of enchantment[4] or ecstasy that only music can induce.

F Some such words are a journey in themselves. The Wolof term *teraanga* is a spirit of hospitality, generosity, and sharing that permeates life in Senegal, where travelers enjoy a warm welcome traditionally extended to guests.

G And Lomas's own lexicon is inspired, in part, by travel. More than two decades ago, a teenaged Lomas spent six months roaming around China—a trip that introduced him to far-ranging cultures and belief systems. "China had such detailed theories about the mind, well-being, and emotional states," he says. "I could definitely appreciate that lots of this fell outside my conceptual horizon."

H "There are real limitations if we only view our emotional lives through the prism of English," he says. It's a belief that he brings to his psychological research. If you want to understand the human mind, Lomas suggests, you have to look beyond your own culture.

[1] Lexicon refers to the entire collection of words in a language or field.
[2] Topography is a geological term that describes the features of an area of land.
[3] Revelry refers to celebration and having fun.
[4] A person feels enchantment when experiencing something extremely beautiful or magical.

WHY LANGUAGE MATTERS 129

Academic competency skills like collaboration, communication, and problem-solving help students develop the skills and behaviors needed to succeed in school and their lives.

CRITICAL THINKING Interpreting Visual Data

When you interpret visual data, look for patterns or correlations (links) between different data sets. Consider the implications of these correlations, and also of the lack of any clear correlation. Lastly, look for anomalies, or exceptions that stand out. Do they tell you anything significant?

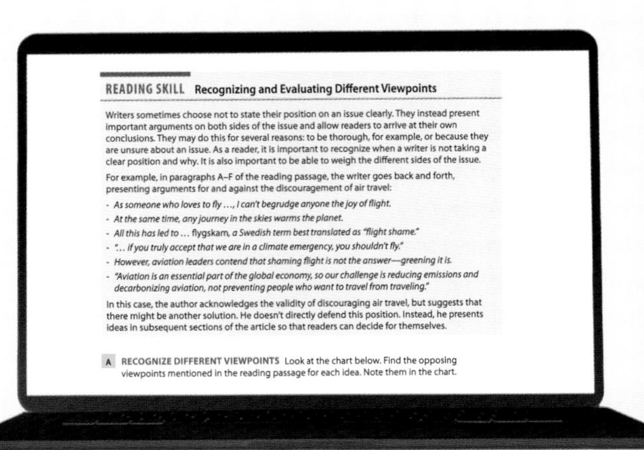

READING SKILL Recognizing and Evaluating Different Viewpoints

Writers sometimes choose not to state their position on an issue clearly. They instead present important arguments on both sides of the issue and allow readers to arrive at their own conclusions. They may do this for several reasons: to be thorough, for example, or because they are unsure about an issue. As a reader, it is important to recognize when a writer is not taking a clear position and why. It is also important to be able to weigh the different sides of the issue.

For example, in paragraphs A–F of the reading passage, the writer goes back and forth, presenting arguments for and against the discouragement of air travel:

- *As someone who loves to fly ..., I can't begrudge anyone the joy of flight.*
- *At the same time, any journey in the skies warms the planet.*
- *All this has led to ... flygskam, a Swedish term best translated as "flight shame."*
- *"... if you truly accept that we are in a climate emergency, you shouldn't fly."*
- *However, aviation leaders contend that shaming flight is not the answer—greening it is.*
- *"Aviation is an essential part of the global economy, so our challenge is reducing emissions and decarbonizing aviation, not preventing people who want to travel from traveling."*

In this case, the author acknowledges the validity of discouraging air travel, but suggests that there might be another solution. He doesn't directly defend this position. Instead, he presents ideas in subsequent sections of the article so that readers can decide for themselves.

A **RECOGNIZE DIFFERENT VIEWPOINTS** Look at the chart below. Find the opposing viewpoints mentioned in the reading passage for each idea. Note them in the chart.

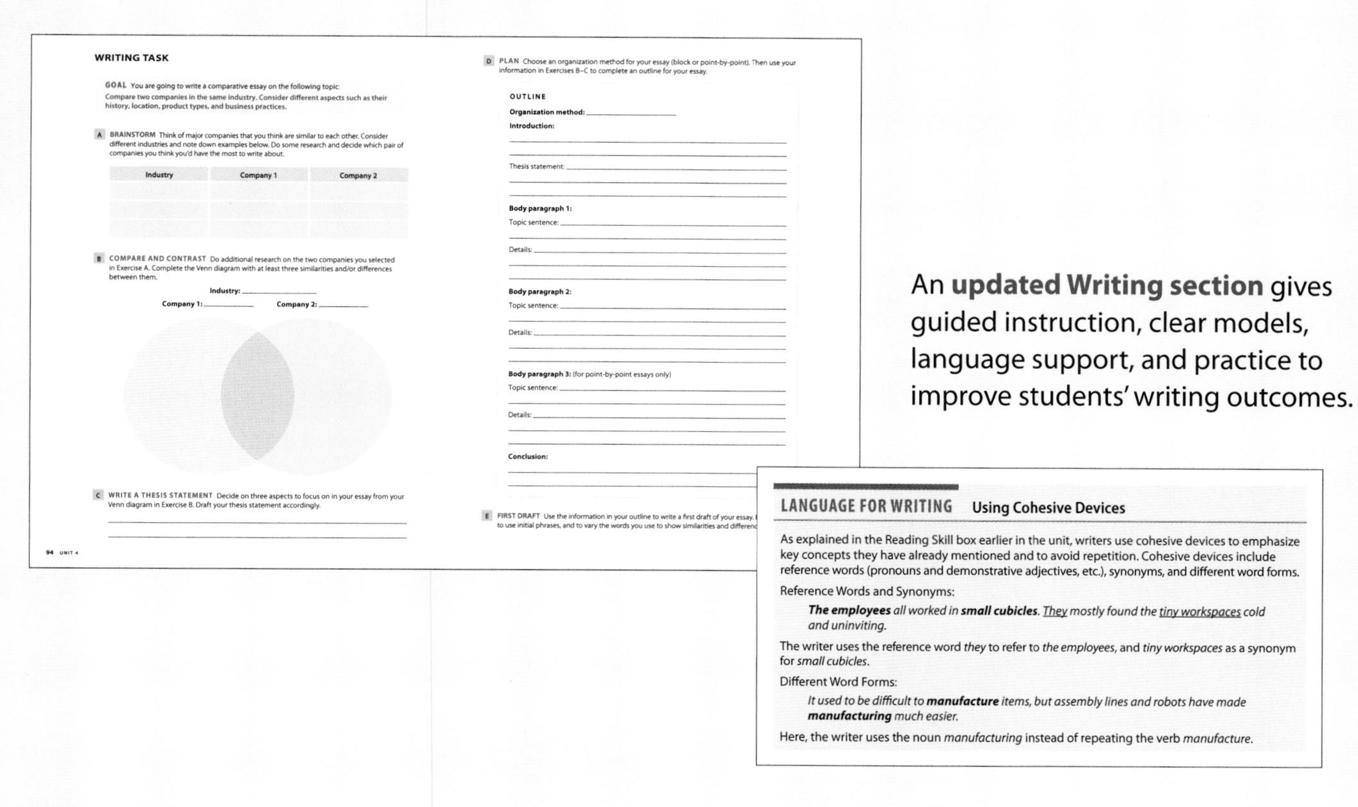

WRITING TASK

GOAL You are going to write a comparative essay on the following topic:
Compare two companies in the same industry. Consider different aspects such as their history, location, product types, and business practices.

A **BRAINSTORM** Think of major companies that you think are similar to each other. Consider different industries and note down examples below. Do some research and decide which pair of companies you think you'd have the most to write about.

Industry	Company 1	Company 2

B **COMPARE AND CONTRAST** Do additional research on the two companies you selected in Exercise A. Complete the Venn diagram with at least three similarities and/or differences between them.

Industry: ____________
Company 1: ____________ Company 2: ____________

C **WRITE A THESIS STATEMENT** Decide on three aspects to focus on in your essay from your Venn diagram in Exercise B. Draft your thesis statement accordingly.

94 UNIT 4

D **PLAN** Choose an organization method for your essay (block or point-by-point). Then use your information in Exercises B–C to complete an outline for your essay.

OUTLINE

Organization method: ____________
Introduction:
Thesis statement: ____________
Body paragraph 1:
Topic sentence: ____________
Details: ____________
Body paragraph 2:
Topic sentence: ____________
Details: ____________
Body paragraph 3: (for point-by-point essays only)
Topic sentence: ____________
Details: ____________
Conclusion:

E **FIRST DRAFT** Use the information in your outline to write a first draft of your essay. to use initial phrases, and to vary the words you use to show similarities and differenc

LANGUAGE FOR WRITING Using Cohesive Devices

As explained in the Reading Skill box earlier in the unit, writers use cohesive devices to emphasize key concepts they have already mentioned and to avoid repetition. Cohesive devices include reference words (pronouns and demonstrative adjectives, etc.), synonyms, and different word forms.

Reference Words and Synonyms:

__The employees__ all worked in __small cubicles__. They mostly found the tiny workspaces cold and uninviting.

The writer uses the reference word *they* to refer to *the employees*, and *tiny workspaces* as a synonym for *small cubicles*.

Different Word Forms:

It used to be difficult to __manufacture__ items, but assembly lines and robots have made __manufacturing__ much easier.

Here, the writer uses the noun *manufacturing* instead of repeating the verb *manufacture*.

An **updated Writing section** gives guided instruction, clear models, language support, and practice to improve students' writing outcomes.

Assessment

Pathways Reading, Writing, and Critical Thinking supports teachers and learners with various forms of assessment, with the goal of helping students achieve real-world success.

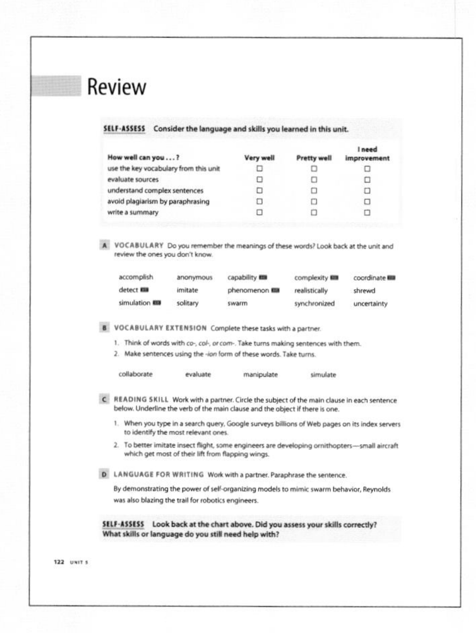

Review

SELF-ASSESS Consider the language and skills you learned in this unit.

How well can you . . . ?	Very well	Pretty well	I need improvement
use the key vocabulary from this unit	☐	☐	☐
evaluate sources	☐	☐	☐
understand complex sentences	☐	☐	☐
avoid plagiarism by paraphrasing	☐	☐	☐
write a summary	☐	☐	☐

A **VOCABULARY** Do you remember the meanings of these words? Look back at the unit and review the ones you don't know.

accomplish, anonymous, capability, complexity, coordinate, detect, imitate, phenomenon, realistically, shrewd, simulation, solitary, swarm, synchronized, uncertainty

B **VOCABULARY EXTENSION** Complete these tasks with a partner.

1. Think of words with *co-, col-,* or *com-*. Take turns making sentences with them.
2. Make sentences using the *-ion* form of these words. Take turns.

collaborate, evaluate, manipulate, simulate

C **READING SKILL** Work with a partner. Circle the subject of the main clause in each sentence below. Underline the verb of the main clause and the object if there is one.

1. When you type in a search query, Google surveys billions of Web pages on its index servers to identify the most relevant ones.
2. To better imitate insect flight, some engineers are developing ornithopters—small aircraft which get most of their lift from flapping wings.

D **LANGUAGE FOR WRITING** Work with a partner. Paraphrase the sentence.

By demonstrating the power of self-organizing models to mimic swarm behavior, Reynolds was also blazing the trail for robotics engineers.

SELF-ASSESS Look back at the chart above. Did you assess your skills correctly? What skills or language do you still need help with?

122 UNIT 5

A **new Review section** provides additional opportunities for formative assessment and encourages students to take control of their learning journey through guided self-assessment.

Opportunities for online assessment on the **new Spark platform** include:

- The NGL Online Placement Test, which places students into the correct level of *Pathways*
- Interactive Online Practice activities and online tests from the Assessment Suite, for formative and summative assessment
- A Course Gradebook that tracks student and class performance against learning objectives, providing teachers with actionable insights to support students' progress

spark

Bring the world to the classroom and the classroom to life with the Spark platform — where you can prepare, teach and assess your classes all in one place!

Manage your course and teach great classes with integrated digital teaching and learning tools. Spark brings together everything you need on an all-in-one platform with a single log-in.

Track student and class performance on independent online practice and assessment. The Course Gradebook helps you turn information into insights to make the most of valuable classroom time.

Set up classes and roster students quickly and easily on Spark. Seamless integration options and point-of-use support helps you focus on what matters most: student success.

CLASSROOM PRESENTATION TOOL

STUDENT'S eBOOK

TEACHER RESOURCES

ONLINE PRACTICE

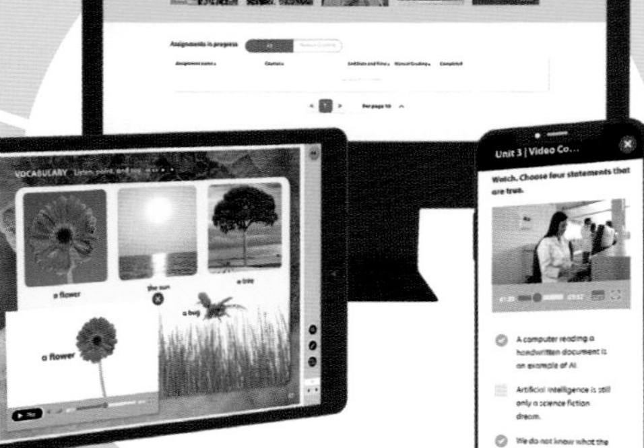

ONLINE PLACEMENT

ASSESSMENT SUITE

ADMIN TOOLS

COURSE GRADEBOOK

Photo credit: ©Brian Yen

*Visit **ELTNGL.com/spark** to learn more*

THE CHANGING WORKPLACE 1

A "telepresence" robot in an office in Toronto, Canada

IN THIS UNIT, YOU WILL:

- Read an article about working with robots
- Watch a video about women in the workforce
- Write about technology and the workplace

THINK AND DISCUSS:

1. In the photo above, an office worker greets a remotely-operated "telepresence" robot. Why do you think this robot was created?
2. Do you think robots like these will become more popular? Why or why not?

EXPLORE THE THEME

Look at the information on these pages and answer the questions.

1. Which decade do you think the photo is from? Why?
2. Which decade in the timeline do you think saw the most important developments? Why?
3. How do you think offices in the future will be different? Give reasons.

The Evolution of Office Work

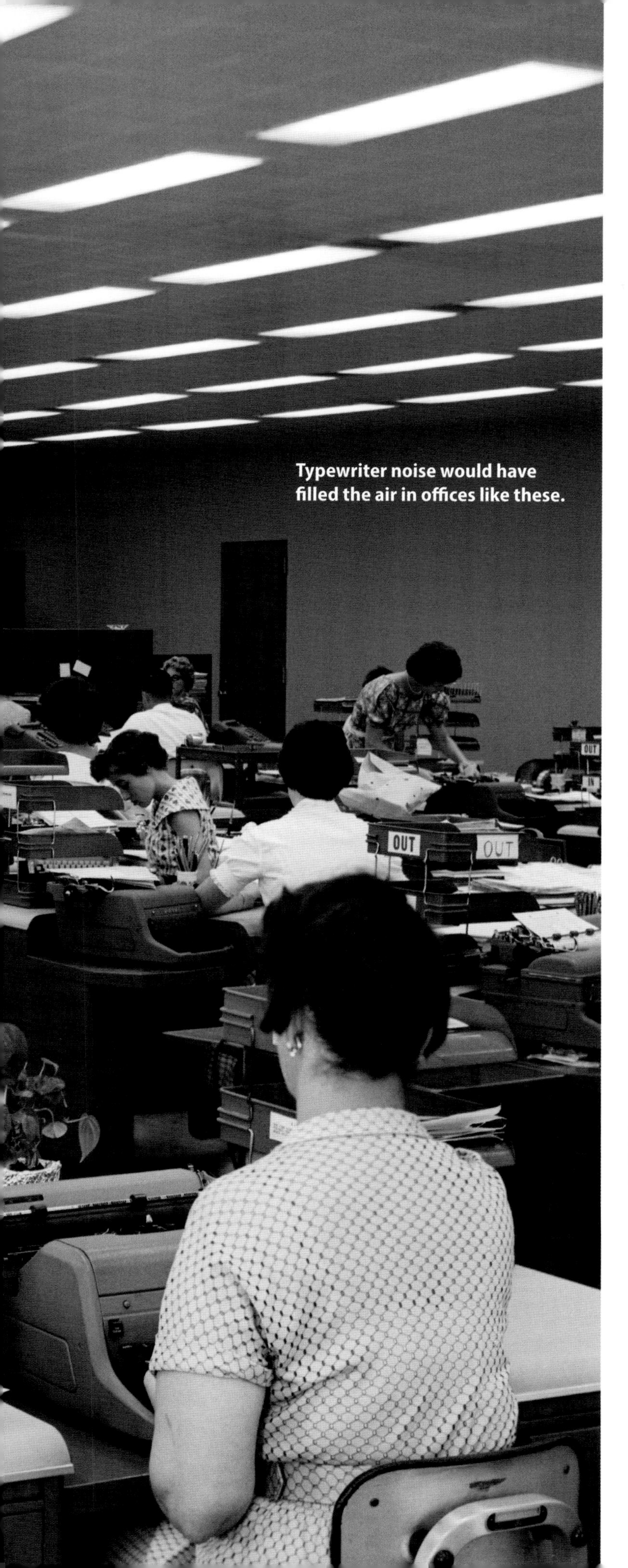

Typewriter noise would have filled the air in offices like these.

Offices may have existed since the 18th century, but they have changed dramatically over time.

1950s More women become office workers. Offices resemble factory floors: employees work in tight rows while managers watch.

1960s Employees work in cubicles—small spaces with partitions to minimize distractions.

1970s Dress codes are loosened. Computers and fax machines begin making their way into offices, replacing typewriters.

1980s Work-life balance becomes a buzzword, and corporate culture becomes a priority. Personal computers become indispensable.

1990s Job-hopping becomes the norm. Companies do more to retain their employees. The internet is born.

2000s Manual work becomes less important. Companies prioritize social and analytical skills.

2010s Globalization results in multinational workforces. Faster internet speeds make telecommuting practical.

2020s Many offices downsize. Hot-desking catches on. Employees no longer have fixed desks: they have shared spaces.

Reading

PREPARING TO READ

A **BUILD VOCABULARY** The words in **blue** are used in the reading passage. Read the text below. Then write the correct form of each word next to its definition.

Today, moving **assembly** lines are a staple of production. However, in the early 1900s, the concept was new—at least in the world of automobile manufacturing. In 1913, Henry Ford, **founder** of the Ford Motor Company, became the first car maker to use this method to manufacture vehicles.

Ford had wanted to **accelerate** car production for a long time. Traditional car assembly was **troublesome**: each worker was responsible for an entire section of the vehicle, which they had to put together manually on a production floor. This meant that they had to be both highly skilled and strong, as the heavy components needed to be dragged across long distances. On average, it took about 12 hours to assemble a single car this way.

Ford's moving assembly line broke the process down into 84 distinct steps. Each worker focused on just one small step—a much simpler, **repetitive** task that was easier to learn, perform, and **master**. This greatly reduced production time: workers could now consistently produce cars at a rate of one every 93 minutes.

Ford's breakthrough had a major **influence** on the automobile industry. It not only reduced production times, but also costs. His success **spurred** other car makers to adopt moving assembly lines in their own factories to remain competitive and meet growing demands.

1. ____________________ (adj) difficult and complicated
2. ____________________ (adj) involving the same action being done many times
3. ____________________ (v) to increase the speed at which something is done
4. ____________________ (v) to encourage someone to take action
5. ____________________ (v) to become highly skilled at something
6. ____________________ (n) the process of building something by putting parts together
7. ____________________ (n) a person who starts a company or an organization
8. ____________________ (n) the ability to effect change in someone or something

B **BUILD VOCABULARY** Complete the sentences below with the correct form of the words and phrases in **blue**. Use a dictionary to help you.

automation (n)	**executive** (n)	**imaginary** (adj)	**incentive** (n)
inevitable (adj)	**maximize** (v)	**relate to** (v)	

1. Today, robots are a part of our everyday lives, not just __________ machines that exist solely in science fiction.
2. If you want to __________ your productivity at the office, try going in early for some quiet time so you can get your work done before everyone else arrives.
3. Despite our very different cultural backgrounds, we find it really easy to __________ each other.
4. Management is offering larger bonuses as a(n) __________ for hitting our sales targets this year.
5. This isn't up to us. It's a decision for the senior account __________.
6. Many factory workers fear that __________ will result in machines taking away manufacturing jobs from people.
7. The company hired far too many people last year, so this year's job cuts were __________.

C **USE VOCABULARY** Discuss these questions with a partner.

1. What are some of the downsides of having to do the simpler, more **repetitive** tasks required of **assembly**-line workers?
2. Think about the skilled mechanics Ford used to hire. How do you think they would have felt about the switch to assembly lines? Can you **relate to** the concerns they may have had?
3. While many people worry that **automation** will result in significant job losses, others argue that it will make up for this by creating new types of jobs. Which side of the argument do you think is more convincing and why?

D **PREDICT** Look at the photos in the reading passage. Then read the title of the reading passage and the first sentence of each paragraph. Answer the questions in your own words. Then read the passage and check your answers.

Critical Thinking

1. What is the reading passage about?

____

____

2. What industries or sectors do you think the reading passage will cover?

____

____

The ROBOT REVOLUTION Has Arrived

By David Berreby

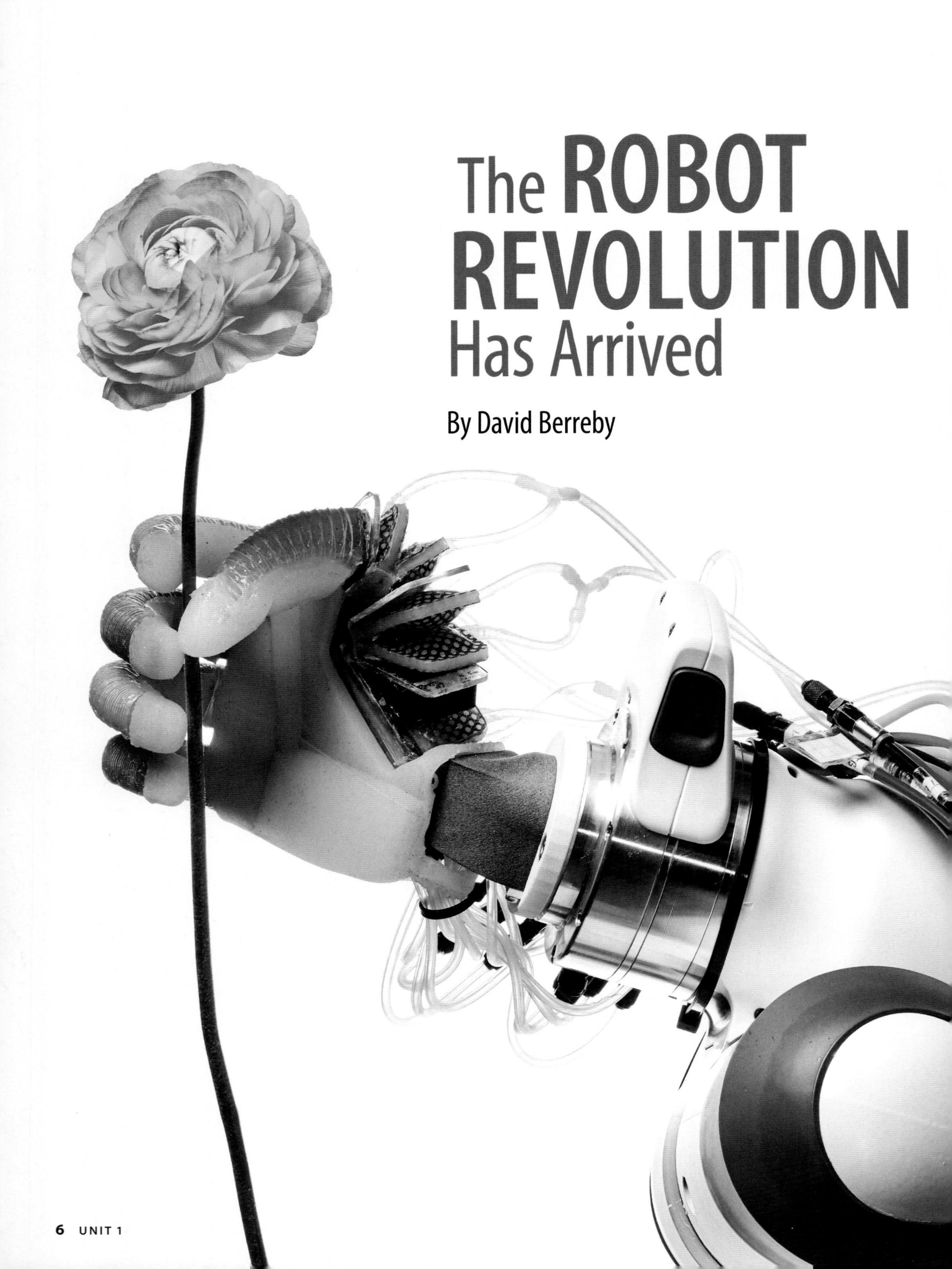

Robots are no longer a thing of science fiction. They are already here.

A The word "robot" was coined by the Czech writer Karel Čapek in 1920, in a play that set the template for a century's machine dreams and nightmares. The robots in that play look and act like people, do all the work of humans—and wipe out the human race before the curtain falls.

B Ever since, **imaginary** robots—from the *Terminator*, to *Astro Boy*, to *Star Wars's* droids—have had a huge **influence** on the plans of robot-makers. They have also shaped the public's expectations of what robots are and what they can do.

C I met a robot on a bright, windy day last January, near Colorado's border with Kansas, in the company of a 31-year-old from San Francisco named Noah Ready-Campbell. To the south, wind turbines stretched to the horizon in uneven ranks, like a silent army of shiny three-armed giants. In front of me was a hole that would become the foundation for another one.

D A Caterpillar 336 excavator was digging that hole—62 feet (19 meters) wide, with walls that sloped up at a 34-degree angle, and a floor 10 feet (3 meters) deep and almost perfectly level. The Cat piled the dug-up earth on a spot where it wouldn't get in the way; it would start a new pile when necessary. Every dip, dig, raise, turn, and drop of the 41-ton machine required firm control and careful judgment.

E The seat in this excavator, though, was empty. The operator lay on the cab's roof. It had no hands; three snaky black cables linked it directly to the excavator's control system. It had no eyes or ears either, since it used lasers, GPS, video cameras, and gyroscope[1]-like sensors. Ready-Campbell, co-**founder** of a San Francisco company called Built Robotics, walked across the dirt, climbed onto the excavator, and lifted the lid of a fancy luggage carrier on the roof. Inside was his company's product—a 200-pound (90-kilogram) device that does work that once required a human being.

F "This is where the AI runs," he said, pointing into the collection of circuit boards, wires, and metal boxes that made up the machine: Sensors to tell it where it is, cameras to let it see, controllers to send its commands to the excavator, communication devices that allow humans to monitor it, and the processor where its artificial intelligence makes the decisions a human driver would. "These control signals get passed down to the computers that usually respond to the joysticks[2] and pedals in the cab."

[1] A **gyroscope** is a device used to stabilize machines and keep them level or upright.
[2] A **joystick** is a lever that people use to electronically control machines.

▲ **A robot helps make change dispensers in a factory in Kazo, Japan.**

G When I was a child in the 20th century, hoping to encounter a robot when I grew up, I expected it would look and act human, like C-3PO from *Star Wars*. Instead, the real robots that were being set up in factories were very different. Today, millions of these industrial machines bolt, weld, paint, and do other repetitive, assembly-line tasks. Often fenced off to keep the remaining human workers safe, they are what roboticist Andrea Thomaz at the University of Texas has called "mute and brute" behemoths.[3]

H Ready-Campbell's device isn't like that. And of course it isn't like C-3PO, either. It is, instead, a new kind of robot, far from human but still smart, adept, and mobile. Once rare, these devices—designed to work with people who have never met a robot—are moving steadily into daily life.

I Even before the COVID crisis added its impetus, technological trends were accelerating the creation of robots that could fan out into our lives. Mechanical parts got lighter, cheaper, and sturdier. Electronics packed more computing power into smaller packages. Breakthroughs let engineers put powerful data-crunching tools into robot bodies. Better digital communications let them store robot "brains" in a computer elsewhere—or connect the minds of hundreds of robots, letting them share a collective intelligence, like bees in a beehive.

[3] **Behemoth** is a term used to describe extremely large creatures or machines.

J Today, robots take inventory[4] and clean supermarket floors. They shelve goods and fetch them for mailing in warehouses. They cut lettuce and pick apples and even raspberries. They help autistic[5] children socialize, and stroke victims regain the use of their arms and legs. Robots now deliver food in Milton Keynes, England, tote supplies in a Dallas hospital, and disinfect hospital rooms in China and Europe.

K According to Daron Acemoglu, an economist at MIT who has studied the effects of robots and other **automation**, there is a particular zeitgeist[6] among many technologists and managers that humans are **troublesome**. Robots, after all, don't need paid vacations or medical insurance. Furthermore, many nations actually encourage automation with tax breaks and other **incentives**. Companies thus save money by cutting employees and adding robots.

L Back at the wind farm site in Colorado, **executives** from the Mortenson Company, a Minneapolis-based construction firm that has hired Built's robots since 2018, told me about a dire[7] shortage of skilled workers in their industry. Built robots dug 21 foundations at the wind farm.

---

[4] To **take inventory** is to update records of the items available in a store or warehouse.
[5] To be **autistic** is to have autism, a neurological condition that often affects social and communication skills.
[6] **Zeitgeist** refers to the mood or spirit of a specific period of time.
[7] If a situation is **dire**, it is extremely urgent.

▼ **A driverless harvesting robot uses suction to pick apples from trees in Washington State, U.S.A.**

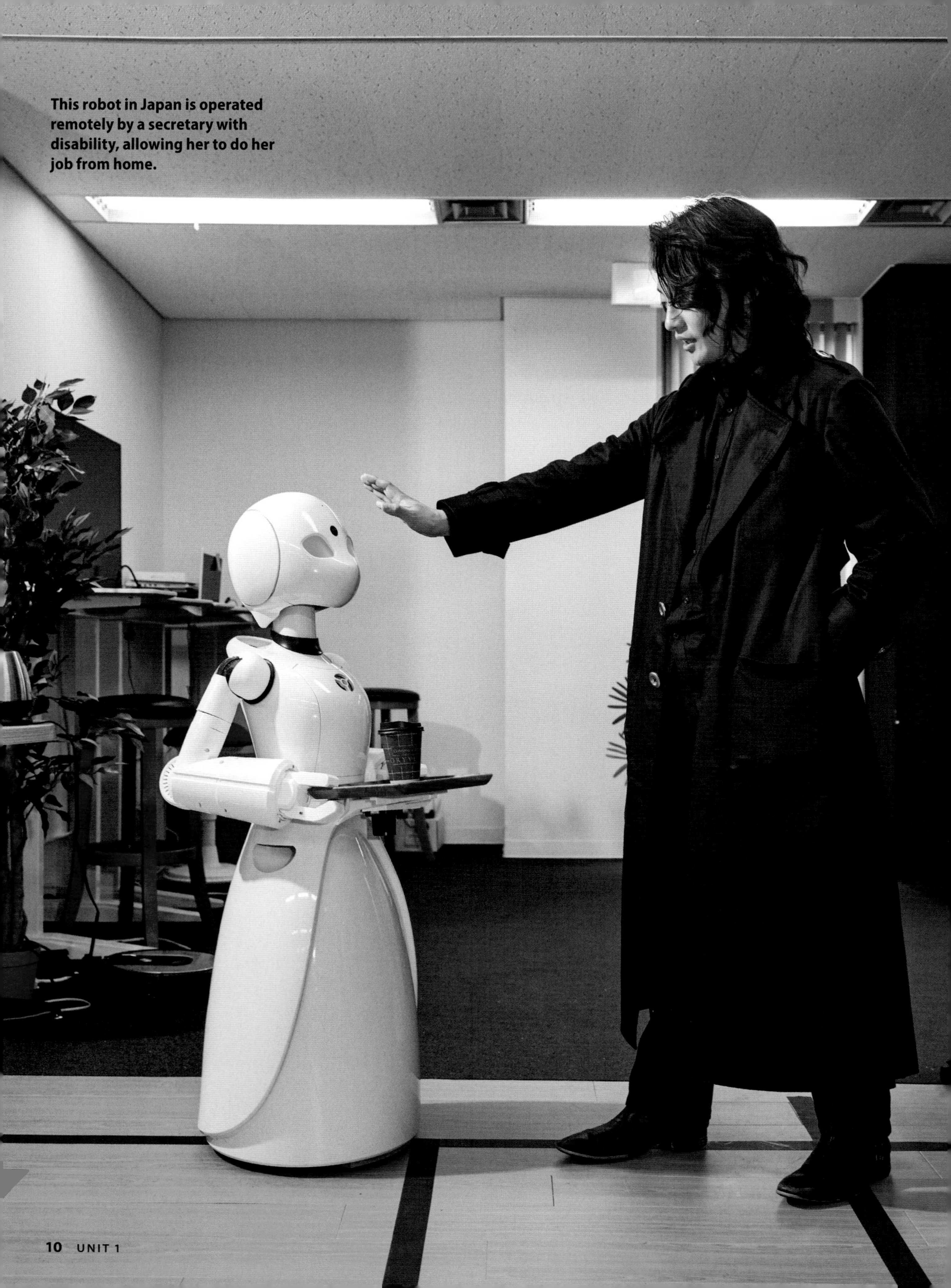

This robot in Japan is operated remotely by a secretary with disability, allowing her to do her job from home.

M "Operators will say things like, Oh, hey, here come the job killers," said Derek Smith, lean innovation[8] manager for Mortenson. "But after they see that the robot takes away a lot of repetitive work and they still have plenty to do, that shifts pretty quickly."

N Once the robot excavator finished the dig we'd watched, a human on a bulldozer[9] smoothed out the work and made ramps. "On this job, we have 229 foundations, and every one is basically the same spec," Smith said. "We want to take away tasks that are repetitive. Then our [human] operators concentrate on the tasks that involve more art."

O Robots can be programmed or trained to do a well-defined task—dig a foundation, or harvest lettuce—better or at least more consistently than humans can. But none can equal the human mind's ability to do a lot of different tasks, especially unexpected ones. None has yet **mastered** common sense.

P Today's robots can't match human hands either, said Chico Marks, a manufacturing engineering manager at Subaru's auto plant in Lafayette, Indiana. "Routing a wiring harness into a vehicle is not something that lends itself well to automation," Marks said. "It requires a human brain and tactile feedback to know it's in the right place and connected."

Q Robot legs aren't any better. In 1996, Manuela Veloso, an AI roboticist at Carnegie Mellon University in Pittsburgh, was part of a challenge to create robots that would play soccer better than humans. She was one of a group of researchers that year who created the RoboCup tournament to **spur** progress. Today RoboCup is a well-loved tradition for engineers on several continents, but no one, including Veloso, expects robots to play soccer better than humans anytime soon.

R "It's crazy how sophisticated our bodies are as machines," she said. "We're very good at handling gravity, dealing with forces as we walk, being pushed and keeping our balance. It's going to be many years before a bipedal[10] robot can walk as well as a person."

S Robots are not going to become artificial people that completely replace us. However, the workplace of the near future will likely be an ecosystem of humans and robots working together to **maximize** efficiency.

T According to Veloso, it is an **inevitable** fact that machines and artificial creatures will become a significant part of our daily lives. The time, she suggests, for us to start accepting them around us like a new species and learning to **relate to** them—the way we do with pets and other humans—is now.

Adapted from "The Robots Are Here," by David Berreby: National Geographic Magazine, September 2020

David Berreby is a science writer whose works have appeared in *The New Yorker, The New York Times Magazine, National Geographic, Nature,* and many other publications.

---

[8] **Lean innovation** refers to the process of getting customer feedback early in order to reduce inefficiency.
[9] A **bulldozer** is a large machine often used in construction to move dirt and heavy items around.
[10] A **bipedal** animal or robot is one that generally walks upright on two feet.

UNDERSTANDING THE READING

A **UNDERSTAND THE MAIN IDEA** Choose the main idea of the reading passage.

a. Robots are a threat to people's jobs because they can do most things better and more consistently than people.

b. Robots won't replace humans because they aren't as maneuverable and haven't yet mastered common sense.

c. Robots will work closely together with human workers, who will continue to remain vital members of the workforce.

B **UNDERSTAND MAIN IDEAS** Match the paragraphs with their main ideas.

1. ____ Paragraph A	a. The robots of today are much better and safer to work with than older robots.
2. ____ Paragraphs C–E	b. Corporations often prefer robots to people.
3. ____ Paragraphs H–J	c. Robots are less capable than people in several ways.
4. ____ Paragraphs K–L	d. Today, robots exist in the real world and do real jobs.
5. ____ Paragraphs M–N	e. The idea of robots has been around for a long time.
6. ____ Paragraphs O–R	f. Human workers appreciate the help robots provide.

C **UNDERSTAND DETAILS** Read the sentences. Choose **T** for true, **F** for false, or **NG** for not given.

1. The Caterpillar 336 excavator was operated by a person.	**T**	**F**	**NG**
2. "Mute and brute" robots are designed to work closely with people.	**T**	**F**	**NG**
3. Ready-Campbell's robots share a collective intelligence.	**T**	**F**	**NG**
4. According to Derek Smith, workers usually don't mind robots taking away repetitive work from them.	**T**	**F**	**NG**

D **UNDERSTAND DETAILS** Complete the sentences. Use no more than two words from the reading passage for each answer.

1. The robots of science fiction ____________ and ____________ like people.

2. Many of the industrial machines used today are ____________ from humans to keep workers ____________.

3. Newer robots are designed to ____________ people who are unused to them.

4. Improvements in technology have allowed more ____________ to be packed into ____________ spaces.

5. Robots can do simple, repetitive work more ____________ than humans, but humans can handle different, ____________ tasks better.

CRITICAL THINKING Recognizing Claims and Counterclaims

In academic writing, writers usually present a main argument and provide evidence to support it. However, good writers also anticipate and address counterclaims. Counterclaims are different positions people have on the same issue. By acknowledging counterclaims—and explaining why they are not valid—writers strengthen their argument. As a reader, it is important to be able to identify counterclaims, and understand why the author chose to include them.

E **RECOGNIZE CLAIMS AND COUNTERCLAIMS** Look at the correct main idea in Exercise A. Then read the excerpts below. Do they support the author's main idea, or is the author acknowledging a counterclaim? Check the correct column for each excerpt.

Critical Thinking

	Main idea	Counterclaim
1. "… there is a particular zeitgeist among many technologists and managers that humans are troublesome."	☐	☐
2. "Operators will say things like, Oh, hey, here come the job killers," …	☐	☐
3. "But after they see that the robot takes away a lot of repetitive work and they still have plenty to do, that shifts pretty quickly."	☐	☐
4. "We want to take away tasks that are repetitive. Then our operators concentrate on the tasks that involve more art."	☐	☐
5. "But none can equal the human mind's ability to do a lot of different tasks, especially unexpected ones."	☐	☐

F **INFER MEANING** Find and underline the following words in the reading passage. Use the context to identify their meanings. Then match each word to its definition.

Critical Thinking

template (paragraph A)	**adept** (paragraph H)	**impetus** (paragraph I)
sturdier (paragraph I)	**tote** (paragraph J)	**tactile** (paragraph P)

1. ____________ very skilled at something
2. ____________ to carry something
3. ____________ relating to the sense of touch
4. ____________ a force that causes something to happen
5. ____________ a model that people refer to or use to do something
6. ____________ tougher and more durable

G **REFLECT** Discuss the questions below in a group.

Critical Thinking

1. What tasks or jobs not mentioned in the reading passage do you think robots would be good at, and why?
2. According to the reading passage, the workplace of the near future will "likely be an ecosystem of humans and robots working together to maximize efficiency." Do you agree? Why or why not?

DEVELOPING READING SKILLS

READING SKILL Understanding Cohesion

Cohesion refers to the way that ideas are linked in a text. Writers use certain techniques (cohesive devices) to refer to ideas mentioned elsewhere in the passage. These techniques include using pronouns (*one[s]*, *another, the other, she, it*), demonstrative pronouns and adjectives (*this, that, these, those*), and synonyms.

In the example from the reading passage below, the writer uses the pronoun *they* to refer to *imaginary robots* in the first sentence:

> *Ever since, imaginary robots . . . have had a huge influence on the plans of robot-makers. They have also shaped the public's expectations of what robots are and what they can do.*

In the next example, the writer uses the demonstrative adjective *that* with the noun *play* in the second sentence to refer to *a play* mentioned in the first sentence:

> *The word "robot" was coined by the Czech writer Karel Čapek in 1920, in a play that set the template for a century's machine dreams and nightmares. The robots in that play . . .*

Note: The referent—the word or idea that is referred to—is not always close to the cohesive device. It may be in a different sentence or even a different section of the text.

A **UNDERSTAND COHESION** Read the sentences. Circle the word or idea that the underlined words or phrases refer to.

1. The Cat piled the dug-up earth on a spot where it wouldn't get in the way; it would start a new pile when necessary. Every dip, dig, raise, turn, and drop of the 41-ton machine required firm control and careful judgment.
2. The seat in this excavator, though, was empty. The operator lay on the cab's roof. It had no hands; three snaky black cables linked it directly to the excavator's control system.

B **UNDERSTAND COHESION** Find the following excerpts in the reading passage. Write the words or ideas that each underlined word or phrase refers to.

1. Paragraph D: . . . where it wouldn't get in the way . . . ____________
2. Paragraph G: Today, millions of these industrial machines bolt, . . . ____________
3. Paragraph H: Ready-Campbell's device isn't like that. ____________
4. Paragraph M: But after they see that . . . ____________
5. Paragraph O: . . . especially unexpected ones. ____________

C **UNDERSTAND COHESION** Read the sentences. What do you think the underlined words refer to, and why? Discuss with a partner.

The workers disliked the robots because they were slower and less precise than them. They were cheaper, though, so the factory owner loved them.

VOCABULARY EXTENSION

WORD PARTNERS *artificial* + Noun

The word *artificial* means human-made, or not naturally occurring. Here are some nouns that collocate with *artificial*. Check any phrases you don't know in a dictionary.

artificial intelligence	*artificial turf*	*artificial light*
artificial limb	*artificial sweetener*	*artificial heart*

A Complete each sentence using the correct form of a noun from the box above.

1. Many people who can't eat sugar use artificial __________ in their drinks.
2. Unlike many artificial __________, the sun's rays reduce stress, improve our moods, and generate vitamin D in our bodies.
3. The machine learned how to perform the task on its own using artificial __________.
4. They're playing the match on artificial __________, not on real grass.
5. She lost her arm in an accident, so she's getting an artificial __________.
6. In extreme cases, doctors are able to temporarily implant an artificial __________ into a patient while waiting for the real organ to arrive.

WORD FORMS *-ize* and *-ization*

You can add *-ize* to certain nouns and adjectives to make verbs. For example, *maximize* means to make maximum use of something, while *socialize* means to be social, or friendly, with people. You can also add *-ation* to *-ize* verbs to make nouns. For example, *maximization* means the process of maximizing something. *Socialization* refers to the process of socializing.

B Complete each sentence using the correct form of a word from the chart below.

Noun/Adjective	custom	familiar	general	visual
Verb with *-ize*	customize	familiarize	generalize	visualize
Noun with *-ation*	customization	familiarization	generalization	visualization

1. He just moved in, so he hasn't __________ himself with the area yet.
2. She thinks all of us like the same things, but that's just a broad __________.
3. I know it's hard to imagine, but you have to try to __________ it.
4. The new product allows for greater __________ to suit individual preferences.

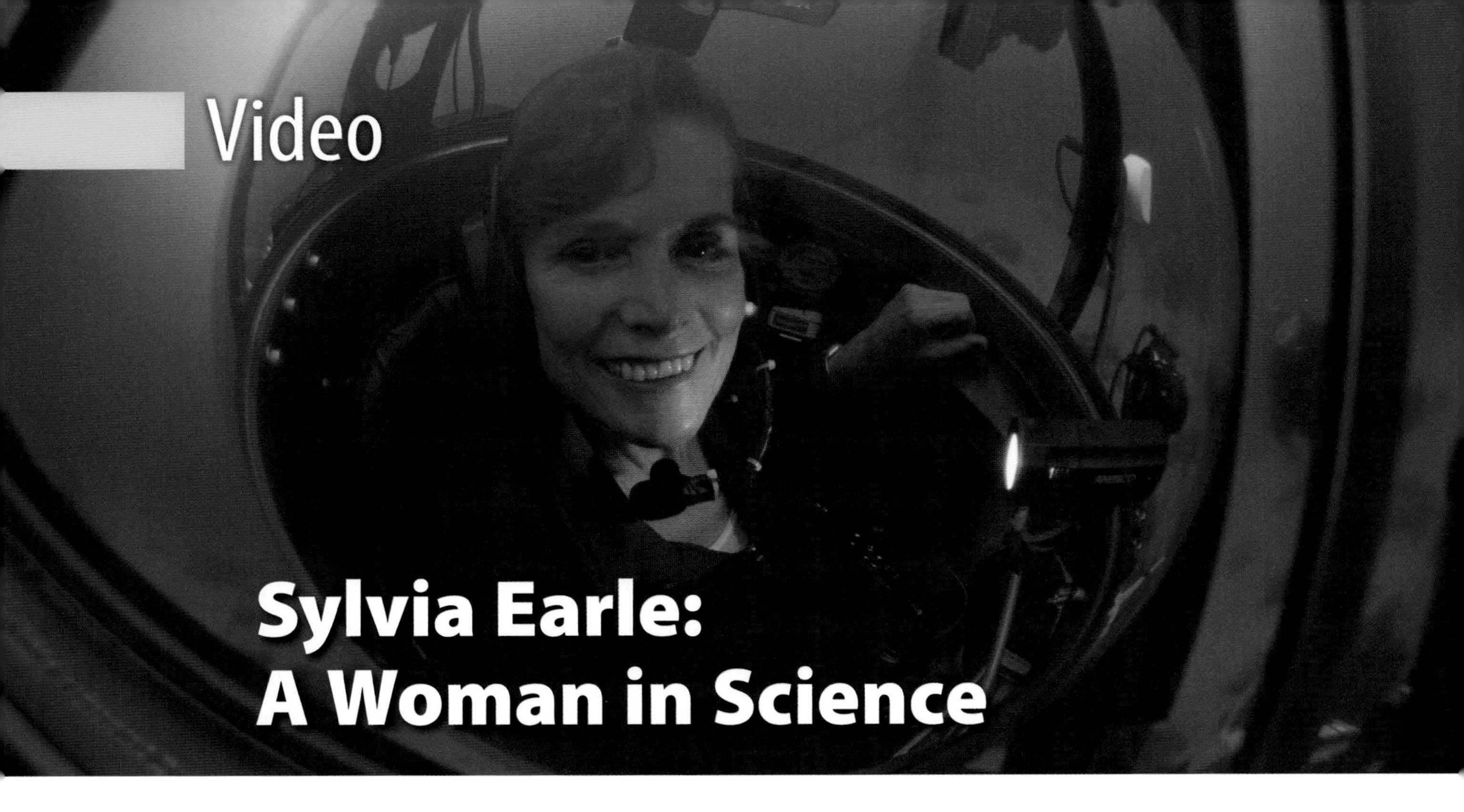

Video

Sylvia Earle: A Woman in Science

Sylvia Earle is a world-renowned marine biologist and a National Geographic Explorer. She has led more than 100 marine expeditions, logged over 7,000 hours underwater, and authored more than 190 publications. In this video, she talks about the struggles she faced as a young woman working in science and the biases that still exist in modern workplaces.

Critical Thinking

A **PREVIEW** Read the paragraph above. In general, do you think it is more difficult for women to find work or gain recognition for their work than men? Why or why not? Discuss with a partner.

B **MAIN IDEAS** ▶ Watch the video. Which of the following are main ideas of the talk? Check (✓) the three correct answers.

- ☐ 1. Earle's parents were not supportive of her career choice.
- ☐ 2. In the past, women were not allowed or encouraged to work in certain fields.
- ☐ 3. The people who hired Earle were looking for female researchers.
- ☐ 4. Today, women are not recognized or rewarded as much as men are for their work.
- ☐ 5. More opportunities exist today for women to pursue careers in scientific fields.

C **DETAILS** ▶ Watch the video again. Choose **T** for true or **F** for false.

1.	Earle's mother often encouraged her to do work usually reserved for men.	**T**	**F**
2.	The job listing Earle responded to specified they were hiring only men.	**T**	**F**
3.	Earle has served on the boards of companies.	**T**	**F**
4.	Earle feels that some women are hired only to give the impression of diversity.	**T**	**F**

Critical Thinking

D **PERSONALIZE** Do gender expectations affect your life decisions? If so, how? Discuss with a partner.

Writing

EXPLORING WRITTEN ENGLISH

A **NOTICE** Read the pairs of sentences. Underline the words and phrases that are different in each pair.

1. a. The individual parts are made separately by different departments. Then, the individual parts are brought together and assembled here.
   b. The individual parts are made separately by different departments. Then, they are brought together and assembled here.
2. a. The internet began as a military application, but it didn't take long for the internet to make its way into people's homes and offices.
   b. The internet began as a military application, but it didn't take long for the innovation to make its way into people's homes and offices.

LANGUAGE FOR WRITING Using Cohesive Devices

As explained in the Reading Skill box earlier in the unit, writers use cohesive devices to emphasize key concepts they have already mentioned and to avoid repetition. Cohesive devices include reference words (pronouns and demonstrative adjectives, etc.), synonyms, and different word forms.

Reference Words and Synonyms:

> ***The employees*** *all worked in* ***small cubicles****. They mostly found the tiny workspaces cold and uninviting.*

The writer uses the reference word *they* to refer to *the employees*, and *tiny workspaces* as a synonym for *small cubicles*.

Different Word Forms:

> *It used to be difficult to* ***manufacture*** *items, but assembly lines and robots have made* ***manufacturing*** *much easier.*

Here, the writer uses the noun *manufacturing* instead of repeating the verb *manufacture*.

B **APPLY** Use cohesive devices to refer to the underlined words in the following sentences. There may be several possible answers for each item.

1. Many people worry that robots will take their jobs. In reality, ____________________ will probably make work a lot easier for humans instead.

2. Computers drastically changed the way work was done. These ____________________ allowed us to calculate quicker, transmit data more easily, and store huge amounts of information.

3. Ford reduced the time needed to manufacture a car by over 10 hours. This ____________________ resulted in lower prices for consumers.

WRITING SKILL Organizing an Essay

An essay is a piece of writing on a specific topic that includes an **introduction**, a **body**, and a **conclusion**.

- The introduction presents general information on the topic and includes a **thesis statement**. The thesis statement presents the main idea of the essay and refers to the main points supporting this idea.
- The body paragraphs support the thesis with facts, details, explanations, and other information. **Transitions** between paragraphs help the reader follow the essay.
- The **conclusion** restates the thesis and leaves the reader with a final thought on the topic.

You usually write an essay in response to an **essay prompt**. The prompt might be an instruction (*Describe/Explain* ...), or it might be a question (*Why ...? To what extent ...? How ...?*). When you respond to a prompt, think about your position on the topic (which will become your thesis statement) and ways to support or explain your position (which may become the topic sentences of your body paragraphs).

C Read the following essay prompt. Then choose the best thesis statement for it. Why is it the best? Discuss your answer with a partner.

What are some ways in which job seekers can make themselves more attractive to employers?

a. Job seekers should make sure that they are attractive to employers.

b. When employers are trying to fill open positions, they usually get dozens, sometimes hundreds, of applications, so it is important to submit an impressive resume.

c. Job seekers can make themselves more attractive to employers by having a professional online presence, writing a good resume, and making a good first impression.

D Check (✓) the three topic sentences that correspond with the correct thesis statement in Exercise C. Then complete the three topic sentences using the transition words in the box.

Finally	First	In addition

☐ 1. ______________, making a good impression from the onset is crucial if you want an employer to consider you for a job.

☐ 2. ______________, applying for as many jobs as possible will increase the likelihood that an employer will notice you.

☐ 3. ______________, writing a good resume is key if you want employers to view your application favorably.

☐ 4. ______________, use colorful language to make sure the achievements you list seem impressive.

☐ 5. ______________, ensure that any information you share about yourself online paints you in a positive light.

E Think of details to support the three topic sentences in Exercise D in your body paragraphs.

1. ____
____
2. ____
____
3. ____
____

F Work with a partner. Discuss the following essay prompt. Think of an appropriate thesis statement, three ideas to support it, and details for each body paragraph.

How can employers improve employee morale in the workplace?

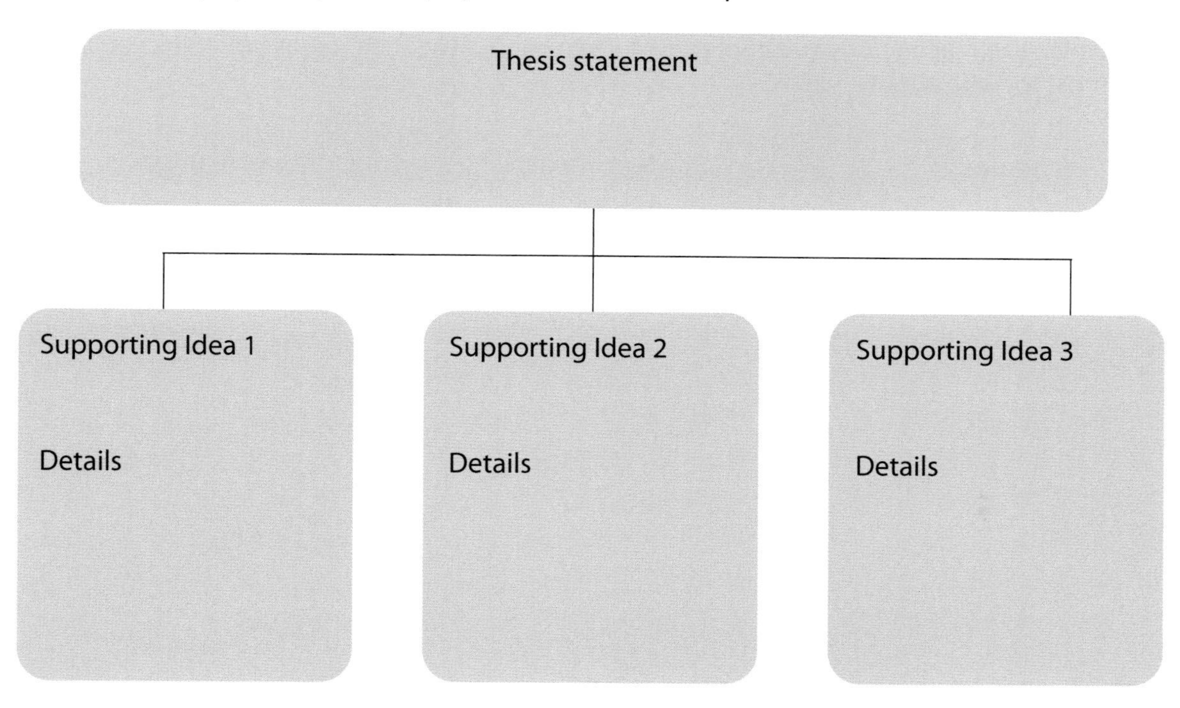

G **VOCABULARY FOR WRITING** The following words can be useful when writing about technology and the workplace. Find the words in the reading passage and use the context to guess their meanings. Then use the words to complete the definitions.

judgment (paragraph D)	**operator** (paragraph E)	**monitor** (paragraph F)
concentrate (paragraph N)	**efficiency** (paragraph S)	

1. A(n) ______________ is the person who drives or runs a machine or a piece of equipment.
2. When you ______________, you focus on one particular thing.
3. ______________ is the ability to make good use of the time and resources available.
4. ______________ is the ability to understand a situation and make good decisions.
5. When you ______________ something, you watch it or regularly check on it.

WRITING TASK

GOAL You are going to write an essay on the following topic:
Describe how an emerging technology will impact jobs in the future.

A **RESEARCH** Research different emerging technologies (other than robots) that you think will have an impact on jobs in the future. Write notes below.

____

____

____

B **SELECT YOUR IDEA** Note your best ideas from Exercise A below. Summarize the ways in which each technology will impact jobs. Then choose the technology you think you'll have the most to write about.

Technology	Positive impacts	Negative impacts

C **WRITE A THESIS STATEMENT** Decide how you want to cover the technology: positively or negatively. Then draft a thesis statement summarizing your position.

____

____

____

D **PLAN** Use your information in Exercises B–C to complete an outline for your essay. Include general information about the topic in your introduction, before the thesis statement.

OUTLINE

Notes for introduction: ______________________________

____

____

Thesis statement: ______________________________

____

____

Body paragraph 1:

Topic sentence: ______________________________

____

Details: ______________________________

____

____

Body paragraph 2:

Topic sentence: ______________________________

____

Details: ______________________________

____

____

Body paragraph 3:

Topic sentence: ______________________________

____

Details: ______________________________

____

Notes for conclusion: ______________________________

____

____

E **FIRST DRAFT** Use the information in your outline to write a first draft of your essay. Remember to make use of cohesive devices to refer to things you have already mentioned, and to avoid repetition.

F **REVISING PRACTICE** The essay below is similar to the one you are writing. Follow the steps to create a better second draft.

1. Add the sentences (a–c) in the most suitable spaces.
   a. Pre-installed games and multimedia programs added an element of fun to computers, and the internet gave users access to a wealth of information.
   b. These amazing machines have served us well in the past, and will no doubt be indispensable to our futures.
   c. One fear people had was that they would not be able to adapt to computers quickly enough.
2. Now fix the following problems (a–c) with the essay.
   a. Use a cohesive device to replace the **bold** words in paragraph B.
   b. Use a cohesive device to replace the **bold** word in paragraph D.
   c. Cross out one unnecessary sentence from the conclusion in paragraph E.

A It's hard to imagine a world without computers. These amazing devices enable countless aspects of modern life and allow us to accomplish incredible things. However, when computers first entered the workplace, many people were afraid of the changes they would bring. History has fortunately proven these fears unfounded: computers have been easier to adapt to than many expected, they have not made work overly repetitive, and they have not replaced human workers.

B _____ Many people feared getting left behind, particularly as more young people who grew up around computers started entering the workforce. However, what **many people** failed to realize was that using a computer wasn't as difficult as they had thought. The commands were more intuitive than many had expected, and this intuitiveness would only increase as computers developed and became even easier to operate.

C In addition, people feared that computers would make work repetitive and mechanical. The machines of the time—with their basic functions and interfaces—were seen by many as uninteresting, and people began to worry that their jobs would become boring. These fears were cast aside as computer interfaces improved and computers became more versatile. _____ As computers got better, it quickly became clear just how immersive they could be.

D Finally, perhaps the biggest fear people had of computers was that they'd simply be replaced by **computers**. It was unclear how much computers could do, and this made people wonder if the skills and experience they had would soon be made irrelevant. Today, we know that computers free us up from having to do repetitive tasks or difficult calculations. They provide frameworks and templates that make our jobs easier, allowing us to focus on the parts of our work that matter most.

E The fear people once had of computers is understandable: they were, after all, powerful machines capable of doing things that humans couldn't. When you think about it, this is interesting—almost funny—because the computers then weren't even very powerful. However, there was no real basis for many of the fears people had. _____

G **REVISED DRAFT** Now use the questions below to revise your essay.

- ☐ Does your introduction provide relevant background information on the topic?
- ☐ Does your thesis state or refer to the main points of your essay?
- ☐ Do your body paragraphs include enough details to fully explain your ideas?
- ☐ Do you use cohesive devices to avoid repetition?
- ☐ Do all your sentences relate to the main idea?
- ☐ Does your concluding paragraph restate the thesis and include a final thought?

H **EDITING PRACTICE** Read the information below. Then find and correct mistakes with cohesive devices in each sentence (1–3).

When using cohesive devices, remember to:
- use pronouns that match the referent in gender and number.
- choose the correct synonym when using a dictionary or thesaurus.

1. One advantage of robots is that it can work non-stop without rest.
2. Automation may help you cut costs, but they may result in a drop in quality.
3. She joined the company in 2016. Since then, the society has hired many other women.

I **FINAL DRAFT** Follow these steps to write a final draft.

1. Check your revised draft for mistakes with cohesive devices.
2. Now use the checklist on page 248 to write a final draft. Make any other necessary changes.
3. Work in pairs and read your partner's final essay. Give feedback on each other's writing.

An employee in a 1980s office using a computer

Review

SELF-ASSESS **Consider the language and skills you learned in this unit.**

How well can you . . . ?	Very well	Pretty well	I need improvement
use the key vocabulary from this unit	☐	☐	☐
recognize claims and counterclaims	☐	☐	☐
understand cohesion	☐	☐	☐
use cohesive devices	☐	☐	☐
organize an essay	☐	☐	☐

A **VOCABULARY** Do you remember the meanings of these words and phrases? Look back at the unit and review the ones you don't know.

accelerate AW	assembly AW	automation AW	executive	founder AW
imaginary	incentive	inevitable AW	influence	master
maximize AW	relate to	repetitive	spur	troublesome

B **VOCABULARY EXTENSION** Complete these tasks with a partner.

1. Take turns making sentences using the words and phrases in the box.

artificial	artificial intelligence	artificial limb

2. Make sentences using both the *-ize* and *-ization* forms of two words from the chart in Exercise B on page 15.

C **READING SKILL** Read the sentences below. Circle what the underlined words refer to.

1. Ford's breakthrough had a major influence on the automobile industry. It not only reduced production times, but also costs.
2. Today, moving assembly lines are a staple of production. However, in the early 1900s, the concept was new . . .

D **LANGUAGE FOR WRITING** Write one or two sentences about robots in the workplace. Use at least one cohesive device. Underline the cohesive device and circle the word or idea that it refers to. Then share your sentences with a partner.

SELF-ASSESS **Look back at the chart above. Did you assess your skills correctly? What skills or language do you still need help with?**

CITY CHALLENGES 2

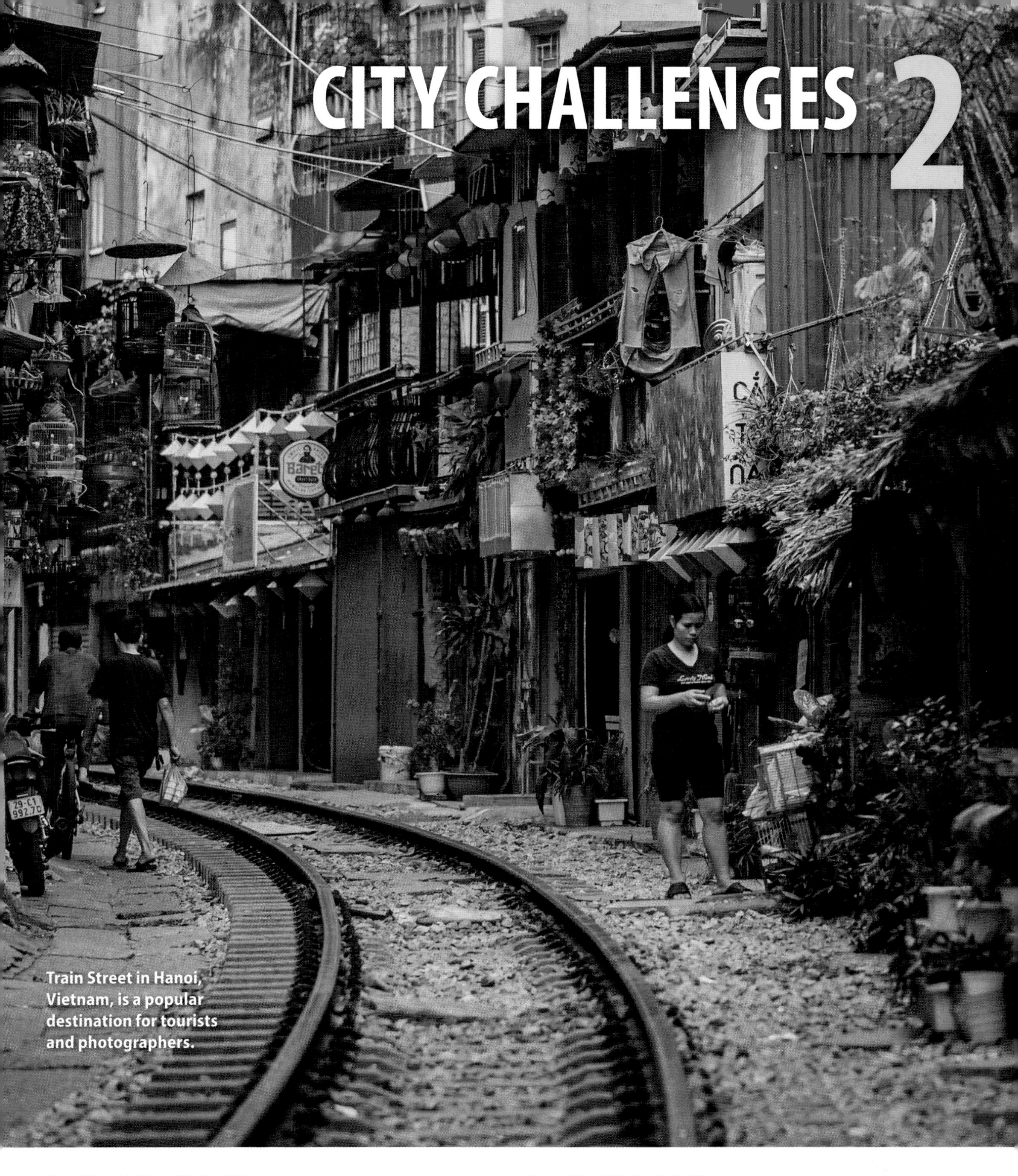

Train Street in Hanoi, Vietnam, is a popular destination for tourists and photographers.

IN THIS UNIT, YOU WILL:

- Read an article about urban wildlife
- Watch a video about a self-cooling building
- Write about a solution to an urban challenge

THINK AND DISCUSS:

1. Hanoi is a modern, thriving city, but the people who live on Train Street have to face unique challenges. Should this street be preserved? Why or why not?
2. Would you enjoy visiting Hanoi's train Street? What about working or living there? Why or why not?

EXPLORE THE THEME

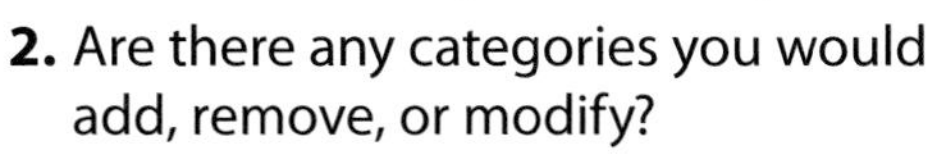

Look at the information on these pages and answer the questions.

1. Which of the six categories do you think is most important? Why?
2. Are there any categories you would add, remove, or modify?
3. Rate a city or town you're familiar with using the six categories.

What Is a Good City?

A bird's-eye view of the Eiffel Tower in Paris, France

Cities are the busiest places on Earth, so keeping them running smoothly is not easy. Historically, many of the world's most famous cities were not just centers of commerce and prosperity; they were also hubs for crime and disease.

Over the decades, these problems have lessened, allowing many cities to mature into major cultural attractions. But what lessons do established cities have to offer newer ones? How should emerging cities strive to improve, and what ideals should they aim for?

Every year, many organizations rate cities around the world using different criteria. One such organization is Resonance Consultancy, which uses six categories to rank cities. Categories like these aren't just tools of assessment: they also offer city planners insight into what makes a city *good*.

METHODOLOGY

Cities are rated based on the six metrics below.

- **PLACE** The quality of a city's natural and built environment, including the sub-categories of Weather, Safety, Neighborhoods & Landmarks, and Outdoors.
- **PRODUCT** A city's key institutions, attractions, and infrastructure, including the sub-categories of Airport Connectivity, Attractions, Museums, University Rankings, Convention Centers, and Pro Sports Teams.
- **PROGRAMMING** The arts and entertainment scene in a city, including the sub-categories of Shopping, Culture, Restaurants, and Nightlife.
- **PEOPLE** The immigration rate and diversity of a city, including the sub-categories of Foreign-Born and Educational Attainment.
- **PROSPERITY** A city's employment rate and its number of corporate head offices, including the sub-categories of Fortune 500 Companies, Household Income, and Income Equality.
- **PROMOTION** The quantity of stories, references, and recommendations shared online about a city, including the sub-categories of Google Search Results, Instagram Hashtags, Facebook Check-ins, and TripAdvisor Reviews.

TOP 10 CITIES

Highlighted rankings (2023)

1. LONDON
1 People — 1 Promotion

2. PARIS
2 Promotion — 3 Product

3. NEW YORK
2 Promotion — 3 Programming

4. TOKYO
2 Programming — 3 Product

5. DUBAI
1 Place — 4 Promotion

6. BARCELONA
5 Product — 6 Place

7. ROME
3 Place — 3 Programming

8. MADRID
6 Programming — 14 Place

9. SINGAPORE
10 Prosperity — 11 Promotion

10. AMSTERDAM
8 Product — 10 People

Reading

PREPARING TO READ

A **BUILD VOCABULARY** The words in **blue** are used in the reading passage. Read the text below. Then write the correct form of each word next to its definition.

Around the world, the pigeon has become **synonymous** with city life. Derived from the rock dove—a similar bird that builds its nest high up on rocky cliffs—it is no wonder pigeons have adapted so well to urban life. Tall buildings with high ledges and small open spaces make an ideal **habitat** for these resourceful birds. The food humans leave behind provides them with a rich and constantly replenishing source of nourishment. And the relative lack of **predators**—like hawks and eagles—means the species is able to thrive and reproduce freely.

Experts who track pigeon populations estimate that there are up to 400 million pigeons living in cities worldwide. Unfortunately, these birds are usually **perceived** as troublesome pests because of the waste they leave behind and the diseases they spread. In order to **minimize** pigeon population growth, some cities like Venice, Bangkok, and Singapore have imposed fines for feeding pigeons. Obviously, this alone won't be enough to completely **eradicate** the problem. In all likelihood, pigeons are here to stay. The best thing we humans could probably do would be to **embrace** them, and adapt to living with them the same way they have adapted to living with us.

1. ______________ (v) to reduce the extent of something
2. ______________ (v) to accept something enthusiastically
3. ______________ (v) to put an end to something
4. ______________ (v) to think of something a certain way
5. ______________ (adj) closely associated with or connected to something
6. ______________ (n) an animal that hunts other animals for food
7. ______________ (n) the natural home of a plant or animal species

A pigeon on a ledge in New York City

B **BUILD VOCABULARY** Complete the sentences below with the correct form of the words and phrases in **blue**. Use a dictionary to help you.

boundary (n)	**consistently** (adv)	**constraint** (n)	**counterpart** (n)
hypothesis (n)	**reliance** (n)	**reversal** (n)	**stem from** (v)

1. Her idea about the changing migration patterns of some of the birds in this city has yet to be proven. For now, it's just a(n) ________________.
2. Together, the river and the mountain range form a clear and natural ________________ that separates the two countries from each other.
3. Many of the locals feel that most of the city's problems ________________ corrupt government officials.
4. In a stunning ________________, the city council announced its decision not to go ahead with the renewal project.
5. Some people regard the pigeon as the flying ________________ of the rat. They both thrive in cities and live on trash.
6. To improve traffic in the city, we need to reduce our ________________ on cars by developing an efficient and comfortable public transportation system.
7. Kyoto is ________________ ranked as one of the best cities to visit in Japan.
8. To grow, the city needs to overcome some natural ________________, like limited space and fresh water.

C **USE VOCABULARY** Discuss these questions with a partner.

1. What are some animals that are commonly found in cities? What makes cities such great **habitats** for these animals?
2. How are the animals that live in your town or city **perceived**? Are they well liked or thought of as pests?
3. How can the problem of pests in a city be **minimized**? Is it possible to **eradicate** pests completely? Why or why not?
4. Are there any wild **predators** that live in your town or city? How much of a threat are they to the people who live there?

D **PREDICT** Look at the photos in the reading passage and read the first sentence of each paragraph. Then answer the questions. Check your answers as you read the passage.

Critical Thinking

1. What urban challenge does the reading passage discuss?
2. How do you think this issue affects people living in cities?
3. What solution(s) to the challenge do you think the reading passage offers?

Wild Cities

By Christine Dell'Amore

A coyote crosses a bridge in Chicago, U.S.A.

Coyotes, bears, raccoons, and other animals are adapting to urban life, resulting in increased contact with humans.

A At first glance, it's a scene that plays out daily in cities across America. A U.S. Postal Service carrier steps out of his mail truck and strides across the street, letters in hand. That much is unremarkable. But this postman either doesn't notice or doesn't seem to care that a hefty American black bear, likely a young male, is sitting a few yards away, vigorously scratching his shedding winter coat.

B Immediately to the left, Interstate 240 roars behind a chain-link fence, apparently just white noise to the bear, which eventually wanders down the sidewalk deeper into this neighborhood barely a half mile from downtown Asheville, North Carolina.

C Along the highway, a team of researchers with the North Carolina Urban/Suburban Bear Study is captivated by another discovery: a deep hollow inside a gnarled silver maple tree. Bear N209, a radio-collared female that's among more than a hundred bears being tracked in a study, hibernated[1] there over the winter, despite the constant rush of vehicles mere feet away.

D "These bears still surprise me," Colleen Olfenbuttel, the state's black bear biologist, shouts over the din of traffic. She holds a ladder steady as a colleague scrambles inside the tree and measures the den. It's the biggest tree den Olfenbuttel has seen in her 23 years of studying black bears. "They're so much more adaptable than we give them credit for."

E Indeed, it's hard to imagine that black bears would take so well to living in Asheville. In this city of about 95,000, nestled in the Blue Ridge Mountains, bears shuffle down residential streets in broad daylight and climb onto people's decks and front porches. Some Asheville residents have **embraced** their furry neighbors, and nearly every person you talk with has a video of their most recent bear encounter.

F The advent of the city bear in Asheville and elsewhere **stems from** a combination of trends, including changes in land use and the tempting buffets[2] available when living near people. These factors have boosted North America's black bear population to nearly 800,000. At the same time, sprawling cities and suburbs have swallowed up large areas of bear **habitat**, leaving the animals little choice but to adapt to living with human neighbors.

G It's a phenomenon happening in urban areas around the world, and it's not unique to black bears. Many mammals that eat a wide variety of foods are moving in and changing their behaviors as they learn urban survival skills.

H Unfortunately, humans and bears don't always live in harmony—even in open-minded Asheville, where bears have killed pets and injured at least one person in recent years. In 2020, a mother bear defending her cubs attacked Valerie Patenotte's dog, which later died. "We understand everyone has to coexist," says Patenotte as we stand on her back deck overlooking the distant mountains. "We just want more space from bears."

---

[1] If an animal **hibernates**, it sleeps through winter to make it through the cold season.
[2] A **buffet** is a large spread of food. People pay a predetermined amount to eat as much of the food as they want.

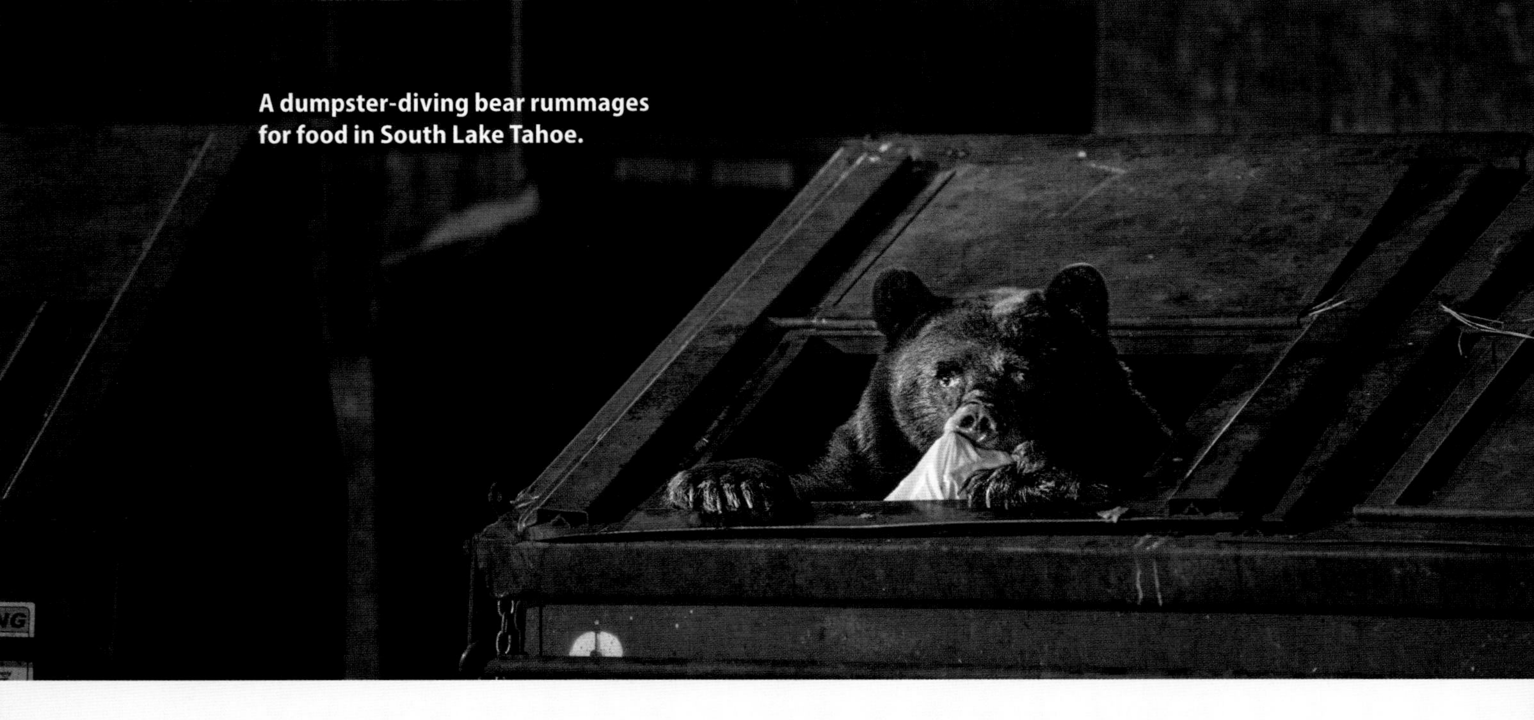
A dumpster-diving bear rummages for food in South Lake Tahoe.

I While black bears have reclaimed about half their former range and now live in some 40 states, coyotes have taken the U.S. by storm in recent decades. They now can be found in every state except Hawaii, and in most major cities. The metropolis most **synonymous** with the urban coyote is Chicago, home to as many as 4,000 of the animals.

J Stan Gehrt, a wildlife ecologist with Ohio State University and the Max McGraw Wildlife Foundation, began studying Chicago's coyotes in 2000, not long after the animals started showing up there. Back then, Gehrt thought his project would last a year. More than two decades later, he's still at it. "We **consistently** underestimate this animal and its ability to adjust and adapt," Gehrt says. "They push the **boundaries** of what we **perceive** to be **constraints**."

K At the beginning of Gehrt's research, he thought coyotes would be restricted to parks and green spaces, but he was wrong. "Now we have coyotes everywhere—every neighborhood, every suburban city, and downtown."

L Indeed, coyotes have succeeded despite our best efforts to **eradicate** them. At least 400,000 are killed each year, about 80,000 by a federal **predator** control. Vehicle strikes are the main cause of death for Chicago's coyotes, but the animals have learned to avoid cars and can even read stoplights.

M Adding to their adaptability is their flexible diet. Coyotes will eat just about anything, from shoe leather to fruit (they can climb fruit trees). According to Gehrt, "Variability[3] is the primary pattern."

N Christopher Schell, an urban ecologist at the University of California, Berkeley, and Julie Young, a wildlife biologist with the U.S. Department of Agriculture, are studying how various diets given to captive coyotes could change the animals' behavior. Their **hypothesis** is that the coyotes eating human food will become bolder around people, which is supported by some anecdotal evidence.[4] Schell and Young theorize that a coyote that eats processed cereal,

[3] **Variability** refers to a lack of consistency or predictable patterns.
[4] **Anecdotal evidence** is evidence that is based on just a few examples or anecdotes (things people say). It is not based on science or data.

for instance, will be hungrier and look for food much more frequently than one that eats a nutrition-dense rabbit for breakfast. Though Gehrt has not noticed such a connection in Chicago coyotes, he notes that a **reliance** on human food does bring coyotes closer to restaurants and homes, which in turn leads to more contact and conflict with people and their pets.

O When zoologist Sarah Benson-Amram first started looking into raccoon behavior and cognition[5] about a decade ago, she figured such a common species would have been studied thoroughly. After all, the bushy-tailed omnivores[6] are pop culture icons, jokingly dubbed trash pandas. Instead, Benson-Amram was shocked to find almost nothing in the scientific literature. A few researchers in the early 1900s had tried to study the clever animals, but gave up when their subjects kept breaking out of their cages.

P So far, she says, her research has confirmed the raccoon's crafty reputation. In an experiment called **reversal** learning, she presented raccoons with a box equipped with a button or foot pedal that, when pressed, released food. After the animals figured out how to get the food, the researchers would switch the buttons and pedals, forcing them to tweak their strategy. Most of the raccoons were able to solve the problem on the first night. To put that into perspective, only one of six coyotes engaged with the box—and not until the 44th night of testing.

[5] **Cognition** refers to how people or animals think and process information in their brains.
[6] **Omnivores** are animals that eat a variety of plant- and animal-based foods.

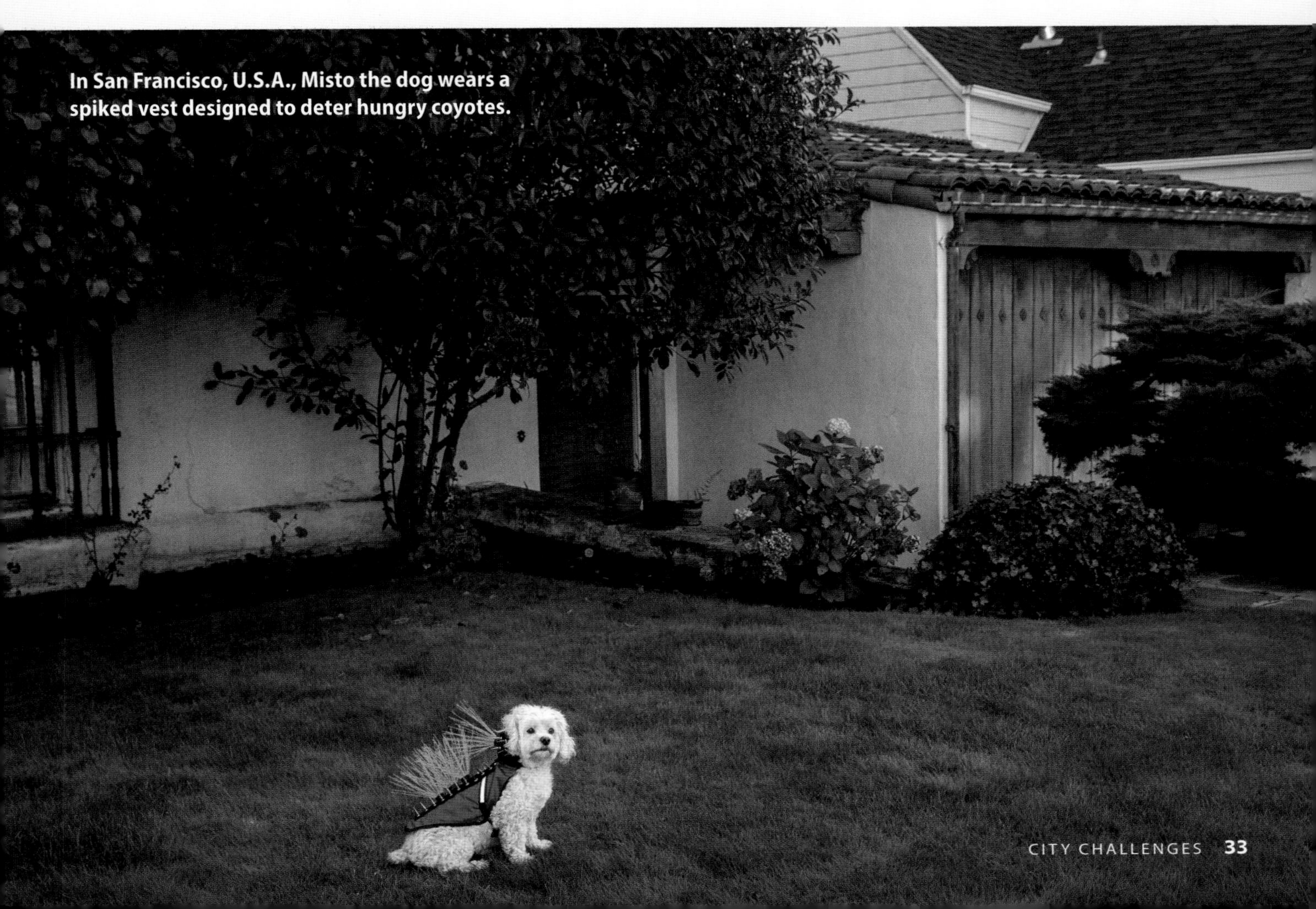

In San Francisco, U.S.A., Misto the dog wears a spiked vest designed to deter hungry coyotes.

Q According to Benson-Amram, now at the University of British Columbia in Vancouver, raccoons have a different survival strategy from coyotes: they're successful by exploiting humans, not avoiding them.

R Like coyotes and bears, raccoons are expanding throughout North American cities. In Washington, D.C., wildlife researchers Kate Ritzel and Travis Gallo wanted to find out whether raccoons living in the city are bolder and more willing to take risks than those in rural areas. They measured this by observing a raccoon's readiness to investigate an unfamiliar object—in this case, bait[7] buried inside a square of wooden stakes.

S The researchers installed more than a hundred automatic cameras throughout the city and rural areas of neighboring Virginia. On a muggy September morning at Fort Totten, Gallo placed the smelly bait—"dead animals in a jar," he called it—while Ritzel strapped a camera to a nearby tree. She would check the videos every two weeks to see which animals had passed through. Her favorite video? A feisty[8] raccoon chasing off a fox.

---

[7] **Bait** is something (typically food) used to lure animals into a trap.
[8] A **feisty** person or animal is one that is small, fiery, and full of energy.

A mother raccoon emerges from a six-inch space between buildings where she is raising her young.

VOCABULARY EXTENSION

WORD PARTNERS Nouns/Adjectives + *constraint*

The noun *constraint* refers to limitations or restrictions. Here are some common collocations with *constraint*:

Noun + *constraint*	**Adjective + *constraint***
time constraint	*financial constraint*
space constraint	*ethical constraint*
resource constraint	*legal constraint*
size constraint	*practical constraint*

A Complete the sentences using the most suitable noun or adjective from the box above.

1. The city won't be able to fund the parade this year due to ______________ constraints.
2. They aren't allowed to do business here anymore because of the ______________ constraints placed on them by the court.
3. Due to rapid growth, the country is facing ______________ constraints. The trade deal it recently signed, however, should provide it with urgently needed water and fuel.
4. The event planners faced many ______________ constraints, such as the need for parking access and shelter in the event of rain.

WORD PARTNERS Words with *counter-*

The prefix *counter-* can mean *against* or *opposite*. It can also mean *complementary*. Here are some examples of words with the prefix *counter-*:

Against/Opposite	**Complementary**
counterattack	*counterpart*
counteract	*counterbalance*
counteroffer	*countersign*

B Complete the sentences using the correct form of the words from the box above.

1. I thought the terms they presented were unreasonable, so I made a ______________ that I believed was fair for everyone.
2. This solution will ______________ the poison, but you need to take it within two hours.
3. Here's the contract with the CEO's signature. Once you have ______________, the deal will be finalized.
4. They make a great team. She's energetic and quick to act, but his cautiousness serves as a great ______________.
5. The army launched a ______________ immediately after their enemy's initial strike.

Video

Turning to Nature

In cities everywhere, the amount of energy used to regulate the temperature inside buildings is staggering. This is not just an expensive problem—it is also an environmental one. Could nature teach us a better, more efficient way to keep buildings cool?

Critical Thinking

A **PREVIEW** Read the paragraph above. Biomimicry refers to imitating nature to solve human problems. Can you think of examples of biomimicry? Discuss with a partner.

B **MAIN IDEAS** ▶ Watch the video. Match the features of the Eastgate Centre with their functions.

1. ______ High thermal mass material
2. ______ Prickly exterior
3. ______ Low-power fan
4. ______ Chimney

a. draws in cool air during the night
b. releases hot air during the day
c. reduces heat gain during the day
d. does not change temperature much

C **DETAILS** ▶ Watch the video again. Write the missing numbers to complete the sentences.

1. Termite nests are about ____________ to ____________ degrees Fahrenheit underground.
2. The Eastgate Centre is about ____________ degrees Fahrenheit during the day.
3. It is about ____________ degrees Fahrenheit during the night.
4. It is about ____________ percent more energy efficient than similar buildings in Zimbabwe.
5. Its climate control system is ____________ percent natural.

Critical Thinking

D **REFLECT** Discuss these questions with a partner.

1. Do you know of any other green buildings like the Eastgate Centre?
2. Would a design like this work where you live? Why or why not?
3. Can you think of other energy-efficient ways to keep buildings cool?

EXPLORING WRITTEN ENGLISH

LANGUAGE FOR WRITING Using Appositives

As you learned in the Reading Skill earlier in this unit, appositives are nouns or noun phrases that give more information about another noun or noun phrase. They help writers avoid unnecessary repetition. They also help reduce the number of short sentences in an essay.

With an appositive:
"These bears still surprise me," Colleen Olfenbuttel, the state's black bear biologist, shouts over the din of traffic.

Without an appositive:
"These bears still surprise me," Colleen Olfenbuttel shouts over the din of traffic. Olfenbuttel is the state's black bear biologist.

Appositives are often separated from the rest of the sentence using commas, dashes, or colons. While commas and dashes are often interchangeable, dashes are more disruptive than commas, and are generally better when you want information to stand out and be noticed.

A NOTICE Read the text. Underline five appositives. Circle the nouns they refer to.

As a schoolboy in Puducherry, a city on India's southeastern coast, Aurofilio Schiavina loved combing the beach, with its nine kilometers of golden sand. In 1991, Schiavina left the city for higher studies in the United Kingdom. However, when he returned in 1999—the year he completed his master's degree in coastal management—the beach had vanished.

Some 30 years ago, Puducherry's sandy shore began to disappear after the construction of an ill-conceived port. The city, an enclave of Tamil Nadu state, soon became a local curiosity: the coastal town without a beach. Today, visitors no longer get to stroll on golden sand. They instead huddle around a long seawall—a stony embankment of concrete and jagged rocks.

Large rocks protect what remains of Puducherry's damaged coast.

B **APPLY** Use appositives to combine the pairs of sentences below. There may be more than one way to combine each pair of sentences.

1. Rosemary Mosco is the author of *A Pocket Guide to Pigeon Watching*. "Pigeons are biological marvels," says Mosco.

   ____

   ____

2. Some cities use reverse osmosis to create clean drinking water. Reverse osmosis is a process that filters out impurities from water.

   ____

   ____

3. The entire beach is covered by breakwaters. These are permanent stone structures that protect the coastline from the ocean.

   ____

   ____

4. The High Line is an elevated pedestrian park in New York City. It is an example of how abandoned infrastructure can be turned into green spaces.

   ____

   ____

WRITING SKILL Structuring a Problem-Solution Essay

A problem-solution essay describes a problem and then offers one or more solutions to it. Here are two ways to structure a problem-solution essay:

Structure 1

Introduction:	Provide context and describe the problem.
Thesis:	Include reference to multiple solutions.
Body paragraph 1:	Solution 1
Body paragraph 2:	Solution 2
Body paragraph 3:	Solution 3
Conclusion:	Evaluate the solutions and make a comment.

Structure 2

Introduction:	Provide context and describe the problem.
Thesis:	State your proposed solution and your reasons.
Body paragraph 1:	Reason 1
Body paragraph 2:	Reason 2
Body paragraph 3:	Reason 3
Conclusion:	Summarize the reasons that support the solution.

Choose the structure you prefer for your essay, then write a suitable thesis statement. Remember, a good thesis has the following characteristics:

- It presents the main idea clearly.
- It refers to your main supporting points.

Review this Writing Skill in Unit 1.

C Read the following pairs of thesis statements. Check (✓) the better thesis statement in each pair. Then discuss your answers with a partner.

1. ☐ a. Green spaces, including parks and gardens, have been shown to improve the lives of city residents.
   ☐ b. Increasing the number of green spaces in a city can improve the mental, physical, and social health of residents.
2. ☐ a. We can combat food insecurity in cities by offering tax credits to supermarkets, organizing mobile farmers' markets, and creating neighborhood gardens.
   ☐ b. Many cities dwellers face food insecurity because they live far away from supermarkets, and thus have inadequate access to healthy and affordable food.

D Look at the correct answers in Exercise C. Which type of problem-solution essay from the Writing Skill box does each thesis statement introduce: structure 1 or structure 2?

Thesis 1: Structure _____ Thesis 2: Structure _____

E Read the sentences from an essay about community service projects. Label the sentences **I** (introduction), **T** (thesis), **B** (body paragraph), or **C** (conclusion). Discuss with a partner how you think the body paragraphs should be ordered.

1. _____ Community service projects include members of the community who are struggling or have been left behind, and offer them a path to reintegrate with their communities.
2. _____ Community service projects lead to actual improvements in quality of life, so residents will be motivated to participate.
3. _____ Community service projects don't just address practical problems; they help people in need and build meaningful bonds that foster a sense of togetherness.
4. _____ In modern, crowded cities, residents are often distant and uncommunicative.
5. _____ Community service projects require teamwork and communication, so participants will bond and get to know each other as they carry out the work.
6. _____ Community service projects are a great way to create a sense of community in cities as they lead to actual improvements, require teamwork, and include members of the community who are struggling.

F **VOCABULARY FOR WRITING** The following words and phrases can be useful when writing about problems and solutions. Write the words and phrases next to their synonyms.

alleviate	cause for concern	implication	inadequate
opt	put into practice	strategy	viable

a. _______________ approach, method
b. _______________ ease, relieve
c. _______________ consequence, significance
d. _______________ problem, issue
e. _______________ decide, choose
f. _______________ apply, implement
g. _______________ feasible, workable
h. _______________ insufficient, flawed

WRITING TASK

GOAL You are going to write a problem-solution essay on the following topic:
Propose one or more solutions to an urban challenge.

A **BRAINSTORM** Read each category in the chart below. Write one possible problem for each category. Then note down one to three possible solutions to each problem.

Category	Problem	Possible solutions
animal-related		
health/well-being		
environmental		
safety		

B **SELECT YOUR IDEA** Review your notes in Exercise A and choose the topic you want to write about. Select the topic with the most compelling solution or solutions.

Review this Writing Skill in Unit 1.

C **WRITE A THESIS STATEMENT** Look at the two thesis statements below. Choose the format that fits your essay structure. Then write your own thesis statement.

Structure 1: Thesis statement includes three possible solutions

Although Canada's goose population is a challenge, it can be controlled by altering their habitats, disturbing their eggs, or simply chasing them away.

Structure 2: Thesis statement includes one solution and three reasons

The best solution for the goose problem in Canada is to simply harass them or chase them away, as it is humane, relatively inexpensive, and usually effective.

Your thesis statement:

___

___

___

D **OUTLINE** Use your information in Exercises A–C to complete an outline for your essay. Include supporting details and a conclusion.

OUTLINE

Introductory paragraph: What is the problem?

____

____

Thesis statement: ____

____

____

Body paragraph 1: What is the first solution/reason?

Topic sentence: ____

____

Supporting details, explanations, examples:

____

____

Body paragraph 2: What is the second solution/reason?

Topic sentence: ____

____

Supporting details, explanations, examples:

____

____

Body paragraph 3: What is the third solution/reason?

Topic sentence: ____

____

Supporting details, explanations, examples: ______________________________

____

____

Concluding paragraph: Review your main points and restate your thesis.

____

____

E **FIRST DRAFT** Use the information in your outline to write a first draft of your essay. Remember to use appositives to provide extra information about nouns and noun phrases, and to use different words and phrases to talk about problems and solutions.

F **REVISING PRACTICE** The essay below is similar to the one you are writing. Follow the steps to create a better second draft.

1. Add the sentences (a–c) in the most suitable spaces.
   a. If the geese can't see or access these areas, they are unlikely to stay.
   b. These resident geese are a challenge for some cities.
   c. Loud noises frighten geese, making them less likely to stay and build nests.
2. Now fix the following problems (a–b) with the essay.
   a. Use an appositive to combine two sentences in paragraph A.
   b. Use an appositive to combine two sentences in paragraph C.

A Canada geese were once endangered but are now thriving, with as many as 7 million living in North America. Canada geese are distinctive birds with black heads and white cheeks. They are usually migratory, meaning they travel to warmer climates during cold weather. However, some Canada geese have stopped making these long journeys, deciding instead to stay through winter. _____ While they can be aggressive, the foremost cause for concern is their droppings, which ruin grassy areas and pollute rivers and lakes. To alleviate this problem, cities have several options: they can alter geese habitats, disturb their eggs, or simply chase them away.

B One way to deter geese is through habitat modification—making areas less attractive as long-term homes. Geese are attracted to shorelines with a direct view onto open grassy areas. _____ Planting tall grasses and vegetation can therefore discourage them from nesting. Some communities have also managed to keep geese away by setting up barriers around the grassy areas. These barriers can be as simple as wires suspended about 18 inches above the ground.

C Addling is another effective way to lower goose populations. Addling is the process of preventing eggs from hatching. The eggs are coated with corn oil, or they are removed from their nests and replaced with dummy eggs. While addling is effective, it does raise ethical concerns for some. In addition, it is labor intensive, requiring three to five trained personnel to find the nest, treat or remove the eggs, and deal with the protective parents.

D Perhaps the best solution to the goose problem is harrassment, which typicallly involves making noise and chasing the geese away. _____ Common noisemakers include lawnmowers and leaf blowers. However, since the geese can get used to hearing just one sound, it is good practice to switch between a variety of noises. Geese don't like being chased either. Communities can drive them off with golf carts and dogs, which are especially effective.

E Migrating Canada geese—flying in their telltale V-formation—often bring pleasure to people on the ground. However, resident geese can pose a multitude of problems. Fortunately, communities aren't helpless. They can effectively deter geese through habitat modification, addling, and harassment.

G **REVISED DRAFT** Now use the questions below to revise your essay.

- ☐ Does your introduction provide relevant background information on the topic?
- ☐ Does your thesis state the main points of the essay?
- ☐ Do you structure your problem-solution essay in a clear, organized way?
- ☐ Do your body paragraphs include enough details to fully explain your ideas?
- ☐ Do all your sentences relate to the main idea?
- ☐ Does your concluding paragraph review the main points of the essay?

H **EDITING PRACTICE** Read the information below. Then find and correct mistakes with appositives in each sentence (1–3).

When using appositives, remember:

- In general, separate appositives from their corresponding nouns or noun phrases using commas, dashes, or colons.
- Add a comma after the appositive if the sentence has not ended.
- Do not use colons to introduce appositives that appear in the middle of sentences.

1. If you look for it, you'll find lots of wildlife here otters, snakes, and even crocodiles.
2. The apartment block a massive structure with large clear windows—is a danger to birds.
3. Geese, large birds known for their aggressive nature are a bit of a problem here.

I **FINAL DRAFT** Follow these steps to write a final draft.

1. Check your revised draft for mistakes with appositives.
2. Now use the checklist on page 248 to write a final draft. Make any other necessary changes.
3. Work in pairs and read your partner's final essay. Give feedback on each other's writing.

Canada geese in Regent's Park, London, U.K.

Review

SELF-ASSESS **Consider the language and skills you learned in this unit.**

How well can you . . . ?	Very well	Pretty well	I need improvement
use the key vocabulary from this unit	☐	☐	☐
understand how information is organized	☐	☐	☐
understand appositives	☐	☐	☐
use appositives	☐	☐	☐
structure a problem-solution essay	☐	☐	☐

A **VOCABULARY** Do you remember the meanings of these words and phrases? Look back at the unit and review the ones you don't know.

boundary	consistently AW	constraint AW	counterpart	embrace
eradicate	habitat AW	hypothesis AW	minimize AW	perceive AW
predator AW	reliance AW	reversal AW	stem from	synonymous

B **VOCABULARY EXTENSION** Complete these tasks with a partner.

1. What collocations do you remember with *constraint*? Take turns making sentences with them.
2. Take turns making sentences with the words below.

counterpart	counteract	counterattack	counterbalance

C **READING SKILL** Work with a partner. Exchange essays and identify two appositives in your partner's essay.

D **LANGUAGE FOR WRITING** Work with a partner. Write two related sentences for your partner to combine using appositives.

SELF-ASSESS **Look back at the chart above. Did you assess your skills correctly? What skills or language do you still need help with?**

ART AND BEAUTY 3

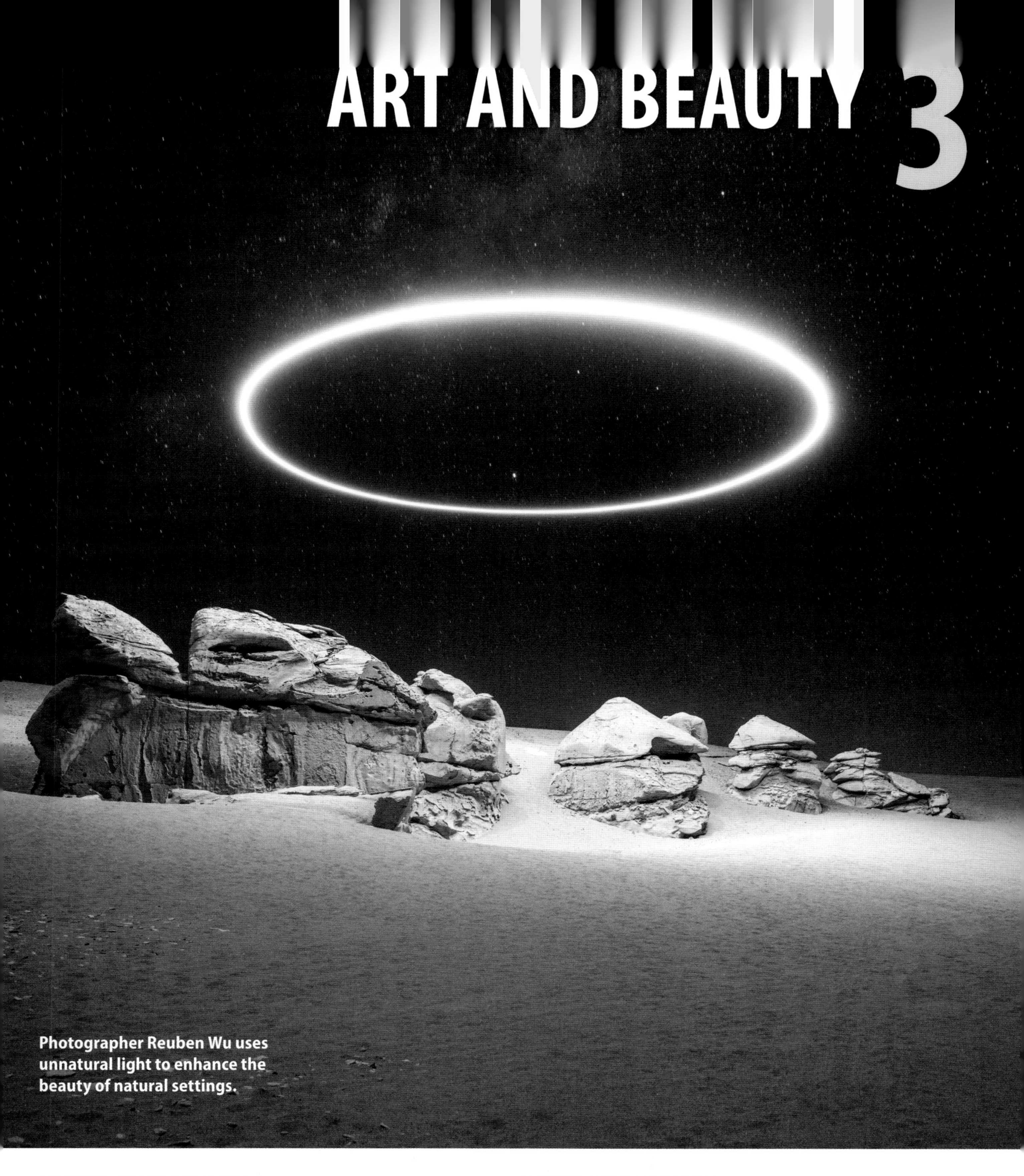

Photographer Reuben Wu uses unnatural light to enhance the beauty of natural settings.

IN THIS UNIT, YOU WILL:

- Read an article about art for three different causes
- Watch a video about a photo contest
- Write about a piece of visual art

THINK AND DISCUSS:

1. Reuben Wu used drones to create the circle of light in the photo above. In what ways does his unusual use of artificial light change the photo?
2. How would you define art? What criteria need to be met for something to be considered art?

EXPLORE THE THEME

Look at the information on these pages and answer the questions.

1. Why does the author choose the title "Art in a New Light"?
2. How does the use of light transform the landscape? How does the photograph make you feel?
3. What are some unconventional art forms that you've seen or read about?

ART in a NEW LIGHT

When we think of art, we often think of great painters and their masterpieces, sculptures carefully chiseled out of stone, or even perfectly composed photographs. For many years, these have been—and perhaps still are—the forms of visual art people are most familiar with. However, they are certainly not the only forms that exist.

Artists are constantly experimenting with new and unusual mediums, and ways to create their works—for example, by using light to transform landscapes and create stunning photographs. The boundaries of art stretch as far as the human mind will allow. As long as artists keep imagining, art will continue evolving in new and magical ways.

Photographer Reuben Wu uses bright lights and dark shadows to profoundly transform this landscape in Milos Island, Greece.

Reading

PREPARING TO READ

A **BUILD VOCABULARY** The words in blue are used in the reading passage. Read the text below. Then write the correct form of each word next to its definition.

Many of the photos of Dutch artist Berndnaut Smilde are of clouds. However, these aren't normal clouds: they're clouds he made himself, inside of buildings. They don't last very long—some disappear after only 10 seconds—but they're definitely not **fake**: they're made of water vapor in the same way actual clouds are.

Smilde's work is part of an **ongoing** art series called *Nimbus*. To create each of his pieces, he first has to find a dramatic architectural environment. He then fills the space with water vapor using a simple spray bottle before using a smoke machine to release tiny particles into the moisture-rich air. These particles **trigger** the formation of small clouds by providing the water vapor with airborne surfaces on which to condense. Once a cloud starts to form, he quickly sculpts it into shape. And when it is finally the right shape and size—usually about six feet tall and ten feet wide—he photographs it in the few seconds it exists, before it dissipates into the air. The end result is **exquisite**—a magical shot of a perfect cloud in a beautiful, seemingly impossible indoor setting.

Smilde's work provides us with an **intimate** look at something that is typically only visible from a long distance away. He likes that his photos elicit strange and **ambiguous** feelings. However, the **impression** he most wants to evoke in his viewers is not the simple wonder of clouds appearing in unusual locations, but a feeling of transience—that his wispy creations exist only for a few seconds before they're gone. "I'm not interested in trying to create something that lasts forever," he says. The art that Smilde makes disappears almost as soon as it is created, rooting each of his pieces not just in a place, but in a specific moment in time.

1. ____________________ (v) to cause a process to begin
2. ____________________ (adj) vague or unclear
3. ____________________ (adj) not real, although it appears to be
4. ____________________ (adj) still happening
5. ____________________ (adj) extremely beautiful or appealing to the senses, in a way that is carefully crafted or delicate
6. ____________________ (adj) close, or deeply personal
7. ____________________ (n) a feeling one has that remains after meeting or encountering a person or thing

B **BUILD VOCABULARY** Complete the sentences below with the correct form of the words in **blue**. Use a dictionary to help you.

analytical (adj)	**conservation** (n)	**envision** (v)	**exhibit** (n)
foremost (adj)	**imply** (v)	**interpretation** (n)	**theoretically** (adv)

1. He didn't say he was angry directly, but he strongly ________________ it.
2. The museum is full of ________________ from all over the world.
3. The meaning of the movie isn't clear. It's open to ________________.
4. Samuel doesn't make decisions based on how he feels. He prefers to take a more ________________ approach.
5. It hasn't been proven experimentally, but ________________, it's possible.
6. Sasha is an active supporter of several wildlife ________________ projects.
7. Their work styles are so different. I can't ________________ them working well together.
8. The guest of honor today is the world's ________________ authority on microbiology.

C **USE VOCABULARY** Discuss these questions with a partner.

1. Have you ever been to an art gallery or display? Which **exhibits** stood out to you? Why?
2. What are some works of art that have left a strong **impression** on you? How did they make you feel ?
3. Are some **interpretations** of art more valid than others? Why or why not? Whose interpretations should matter most?

D **PREDICT** Read the title of the reading passage. Then look at the photos. How do you think the art discussed in the passage makes an impact? Check your ideas as you read the passage.

Critical Thinking

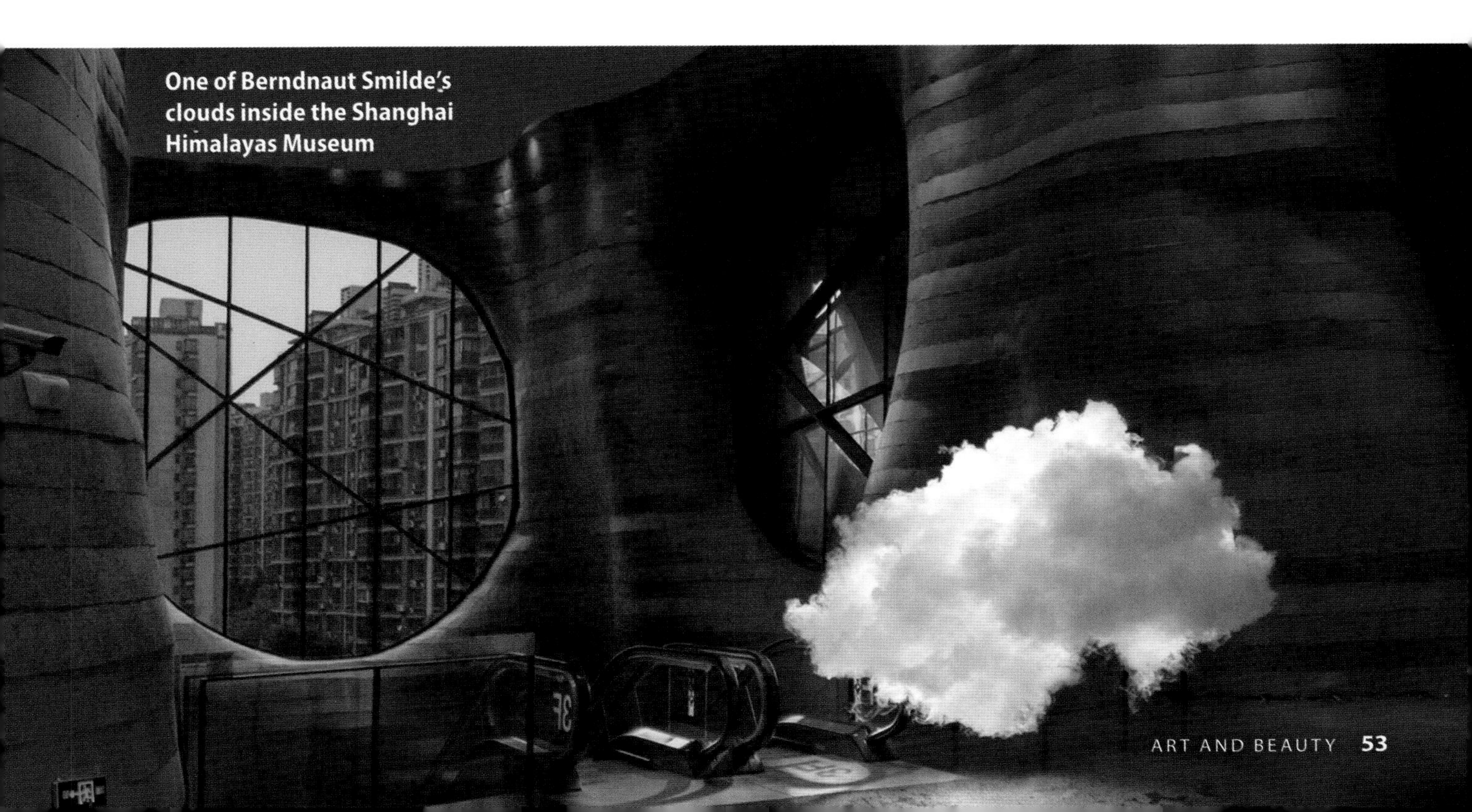

One of Berndnaut Smilde's clouds inside the Shanghai Himalayas Museum

Making an Impact Through **Art**

The eyes of the African wild dog in this painting have the ability to draw viewers in.

Art has the power to inspire and effect change, as evidenced by these three examples.

ART FOR CONSERVATION

A Stare into the eyes of *The Watcher*, British artist Sophie Green's portrait of an African wild dog, and you'll see there's something reflected. A triangular outline of a distant mountain perhaps, or maybe a termite mound on the savanna.[1] Something the animal is looking at, in any case, that draws and locks your own gaze. And by the time it does, you realize that the animal is actually now looking at you.

B The effect is striking: a strangely **intimate** moment with one of the planet's most beleaguered[2] mammals emerging from the shadows. But of course, it's not really an animal; just a very realistic painting of one.

C "That's always been my aim," says Green. "I want my artwork to be a window into another ecosystem. So people can feel they're face to face with the animal, rather than looking through a lens or at just another picture. Most people don't get that experience unless they go on a safari or an expedition. I kind of want my artwork to be that experience for them."

D Green's 14-piece exhibition—entitled *Impermanence: The Art of Conservation*—was initially **envisioned** to feature only polar animals, but Green says she quickly realized she was painting herself into a corner—conservation issues, human encroachment, and climate change affect animals all over the world, so she started to branch out. Hence images of balletic humpbacks, a great white shark, penguins, an African lion—and that African wild dog, amongst others.

E Green claims her art is not rooted in creativity. "I'm quite detail-focused, it's just my personality type. I would say I'm more **analytical**. I prefer something to be exact and precise."

F She says she paints in acrylic and adds that it's an unusual medium in hyper-realism. "It dries very quickly, but weirdly I prefer that," she says. "The way I build depth is with layer after layer after layer, and I do it quickly. It creates more of a depth perception."

G This lends itself to the hyper-real quality of her **exhibits**. "In watercolor, you work light to dark; you work dark to light in oil and acrylic. It's less a physical thing, more of a light perception. Light value on top of dark values kind of gives the **impression** of being in three dimensions."

---

[1] **Savanna** refers to large grassy plains in the African continent.
[2] If something is **beleaguered**, it is in a very difficult situation.

H Green adds that hope is an embedded theme in her collections and is also the source of her collection's **ambiguous** title.

I "The name *impermanence* is open to **interpretation**—it kind of **implies** the impermanence of certain species and ecosystems," she says. "But it could also represent the impermanence of our problems. There's a dark side, but there can also be a light side."

Adapted from "This artist's animal paintings bridge a gap between photography and reality," by Simon Ingram: National Geographic, October 2022

Simon Ingram is a writer for *National Geographic* and other well-known publications. He is also an editor and a photojournalist.

ART AS ACTIVISM

J It started as a countercultural art movement in 2001. After years studying at the Academy of Fine Arts, Kinshasa—following teachers' advice on creating work with "proper" materials, such as resin and plaster of Paris—some students in the Democratic Republic of the Congo (DRC) decided to do something different. They created art with what was in their immediate environment, including tires, exhaust pipes, foam, plastic bottles, antennas, tins that had held milk or paint, feathers, CDs, rubber slippers, and other discarded items.

K This work, the artists believed, felt familiar to a Congolese audience and spoke to a particularly egregious[3] aspect of Congolese life: waste. Waste generated locally by citizens. Waste dumped in the country by hyper-consumerist nations. Waste **triggered** by the endless extraction of resources from the DRC's earth, or the rapacious[4] collection of the same above land.

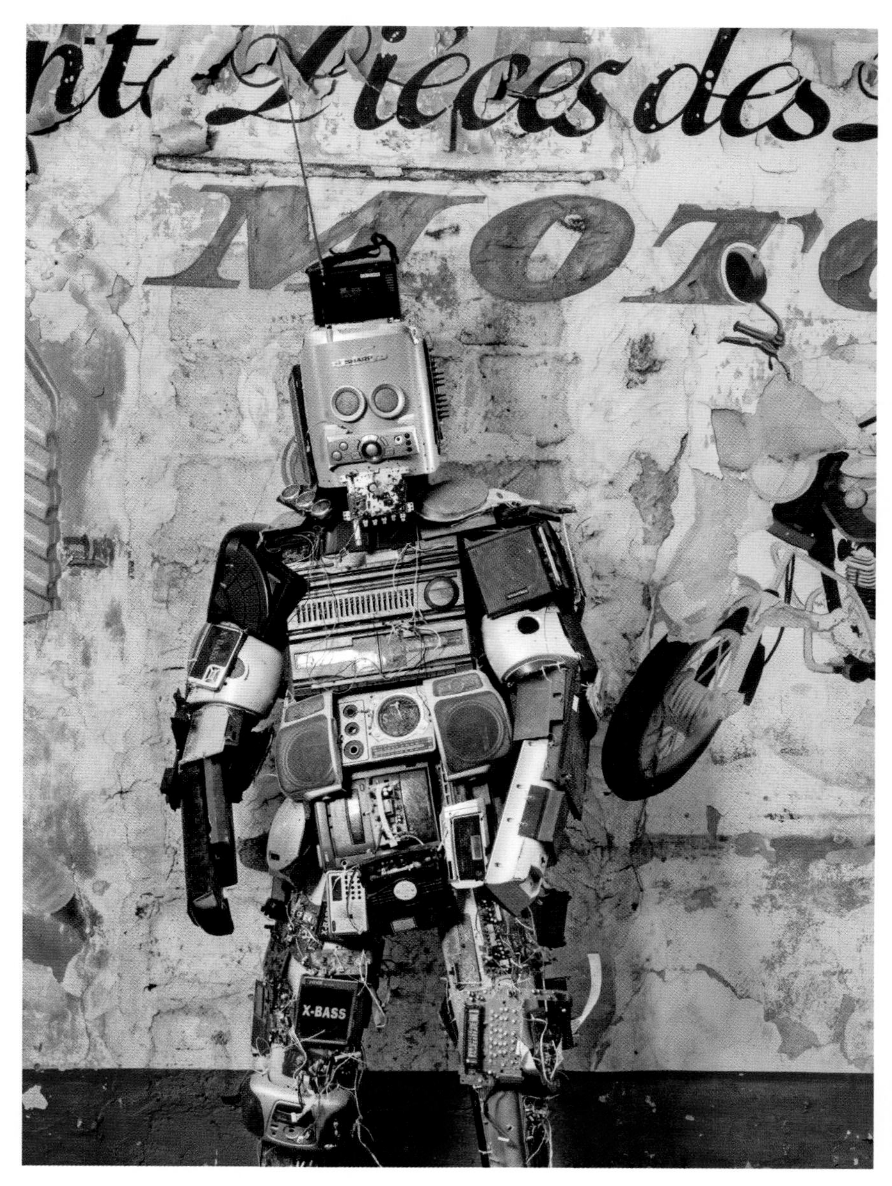

▲ ***Robot Annonce*, a wearable sculpture by Jared Kalenga made using old radio parts**

L In Kinshasa, gutters are brimming with nonrecyclable plastic bottles. Markets are awash with second- and third-hand goods, castoffs from high-income countries. In areas where international companies mine for cobalt—a precious component of smartphone batteries—frequent discharges contaminate river systems and surrounding life. By repurposing waste to create sculpture and performance art, the artists wanted to dial up the public's acuity[5] toward an **ongoing** emergency. Waste also provided the artists with an opening to comment on other fraught[6] sociopolitical issues.

---

[3] If an action is **egregious**, it is wrong and offensive.
[4] Someone who is **rapacious** is very greedy.
[5] **Acuity** refers to the sharpness of one's thoughts, vision, or hearing.
[6] If something is **fraught**, it is stressful or causes anxiety.

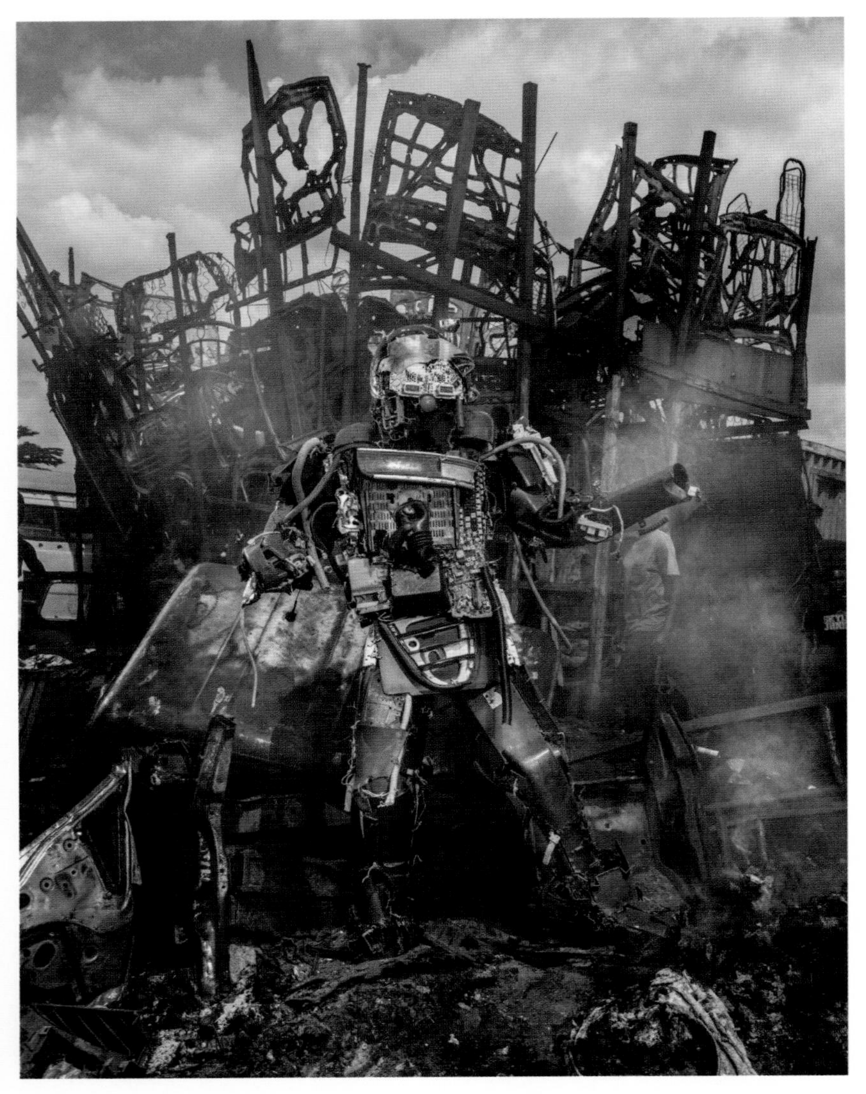

▲ **A figure made from automobile parts by Precy Numbi**

M *Robot Annonce*, for example, is a wearable sculpture by Jared Kalenga made of broken radio parts. It seeks to raise awareness about the ever-spreading reach of fake news. Precy Numbi's figure made out of automobile parts is a way of protesting the millions of "garbage cars" imported into Africa every year—secondhand vehicles that discourage the growth of the continent's own auto industry. And *Femme Électrique*, Falonne Mambu's creation made of electric wires, is double-edged. It speaks to the paucity of electric power service in the DRC and, simultaneously, what goes on in the dark: assaults and kidnappings. Mambu's inspiration for the work was drawn from periods in her life when she was homeless.

N These socially conscious creators who turn refuse into protest art "are out here pushing limits," says Yvon Edoumou, founder of the Galerie Malabo in Kinshasa. "We don't see a lot of that."

Adapted from "Transforming Trash Into Protest Art," by Ayodeji Rotinwa: National Geographic Magazine, June 2022

Ayodeji Rotinwa is a writer, editor, and journalist whose work has appeared in *National Geographic Magazine* and other well-known publications.

ART FOR SCIENCE

O The art of origami has existed in Japan since at least the 17th century. Initially, origami models were simple and used largely for ceremonial purposes. But in the mid-20th century, origami master Akira Yoshizawa helped elevate paper folding to a fine art, breathing life and personality into each creature he designed.

P In the late 1950s, Yoshizawa's delicate forms inspired Tomoko Fuse, now one of the **foremost** origami artists in Japan. Her father gave her Yoshizawa's second origami book when she was recovering from diphtheria[7] as a child. Fuse methodically crafted every model, and she's been entranced with origami ever since. "It's like magic," she says. "Just one flat paper becomes something wonderful."

Q Among her many achievements, Fuse is famous for her advances in modular[8] origami, which uses interlocking units to create models with greater flexibility and potential complexity. But she thinks of her work as less about creation than about discovering something that's already there. She describes her process as if she's watching from afar, following wherever the paper leads her. "Suddenly, beautiful patterns come out."

R Indeed, origami taps into patterns that echo throughout the universe, seen in natural forms such as leaves emerging from a bud, or insects tucking their wings. For these **exquisite** folds to become scientifically useful, however, researchers must not only discover the patterns but also understand how they work. And that requires math.

S Putting numbers to origami's intriguing patterns has long driven the work of Thomas Hull, a mathematician at Western New England University in Springfield, Massachusetts. Hull still remembers unfolding a paper crane at age 10 and marveling at the ordered creases[9] in the flat sheet. There are rules at play that allow this to work, he recalls thinking. Hull and others have spent decades working to understand the mathematics governing the world of origami.

[7] **Diphtheria** is a serious health condition that affects breathing and swallowing.
[8] If something is **modular**, it is made of components that can be easily attached or detached.
[9] **Creases** are the lines created by folding something.

Mathematicians do not fully understand the math behind the curving folds of this origami structure.

This golden disc—a light shield for telescopes in space—is designed to fold into a cylinder for launch.

T In his office are an array of models that are folded in intriguing shapes or move in unexpected ways. One is an impossible-looking sheet folded with ridges of concentric[10] squares, which cause the paper to twist in an elegant swoop known as a hyperbolic paraboloid. Another is a sheet folded in a series of mountains and valleys called the Miura-ori pattern, which collapses or opens with a single tug. Dreamed up by astrophysicist Koryo Miura in the 1970s, the pattern was used to compact the solar panels of Japan's Space Flyer Unit, which launched in 1995.

[10] **Concentric** shapes surround each other, and increase in size the further out they get.

U Origami is now pushing the limits of what scientists think is possible, particularly at the tiniest of scales. At the University of Pennsylvania's Singh Center for Nanotechnology, Marc Miskin, an electrical engineer, has been crafting an army of robots, each no bigger than a speck of dust. Such small bots require big creativity. At tiny scales, forces like friction are enormous: gears don't turn, wheels don't spin, and belts don't run. That's where origami comes in. Fold patterns will bend and move the same way at any size, at least theoretically.

V Miskin sees a world of possible ways these tiny bots could be used, from manufacturing to medicine. And the venerable[11] art form of origami has provided him and other innovators with a new tool kit to ignite the imagination and create technologies once thought impossible.

Adapted from "The Future Is Folded," by Maya Wei-Haas: National Geographic Magazine, February 2023

Maya Wei-Haas is an award-winning science writer with a particular interest in rocks and reactions. She holds a Ph.D. in Earth Science from the Ohio State University, and is a staff writer for *National Geographic Magazine.*

[11] If something is **venerable**, it is highly revered or respected.

This robot, designed to twist as it folds and unfolds, could propel itself inside our bodies to deliver drugs to specific organs.

UNDERSTANDING THE READING

A **UNDERSTAND MAIN IDEAS** How do the art forms in the reading passage make an impact? Choose the correct answers.

1. Sophie Green's hyper-realistic paintings ____.
   a. promote conservation by allowing people to connect with animals
   b. educate people about animals by highlighting their amazing traits
2. The art made from waste material in the DRC ____.
   a. raises the international profile of the country
   b. raises awareness of urgent issues
3. The art of origami ____.
   a. teaches scientists how plants and animals move in nature
   b. provides scientists with a new way to design products

B **UNDERSTAND DETAILS** Match the parts to complete the descriptions.

1. ____ The Watcher	a. highlights the spread of misinformation in the media.
2. ____ Impermanence	b. was made use of in a space vehicle.
3. ____ Robot Annonce	c. has eyes that attract the viewer's gaze.
4. ____ Femme Électrique	d. draws attention to a country's unreliable power supply.
5. ____ The Miura-ori pattern	e. is a collection of 14 paintings of animals.

C **UNDERSTAND DETAILS** Read the sentences. Choose **T** for true, **F** for false, or **NG** for not given.

1. Sophie Green prides herself on her creativity.	**T**	**F**	**NG**
2. Green prefers paints that dry quickly.	**T**	**F**	**NG**
3. Most of the waste products in the DRC are from other nations.	**T**	**F**	**NG**
4. Precy Numbi wants his country's auto industry to slow the rate of manufacturing.	**T**	**F**	**NG**
5. At large scales, gears and wheels work better than fold patterns.	**T**	**F**	**NG**

Critical Thinking

D **SUMMARIZE** Write down briefly what each person does or did. Paraphrase your answers.

1. Jared Kalenga ____________________.
2. Yvon Edoumou ____________________.
3. Akira Yoshizawa ____________________.
4. Tomoko Fuse ____________________.
5. Thomas Hull ____________________.
6. Koryo Miura ____________________.
7. Marc Miskin ____________________.

E **INFER MEANING** Find and underline the italicized words in the reading passage. Use the context to identify their meanings. Then choose the correct words to complete the definitions.

Critical Thinking

1. Paragraph D: An *encroachment* is when someone gradually **gives up / takes over** land or space.
2. Paragraph G: If something *lends itself* to a process or task, it is **suitable** / **inappropriate** for that process or task.
3. Paragraph I: The word *impermanence* refers to how everything will **eventually change / always stay the same**.
4. Paragraph K: When you make an *extraction*, you **add / remove** something.
5. Paragraph M: When we experience *paucity,* we have **too little** / **too much** of something.
6. Paragraph M: If you do two things *simultaneously*, you do them **one after the other / at the same time**.
7. Paragraph P: If you're *entranced*, you are **introduced to**/ **fascinated by** something.

CRITICAL THINKING Applying Ideas

Taking ideas from a reading passage and applying them to other contexts can help you better evaluate the information you read. For example, you can apply an author's or artist's opinion to your own experiences in order to help you better understand the opinion, or decide how much you agree or disagree with it.

F **APPLY IDEAS** Think about your own experiences and discuss the questions with a partner.

Critical Thinking

1. The reading passage states, "Art has the power to inspire and effect change." Do you agree with this statement?
2. Go online and look for examples of art that have effected change in the world. Explain how the art has impacted people or inspired them to action.
3. What are some commonly found waste items in your town or city? How could they be used to create art?
4. If you had to highlight a social issue using art, what issue would it be? What art form would you choose?

G **REFLECT** Look at the photos in the reading passage again. Discuss with a partner.

Critical Thinking

1. Which work of art do you find the most beautiful or impressive? Why?
2. Which work of art do you find the most thought-provoking? Why?
3. Which has the most power to effect change: Green's hyper-realistic paintings, the sculptures from the DRC, or the origami art form? Why?

DEVELOPING READING SKILLS

READING SKILL Using a Concept Map

A concept map is a type of graphic organizer. It helps you see how main ideas and details in a reading passage relate to each other. Taking notes in a concept map can help you remember information from a passage and understand better how the information is connected, so you can use it later in a discussion, writing assignment, or test.

When creating a concept map, start with the title or a description of your overall focus in the center box. Then place your main ideas in separate boxes branching off from the center. Sub-points should branch off from main ideas in separate boxes, and so on. Each box should contain just one idea. Be concise, use abbreviations, and leave out unimportant information.

A **USE A CONCEPT MAP** Complete the concept map with information from the reading passage.

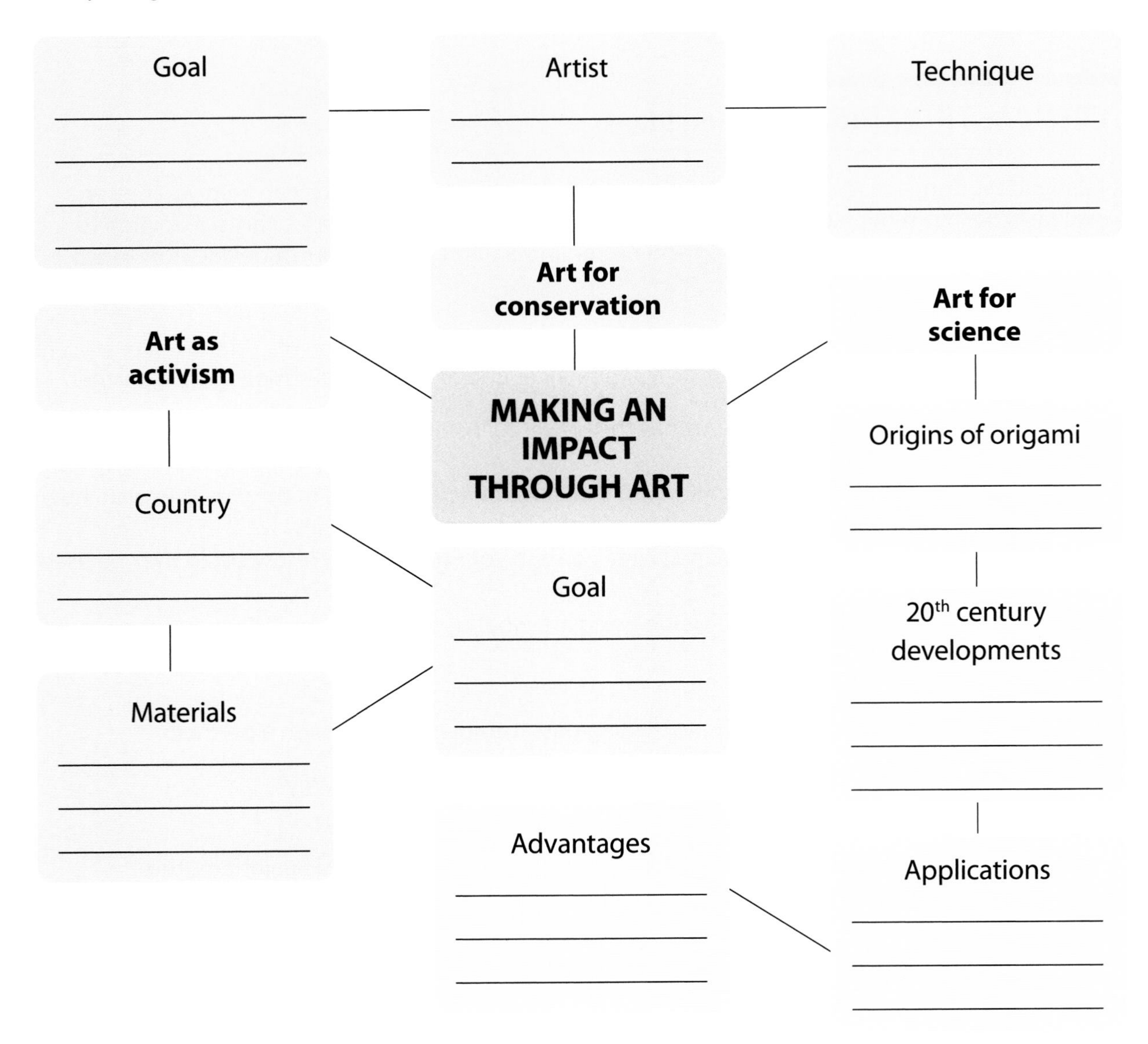

B **USE A CONCEPT MAP** Now look back at the reading passage in Unit 2. Create a concept map to summarize the key ideas relating to wildlife in cities.

VOCABULARY EXTENSION

WORD LINK *ambi-*

The prefix *ambi-* usually means *both* or *two*, though it can also imply *several* or *many*. However, not all words with the prefix have as clear a link to these meanings. Here are some examples of words starting with *ambi-*:

ambiguous: having more than one interpretation
ambidextrous: being able to use both hands equally well
ambivert: a person who is equally introverted and extroverted
ambivalent: having two very different feelings about something
ambience: the mood and feel of one's surroundings

A Complete each sentence with the correct word from the box above.

1. Both options have strong benefits and drawbacks, so I'm ________________ about the best way forward.
2. Keiko's broken arm isn't as much of a problem for her as it would be for other people because she's completely ________________.
3. The restaurant is cozy and always plays good music. I really love the ________________.
4. The author wanted to keep readers guessing, so she opted for a deliberately ________________ ending to her novel.
5. Farhad doesn't mind parties, but he loves being alone, too. He's an ________________.

WORD PARTNERS *trigger* + Noun

Here are some words and phrases that commonly partner with the verb *trigger*:

Illnesses: *asthma, allergies, heart attack*
Events: *investigation, attack, explosion*
Feelings: *memory, need, thought*
Reactions: *reaction, response, backlash*

B Complete each sentence with the correct form of a word from the box above. More than one answer may be possible.

1. Old songs often trigger ____________________ of people and places from long ago.
2. Small particles make my skin itch, so a day in a dusty city will definitely trigger my ____________________.
3. The chemical reaction triggered a(n) ____________________ that destroyed several vehicles in the area.
4. The mayor's unpopular decision triggered a(n) ____________________ from protesters.

Video

A woman uses her phone on a train in Hong Kong, China.

Photo Contest

Each year, National Geographic invites amateur photographers to enter their photos into a competition. Thousands are submitted every year, but only a handful of winners are chosen, including Brian Yen, whose grand prize-winning photo you see above.

Critical Thinking

A **PREVIEW** Look at the photo above. Is there anything you like or dislike about it? Does it tell you a story, or leave you with any strong feelings? Discuss with a partner.

B **MAIN IDEAS** ▶ Watch the video. What aspects did the judges consider when assessing the photos? Check (✓) the five correct answers.

- ☐ a. It focuses on one main element.
- ☐ b. It touches the viewer emotionally.
- ☐ c. It is good technically.
- ☐ d. It has good composition.
- ☐ e. It looks natural.
- ☐ f. It shows something in a new way.
- ☐ g. It makes good use of color and light.
- ☐ h. It captures something rare.

C **DETAILS** ▶ Watch the video again. Match the photos with the statements.

1. _____ basketball court
2. _____ swimming pool
3. _____ owl
4. _____ wildebeests
5. _____ train

a. It took time for the judges to appreciate it.
b. The judges had divided opinions about it.
c. The judges felt it had a calming effect.
d. A judge felt that it offered a new perspective.
e. The judges felt it wasn't good enough technically.

Critical Thinking

D **APPLY** Consider the qualities of a good photo mentioned by the judges. Which photo in the video do you think is best? Discuss your choice with a partner.

EXPLORING WRITTEN ENGLISH

LANGUAGE FOR WRITING Using Relative Clauses

Relative clauses give more information about nouns. They are a good way to add details and vary your sentence types. In addition to *who*, *which*, and *that*, you can also introduce relative clauses using *when*, *where*, and *whose*. There are two types of relative clauses:

Restrictive relative clauses give essential information about a noun. If you take away the clause, the sentence doesn't fulfill its main function as essential details are lost. For example:

Mambu's inspiration for the work was drawn from periods in her life when she was homeless.

Nonrestrictive relative clauses give nonessential or additional information. Even if you remove the clause, the sentence still works. For example:

Dreamed up by astrophysicist Koryo Miura in the 1970s, the pattern was used to compact the solar panels of Japan's Space Flyer Unit, which launched in 1995.

Relative clauses can appear in the middle or at the end of sentences:

The person who took the photo above was Brian Yen.

Brian Yen, whose photo you see above, was one of the winners.

One of the winners was Brian Yen, whose photo you see above.

When using nonrestrictive relative clauses, remember:

- Use a comma before nonrestrictive relative clauses at the end of sentences.
- Use commas before and after nonrestrictive relative clauses in the middle of a sentence.
- Use *which* rather than *that* when referring to objects in nonrestrictive clauses.

See the Grammar Reference on page 249

A NOTICE Read the sentences (a–d) below. Then answer the questions (1–3).

a. Japan is the land where origami first originated.
b. Fuse was influenced by Yoshizawa, whose work elevated origami to a fine art.
c. The Miura-ori pattern was put to scientific use in 1995, when Japan's Space Flyer Unit was launched.
d. Robots that make use of fold patterns can theoretically work at tiny scales.

1. What noun does each underlined clause describe?
2. What words are used to introduce the underlined clauses?
3. Which sentences still fulfill their main functions even with the underlined clauses removed? Why?

B APPLY Combine each pair of sentences using restrictive or non-restrictive relative clauses. More than one answer may be possible.

1. Sophie Green prefers to use acrylic paint. Her paintings are hyper-realistic.

____

____

2. Berndnaut Smilde photographs indoor clouds. He creates them using water vapor and a smoke machine.

____

____

3. The impact of waste is felt strongly by the Congolese artists. Their work brings attention to the issue.

____

____

4. Vincent van Gogh was strongly influenced by Japanese art. He made copies of several Japanese prints and paintings.

____

____

C **REFLECT** Think of three artists, art forms, or works of art. Write sentences about how they make you feel, or what you find interesting or admirable about them. Use a relative clause in each sentence.

1. ____

____

2. ____

____

3. ____

____

WRITING SKILL Supporting a Thesis

Review this Writing Skill in Units 1 and 2

As you read in Units 1 and 2, a thesis statement expresses the main idea of an entire essay. Each body paragraph in an essay then provides details for and explanations of this main idea. To effectively support a thesis statement, do the following:

- Describe one key point of your thesis in the topic sentence of each body paragraph.
- Order your body paragraphs to match the order of ideas in your thesis statement.
- Provide enough details (facts and examples) to develop the idea of each topic sentence.

D Read this excerpt from an introduction to an essay on Frank Lloyd Wright's famous building Fallingwater. Underline the key concepts in the thesis statement.

The term organic architecture, which was coined by the American architect Frank Lloyd Wright, applies to structures that create a sense of harmony with the natural world. Fallingwater, a house designed by Wright in 1935, is a perfect example of organic architecture due to the way it fits with its natural surroundings and its use of natural building materials.

Thesis Statement

Fallingwater, designed by Frank Lloyd Wright

E Check (✓) the two best topic sentences for the body paragraphs of the essay.

☐ a. The way Fallingwater is assimilated into its natural environment is an example of organic architecture.

☐ b. Located in the Laurel Highlands in southwest Pennsylvania, Fallingwater is surrounded by trees, streams, and waterfalls.

☐ c. Fallingwater was built by local craftspeople who collected sandstone and other materials native to the area.

☐ d. The organic approach is also evident in the way Wright used natural materials to build Fallingwater.

F Read the notes below. Which of the two correct topic sentences in Exercise E does each note best support? Write the correct letter (a–d).

1. _____ exterior color matches color of surrounding rocks
2. _____ built from stones found in local area
3. _____ living room fireplace incorporates boulders from a nearby building site
4. _____ house is built around a tree

G **VOCABULARY FOR WRITING** The following words and expressions can be useful when writing about visual art forms. Match each word to its definition. Use a dictionary to help you.

1. _____ balance — a. the quality of being delicate, or not immediately obvious
2. _____ composition — b. an idea that recurs and extends through a piece of art
3. _____ theme — c. the material of artistic expression, such as paint or clay
4. _____ medium — d. the even distribution of elements throughout a piece of art
5. _____ striking — e. noticeable; impressive
6. _____ subtlety — f. the framing and arrangement of the elements in a piece of art

WRITING TASK

GOAL You are going to write an essay on the following topic:

Evaluate a piece of visual art (e.g., a painting, photograph, or sculpture) using different criteria.

A **BRAINSTORM** Choose a piece of visual art. Evaluate the piece of art using the two criteria below, as well as three more criteria of your own choosing. Select your criteria from the Video section or elsewhere in this unit, or research *aesthetic criteria for evaluating art* online.

Name of piece of art:

Type of visual art:

Medium:

Theme:

Aesthetic Criteria	Details
1. Skill and Technique	
2. Composition	
3.	
4.	
5.	

Review this Writing Skill in Unit 1

B **ORGANIZE IDEAS** Look at your chart in Exercise A. Circle the three criteria you have the most to write about. Then list them below in the order you will write about them in your essay.

1. ______________________________
2. ______________________________
3. ______________________________

C **WRITE A THESIS STATEMENT** Write a thesis statement for your essay. Include in your thesis your three criteria in Exercise B.

____

____

____

D **PLAN** Use your information in Exercises A–C to complete an outline for your essay. Remember that each topic sentence should support a reason, example, or argument made in your thesis statement.

OUTLINE

Notes for introduction: ____________________

____

Thesis statement: ____________________

____

____

Body paragraph 1:

Topic sentence: ____________________

____

Details: ____________________

____

____

Body paragraph 2:

Topic sentence: ____________________

____

Details: ____________________

____

____

Body paragraph 3:

Topic sentence: ____________________

____

Details: ____________________

____

____

Notes for conclusion: ____________________

____

____

E **FIRST DRAFT** Use the information in your outline to write a first draft of your essay. Remember to use restrictive and nonrestrictive relative clauses to vary your sentence types and make your essay more interesting.

F **REVISING PRACTICE** The essay below is similar to the one you are writing. It uses a set of criteria to evaluate a building. Follow the steps to create a better second draft.

1. Add the sentences (a–c) in the most suitable spaces.
    a. The entire library is on one level, and it has an open design—there are no interior walls or dividers.
    b. The large windows are framed in copper, which contrasts interestingly against the light gray color of the granite structure.
    c. It is known to be resistant to the effects of both the environment and pollution.
2. Now fix the following problems (a–c) with the essay.
    a. Fix a problem with a nonrestrictive relative clause in paragraph B.
    b. Fix a problem with a nonrestrictive relative clause in paragraph D.
    c. Delete an unrelated idea in paragraph D.

A What makes a building great? For many, aesthetics are most important. However, according to architect Marcus Vitruvius Pollio of ancient Rome, there are two more principles to consider: durability (how strong and long-lasting a structure is) and function (how well the structure serves its purpose). In my city, one building stands out for the way it satisfies all three criteria. The Rostonville Library is an example of great architecture because it is durable, functional, and aesthetically pleasing.

B The Rostonville Library is extremely durable because it is built primarily of granite, that is an extremely strong material. _____ Granite structures are stable and resistant to vibrations too, so the Rostonville Library will likely be able to withstand earthquakes and other disasters. Because of the sturdy materials used to build the library, there is little doubt that the building will be able to stand the test of time.

C The Rostonville Library is also great at fulfilling its main function, which is to provide free access for members of the community to a variety of print and digital information. The library is designed to be easily accessible to all. _____ In addition, large windows around the facility let in plenty of natural light, which makes reading and locating different sections within the library easy.

D Finally, the Rostonville Library is beautiful. Aesthetically pleasing details make it attractive, both inside and out. _____ An array of plants which are all native to the area and allowed to grow freely, cascade down the sides of the building from a rooftop garden. These features soften the structure's lines and help it blend into its surroundings. The library was built next to the city park, which is also home to many native plants.

E Because of its durability, functionality, and beauty, the Rostonville Library is a great structure. By adhering to Vitruvius's principles, the building helps make its urban surroundings pleasant. It provides peace, comfort, and joy to the people who use it, and it will continue to do so for many years to come.

G **REVISED DRAFT** Now use the questions below to revise your essay.

- ☐ Does your introduction provide relevant background information on the topic?
- ☐ Does your thesis state the main points of the essay?
- ☐ Do your body paragraphs have clear and concise topic sentences?
- ☐ Do your body paragraphs include enough details to fully explain your ideas?
- ☐ Do you use restrictive and nonrestrictive relative clauses correctly?
- ☐ Do all your sentences relate to the main idea?
- ☐ Does your concluding paragraph have a summary statement and a final thought?

H **EDITING PRACTICE** Read the information below. Then find and correct mistakes with nonrestrictive relative clauses in each sentence (1–3).

> When using nonrestrictive relative clauses, remember to:
> - use one comma before a nonrestrictive relative clause that appears at the end of a sentence.
> - use two commas, one before and one after, when the nonrestrictive relative clause appears in the middle of a sentence.
> - use *which* (not *that*) for objects in nonrestrictive relative clauses.

1. This is an excellent example of good composition which is the way elements are arranged in a piece of visual art.
2. The importing of old second-hand vehicles, that is a big problem throughout the African continent, discourages the growth of the DRC's own auto industry.
3. Origami, which is an artform involving the folding of paper to make models originated in Japan in the 17th century.

I **FINAL DRAFT** Follow these steps to write a final draft.

1. Check your revised draft for mistakes with relative clauses.
2. Now use the checklist on page 248 to write a final draft. Make any other necessary changes.
3. Work in pairs and read your partner's final essay. Give feedback on each other's writing.

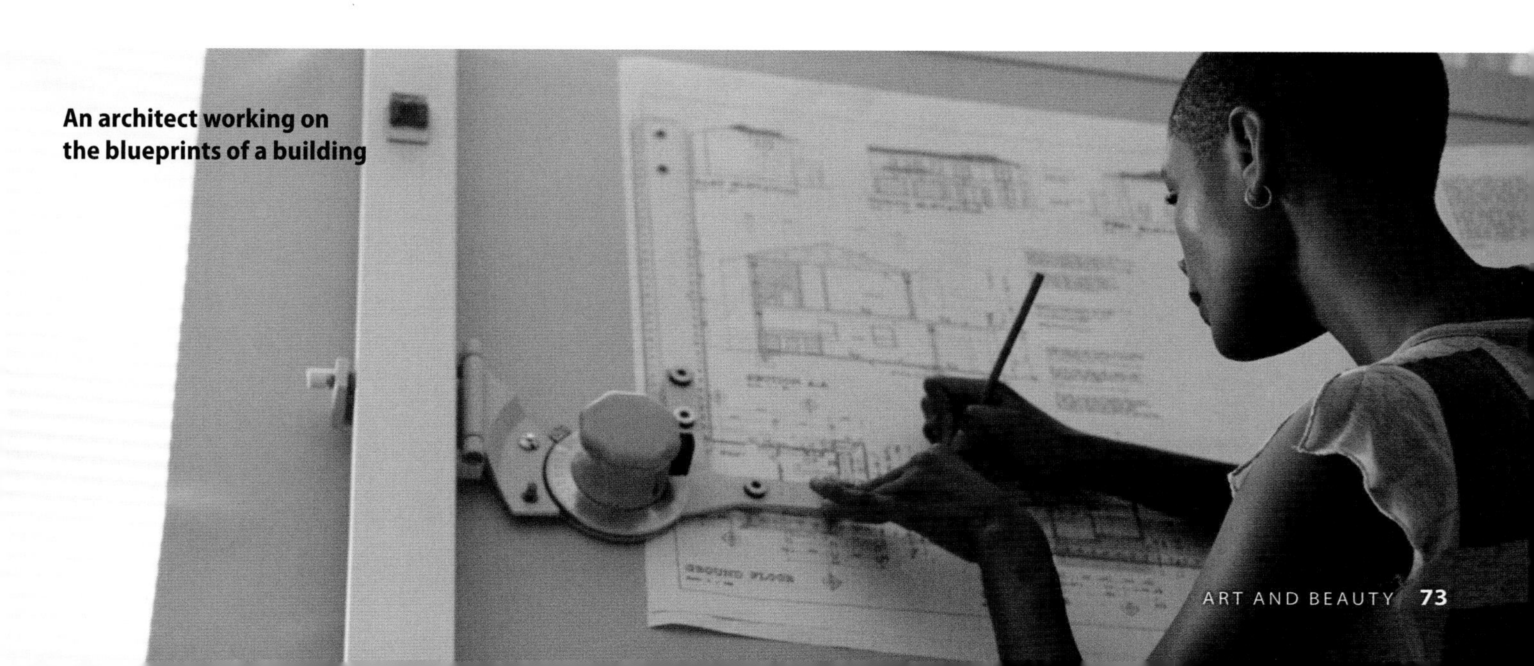

An architect working on the blueprints of a building

Review

SELF-ASSESS **Consider the language and skills you learned in this unit.**

How well can you . . . ?	Very well	Pretty well	I need improvement
use the vocabulary from this unit	☐	☐	☐
apply ideas	☐	☐	☐
use a concept map	☐	☐	☐
use relative clauses	☐	☐	☐
support a thesis	☐	☐	☐

A **VOCABULARY** Do you remember the meanings of these words? Look back at the unit and review the ones you don't know.

ambiguous AW	analytical AW	conservation AW	envision	exhibit AW
exquisite	fake	foremost	imply AW	impression
interpretation AW	intimate	ongoing AW	theoretically AW	trigger AW

B **VOCABULARY EXTENSION** Complete these tasks with a partner.

1. Take turns making sentences with the words in the box.

ambidextrous	ambience	ambiguous	ambivalent

2. What are some collocations with the verb *trigger*? Take turns making sentences with them.

C **READING SKILL** Make a concept map of your essay on a separate piece of paper. Share it with a partner.

D **LANGUAGE FOR WRITING** Write two sentences about a piece of art from this unit. In your first sentence, use a restrictive relative clause. In your second sentence, use a nonrestrictive relative clause.

1. ____

____

2. ____

____

SELF-ASSESS **Look back at the chart above. Did you assess your skills correctly? What skills or language do you still need help with?**

RETHINKING TRANSPORT 4

A train carries passengers over a street in Wuppertal, Germany.

IN THIS UNIT, YOU WILL:

- Read an article about the business of air travel
- Watch a video about driverless transportation
- Write about two companies from the same industry

THINK AND DISCUSS:

1. The photo above shows a suspension railway in Wuppertal, Germany. What advantages do suspension railways have over traditional trains or trams?
2. What changes to public and private transportation would you like to see in your town or city?

EXPLORE THE THEME

Look at the information on these pages and answer the questions.

1. In what ways are electric cars better than gas-powered cars?
2. What factors are leading to the increase in demand of electric cars?
3. Would you choose an EV over a gas-powered car? Why or why not?

Going Electric

The automobile industry is on the verge of change. The internal combustion engine that drives most vehicles has allowed us to transform the world, but its toxic by-products have left a heavy mark on the health of the planet.

CHARGING AHEAD

In 2021, EVs accounted for just 4 percent of global car sales. This will change with increased government support, improvements in battery cost and technology, more public and private charging ports, and new electric versions of popular car and truck models.

MORE CHARGING PORTS

More charging stations are being built. Ports are being added to existing gas stations.

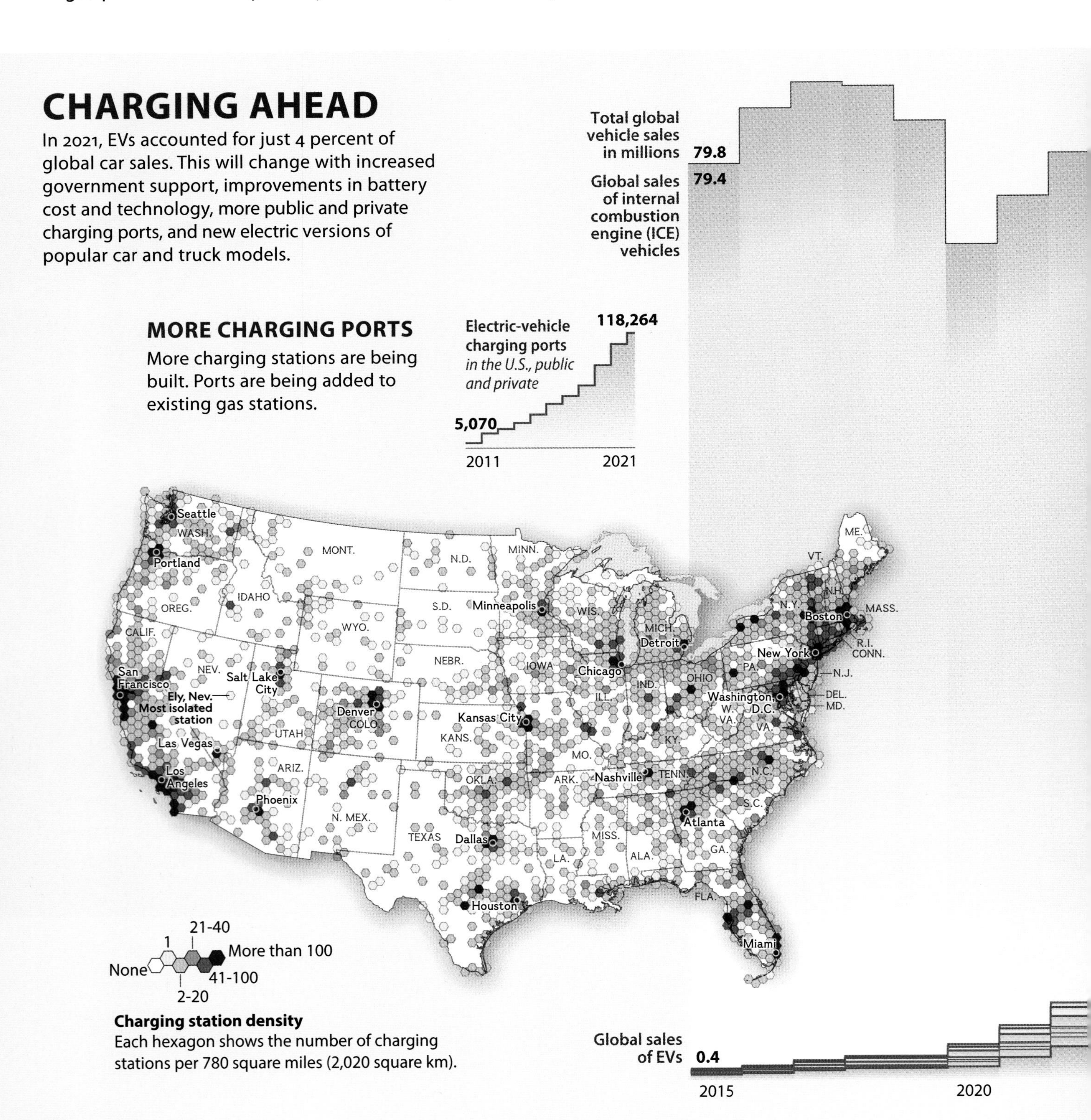

Charging station density
Each hexagon shows the number of charging stations per 780 square miles (2,020 square km).

Fortunately, a promising alternative has arrived. Electric vehicles (EVs) produce no emissions and offer greater fuel efficiency than their gas-powered predecessors. In addition, EVs are able to use energy generated from greener renewable sources.

While more needs to be done to make battery manufacturing cleaner, the advantages of EVs are hard to deny—so expect to see a surge in EV sales in the years to come.

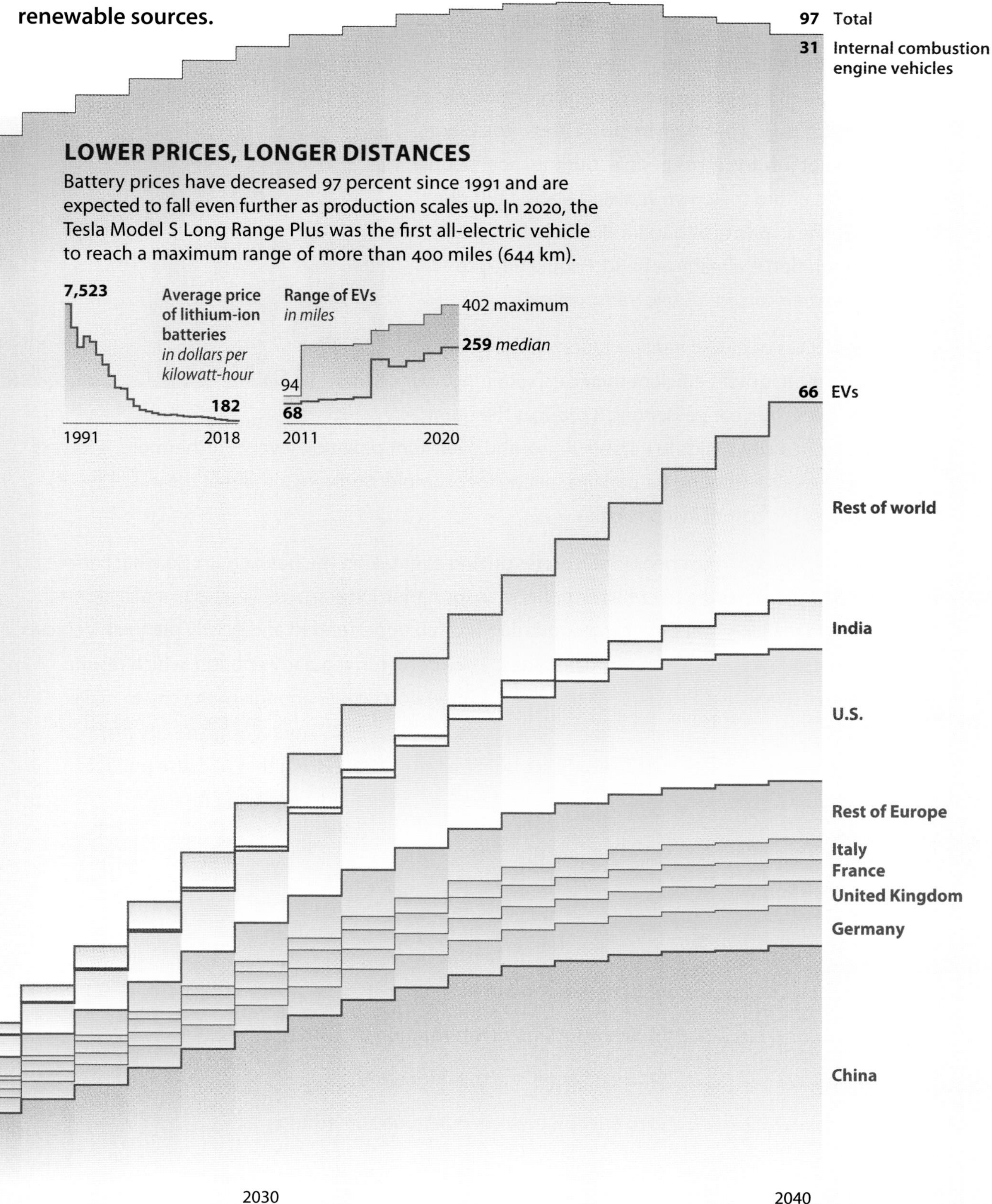

Reading

PREPARING TO READ

A **BUILD VOCABULARY** The words in **blue** are used in the reading passage. Read the text below. Then write the correct form of each word next to its definition.

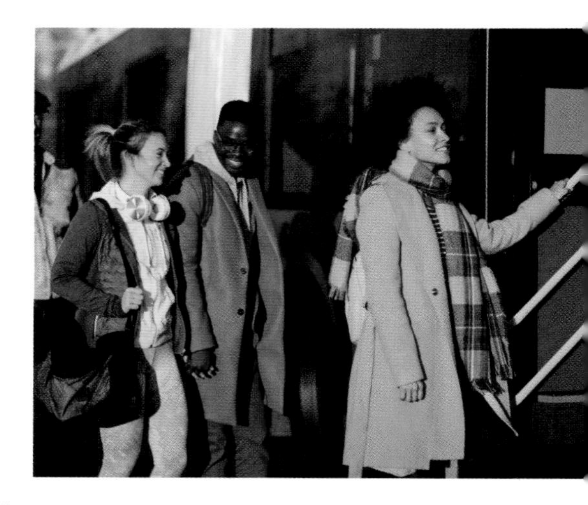

Nobody likes a traffic jam. They lead to delays, **disruptions**, pollution, and stress. Unfortunately, congestion is a problem in most cities—the places with not just the most people, but the most people able to afford their own vehicles. Many cities don't have the **capacity** to handle all this traffic. Luckily, the solution is already at hand: People need to **swap** their cars for public transportation.

Advocates of public transportation cite several benefits. It is more efficient than cars, requiring much less fuel per passenger. It reduces the number of cars in a city, which lowers air, noise, and even light pollution levels. Furthermore, it lowers stress levels—fighting for parking spaces, for example, becomes a thing of the past. Plus, it reduces the cost of living in cities.

Clearly, though, most people still prefer driving over taking the bus or train. So what can we do to **urge** more people to embrace public transportation? The answer is simple: make it better. The sad reality is that public transportation is often underfunded and poorly planned. Vehicles are sometimes old and under-maintained. They don't run regularly enough, which results in **excessive** waiting times. And their routes often don't cover enough of the city to make them viable. It's important that public transportation officials work **alongside** city planners and invest sufficiently in solving these problems. It's worth noting that because public transportation is also a source of revenue, a good system ends up paying for itself.

1. ________________ (adj) too much
2. ________________ (n) the maximum something can contain or do
3. ________________ (prep) together with
4. ________________ (n) a person who publicly supports a cause or an idea
5. ________________ (n) the disturbing or interruption of a process
6. ________________ (v) to exchange one thing for another
7. ________________ (v) to encourage someone to do something

B **BUILD VOCABULARY** Complete the sentences below with the correct form of the words in **blue**. Use a dictionary to help you.

aviation (n)	**campaign** (n)	**catch on** (phr)	**committee** (n)
competitive (adj)	**conversion** (n)	**dilemma** (n)	**elite** (adj)

1. Members of the ________________ class in this city are unlikely to switch from cars to buses and trains, no matter how much public transportation improves.
2. Pilots and airport staff are just some of the people working in the ________________ industry.
3. Car makers who sell only gas-powered vehicles will struggle to remain ________________.
4. If prices continue to fall at this rate, it won't take long for EVs to ________________ in this city.
5. They've assembled a(n) ________________ to replan bus routes in the city.
6. The mayor launched a(n) ________________ aimed at getting people to drive less.
7. The ________________ of grain into biofuels such as ethanol is a relatively simple process.
8. Biofuels present us with a(n) ________________: should we be turning food into fuel?

C **USE VOCABULARY** Note answers to the questions below. Then discuss with a partner.

1. Are there any **committees** you can join in your school or workplace? What are their goals?

____

____

2. How often do **disruptions** to public transportation occur in your town or city?

____

____

3. In a world that's becoming increasingly environmentally conscious, what are some things car makers could do to remain **competitive**?

____

____

D **PREDICT** Work with a partner. What are some things the aviation industry can do to make flying greener? Check your ideas as you read the passage.

Critical Thinking

____

____

____

____

Green Air Travel

By Sam Howe Verhovek

A model of a Flying-V airplane undergoes wind tunnel testing at the Delft University of Technology in the Netherlands.

Can the aviation industry reinvent itself to make flying less harmful to the environment?

A As someone who loves to fly and never tires of looking at landmarks below, clouds alongside, or stars above, I can't begrudge anyone the joy of flight. At the same time, any journey in the skies warms the planet. Some experts peg air travel as the source of up to 5 percent of the human contribution to global warming today.

B That figure will likely climb as passenger and freight[1] air traffic grows, and as other activities like land transportation and construction become more energy efficient. All this has led to a movement urging people not to fly or at least to fly a lot less, a campaign with a name that has caught on in Europe and is becoming familiar elsewhere: *flygskam*, a Swedish term best translated as "flight shame."

C "Hour for hour, there is just about nothing you as an individual can do that's worse for the health of the planet than to sit on an airplane," says Peter Kalmus, an astrophysicist turned NASA climate scientist who hasn't flown since 2012. "The hard fact that most people haven't accepted yet is that we don't need to fly, and if you truly accept that we are in a climate emergency, you shouldn't fly."

D In July, France adopted a ban on all domestic air trips that can be made by train in less than two and a half hours. In the United Kingdom, the official Committee on Climate Change jolted the elite world of the most active fliers by proposing "a ban on air miles and frequent flyer loyalty schemes that incentivize excessive flying."

E However, aviation leaders contend that shaming flight is not the answer—greening it is.

F "Aviation is an essential part of the global economy, so our challenge is reducing emissions and decarbonizing aviation, not preventing people who want to travel from traveling," says Sean Newsum, the director of aviation sustainability strategy for Boeing. "That's really our foundational belief as an industry at this point."

G Among the potential paths to green salvation for air travel, the quickest might be down a gravel road deep in the woods of central Georgia, leading to a hulking complex called the Freedom Pines Biorefinery. There I meet Curt Studebaker, a lanky, friendly young chemical engineer who is in the business of turning waste—all kinds of waste—into sustainable aviation fuel (SAF).

H "The amazing thing is, once you get it right, it's really a better fuel even than Jet A," the standard kerosene fuel in U.S. aviation, Studebaker tells me. "It's actually cleaner."

I For now, SAFs are still blended with standard fuel. But they are cast as the giant first step toward shrinking aviation's carbon footprint.[2] The challenges? First, it's very expensive. This alternative fuel costs two to six times more than

[1] **Freight** refers to cargo that is transported in bulk by land, air, or sea.
[2] **Carbon footprint** refers to the amount of greenhouse gases a person, group, or industry releases into the atmosphere.

Researchers at the Technical University of Munich study how algae might be used to create biofuels.

kerosene, and although more flights are using SAFs, it all adds up to little more than a drop in the bucket—well under 0.1 percent of the 95 billion gallons of fuel the industry used in 2019. Second, the industry can't rely on the easiest, cheapest sources for **conversion**: crops. If fuel producers were to gobble up land and water more urgently needed for food, air travel would simply trade one environmental black eye for another.

J Proponents contend that if SAF production were built to the scale needed to serve the bulk of aviation needs, the price would drop precipitously,[3] becoming **competitive** with kerosene. But getting to scale is a classic chicken-or-egg **dilemma**. Unless there's demand, supply won't grow; but because the current supply is so small and costly, it's hard to stimulate demand. That's where the problem becomes political: the solution could be a carbon tax on kerosene or a requirement that SAFs account for a percentage of all aviation fuel.

K "Basically, there has to be a humongous ramp-up to SAFs," says Paul Stein, chief technology officer of Rolls-Royce, the British manufacturer whose next-generation UltraFan, the biggest and one of the most efficient jet engines ever, is designed to use the alternative fuel. "But industry is generally behind a SAF mandate.[4] And certainly our position as a company is, yes! We need more SAFs. It would be a huge contribution to the planet."

---

[3] If something drops **precipitously**, it drops quickly and by a large amount.
[4] A **mandate** is an official ruling or order passed on from a high authority.

L At Airbus headquarters in the south of France, there is a flying machine made of composite materials[5] resembling no airliner that has ever taken to the skies, at least outside of science fiction movies or UFO[6] sightings. The plane, known as Maveric, is a model aircraft with a 3.2-meter wingspan. For Airbus, Maveric's design could hold the answer to this intriguing question: Is there a more efficient—greener—way to design an airliner?

M For all kinds of reasons, the modern aircraft manufacturing industry does not easily lend itself to the **disruption** that can so suddenly upend conventional thinking in other industries. A true game changer of an airliner will take many, many years to develop and more years to weather the gauntlet of safety tests involved in certification for commercial service.

N Yet the so-called blended wing body design employed by Maveric—although with major technical challenges to overcome—could yield as much as a 40 percent reduction in carbon emissions compared with today's planes. The main advantage of the streamlined design is that the entire aircraft functions much like a wing, reducing drag[7] and making it much easier to generate lift. In the Netherlands, researchers at the Delft University of Technology used similar principles in designing Flying-V, an aircraft that looks very much like a boomerang.[8]

---

[5] **Composite materials** are made by combining materials with different properties.
[6] **UFO** stands for "unidentified flying object." The term refers to aircraft that are unrecognizable or thought to be from outer space.
[7] **Drag** is the wind resistance that airplanes and other vehicles experience when moving at speed.
[8] **Boomerangs** are small V-shaped objects from Australia that return when thrown correctly.

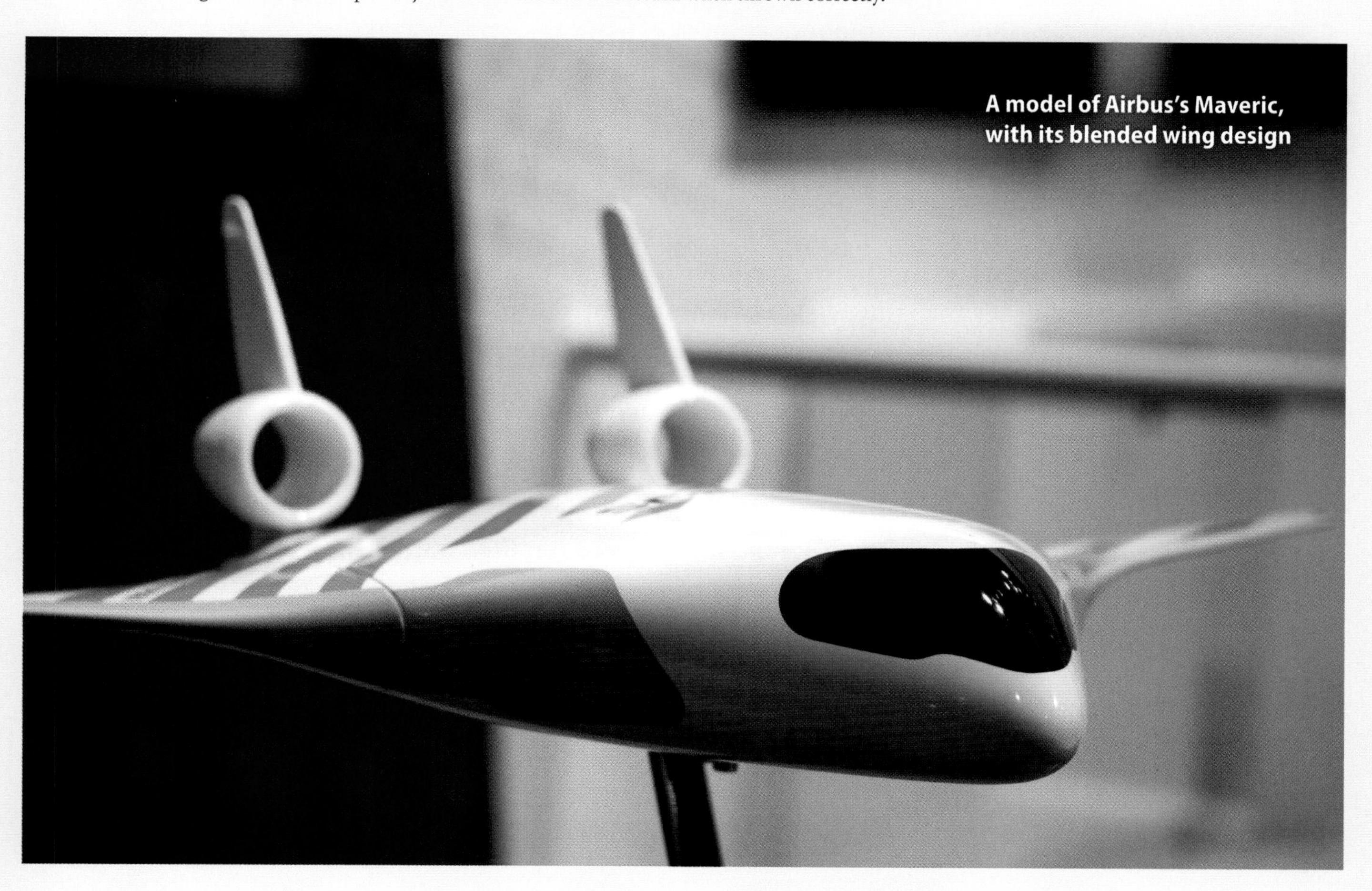
A model of Airbus's Maveric, with its blended wing design

O In 2020, Airbus went a step further and created a major stir in the industry by announcing it was working on a line of aircraft with a stunning capability: zero-emission flight. A Maveric variant and two smaller tube-and-wing airliners, it said, would operate on hydrogen fuel. The main by-product? Water vapor.

P As is true with electric automobiles, zero emission doesn't necessarily mean zero pollution. Just as it matters where the electricity comes from to charge the car's battery, Airbus's approach begs the question of how to create and store hydrogen fuel.

Q Most hydrogen used today comes from fossil fuels. But so-called green hydrogen, in which clean electricity is used to separate water into hydrogen and oxygen, is the holy grail. **Advocates** say that technological progress and scaling up will bring green hydrogen its day in the sky.

R In the central California farm town of Hollister, a stubby banana-yellow aerial vehicle with 13 rotors whirls around. It has no pilot.

S The self-flying electric plane may be an oddity today, but its inventors expect it to be a commonplace feature of tomorrow—the aerial taxi. As more than one evangelist for the urban air mobility industry puts it, "Think: Uber meets Tesla in the sky."

T Their company, called Wisk, is just one of many aspiring entrants, although with major chops: It has financial backing from Boeing and Kitty Hawk, the aviation start-up founded by Google's Larry Page. Its vision is a world in which taking a flying taxi will be as easy and affordable as an automobile ride is today—and safer to boot.

U "This is not the Wild West," Gary Gysin, Wisk's chief executive, tells me when I visit the company's hangar.[9] "We will absolutely meet the incredibly stringent safety standards already set for the aviation industry. We have to—nobody's flying anywhere until the FAA (the Federal Aviation Administration) says so."

V Just when this particular industry might take off is, well, up in the air. Gysin says the industry likely will start by shuttling people among airports and "vertiports," which might be a landing pad atop a Manhattan apartment building, or a parking lot in a Los Angeles suburb.

W Just how strong a public backlash to the idea of air taxis there might be is hard to say. But electric-powered flight, while still severely limited by battery weight and **capacity**, is happening on another front. One intriguing approach is in British Columbia, Canada, where a commuter seaplane operator is retrofitting[10] its workhorse fleet of 60-year-old de Havilland Beavers and Otters, **swapping** out gas-fired piston engines for electric motors.

[9] A **hangar** is a place where airplanes are kept.

[10] **Retrofitting** is the act of customizing a finished product by installing new parts, in a way not intended by the manufacturer.

Harbour Air's battery-powered sea plane gets its power from a hydro-electric dam.

x Greg McDougall, Harbour Air's founder and chief executive, piloted the December 2019 initial test run on the first such plane. "We're proud to be the first airline in the world to offer completely clean electric flight, fueled by our province's sustainable hydropower," McDougall tells me. "But I'm not doing this just because I'm some wild-eyed environmentalist hippie. I am a businessman. This is going to lower my costs, which is going to lower the cost of everyone's tickets."

Adapted from "How Green, How Soon?" by Sam Howe Verhovek: National Geographic Magazine, October 2021

Sam Howe Verhovek is a writer whose articles have appeared in many major publications. He is also a journalist, a professor, and the author of the book *Jet Age: The Comet, the 707, and the Race to Shrink the World.*

UNDERSTANDING THE READING

A **UNDERSTAND MAIN IDEAS** Choose the correct heading for each section in the reading passage.

1. _____ Paragraphs A–F
2. _____ Paragraphs G–K
3. _____ Paragraphs L–O
4. _____ Paragraphs R–X

a. Electric Flights
b. Using Greener Energy
c. Air Travel and the Environment
d. Designing Better Planes

B **UNDERSTAND DETAILS** Complete the sentences. Use no more than two words from the reading passage for each answer.

1. Freedom Pines Biorefinery uses _______________ to create sustainable aviation fuel.
2. Rolls-Royce produced a large and _______________ jet engine that is designed to run on alternative fuel.
3. Airbus is designing airplanes that experience less _______________ and more _______________.
4. Wisk wants its planes to function as _______________ that fly.
5. The FAA ensures that airplanes meet _______________.
6. Harbour Air uses clean electricity that is generated using _______________.

C **UNDERSTAND DETAILS** Note answers to the questions below. Then discuss with a partner.

1. What is the strategy of the *flygskam* campaign?

____

____

2. Why do you think some countries have proposed a ban on frequent flyer loyalty schemes?

____

____

3. How can government intervention make SAFs more viable?

____

____

4. What has to happen for hydrogen to be considered green?

____

____

5. Why might there be a public backlash against air taxis?

____

____

D **INFER MEANING** Find and underline the following words in the reading passage. Use the context to identify their meanings. Then match each word to its definition.

Critical Thinking

1. ____ **begrudge** (paragraph A)
2. ____ **incentivize** (paragraph D)
3. ____ **proponent** (paragraph J)
4. ____ **humongous** (paragraph K)
5. ____ **variant** (paragraph O)
6. ____ **aspiring** (paragraph T)

a. a slightly different version of something
b. extremely large
c. to offer some sort of reward for doing something
d. to give or allow something reluctantly
e. eager to take on a role or accomplish something
f. someone who supports a cause or an idea

CRITICAL THINKING Understanding Multiword Phrases

Some words are commonly grouped together to make multiword units or phrases. In these phrases, words often have different meanings than they do when they are used individually. It is important to learn these words as units and to use context to help you understand what they mean.

E **UNDERSTAND MULTIWORD PHRASES** Find and underline the following multiword phrases in the reading passage. Then choose the best meaning for each phrase.

Critical Thinking

1. If something is a **drop in the bucket**, it has a very ____ impact on something. (paragraph I)
   a. large
   b. small
2. A **chicken-or-egg** situation is one in which ____. (paragraph J)
   a. two things can happen, but not at the same time
   b. neither thing can happen unless the other thing happens first
3. If something is a **game changer**, it ____. (paragraph M)
   a. changes the way that something has been done for a long time
   b. changes the rules and makes a game impossible to play anymore
4. **Begs the question** means ____. (paragraph P)
   a. to beg someone to ask a question for you
   b. to raise an obvious question
5. **To boot** means ____. (paragraph T)
   a. as well, or in addition
   b. because of, or as a result of

F **EVALUATE** Think about the new ideas mentioned in the reading passage. Which do you think is the best? Consider the environmental impact, cost, ease of use and implementation, practicality, and safety of each solution. Discuss your ideas in a group.

Critical Thinking

DEVELOPING READING SKILLS

READING SKILL Recognizing and Evaluating Different Viewpoints

Writers sometimes choose not to state their position on an issue clearly. They instead present important arguments on both sides of the issue and allow readers to arrive at their own conclusions. They may do this for several reasons: to be thorough, for example, or because they are unsure about an issue. As a reader, it is important to recognize when a writer is not taking a clear position and why. It is also important to be able to weigh the different sides of the issue.

For example, in paragraphs A–F of the reading passage, the writer goes back and forth, presenting arguments for and against the discouragement of air travel:

- *As someone who loves to fly . . ., I can't begrudge anyone the joy of flight.*
- *At the same time, any journey in the skies warms the planet.*
- *All this has led to . . .* flygskam, *a Swedish term best translated as "flight shame."*
- *". . . if you truly accept that we are in a climate emergency, you shouldn't fly."*
- *However, aviation leaders contend that shaming flight is not the answer—greening it is.*
- *"Aviation is an essential part of the global economy, so our challenge is reducing emissions and decarbonizing aviation, not preventing people who want to travel from traveling."*

In this case, the author acknowledges the validity of discouraging air travel, but suggests that there might be another solution. He doesn't directly defend this position. Instead, he presents ideas in subsequent sections of the article so that readers can decide for themselves.

A **RECOGNIZE DIFFERENT VIEWPOINTS** Look at the chart below. Find the opposing viewpoints mentioned in the reading passage for each idea. Note them in the chart.

Idea	Arguments for this idea	Arguments against this idea
SAFs		
Hydrogen fuel		
Battery power		

B **EVALUATE DIFFERENT VIEWPOINTS** Look at your notes in Exercise A. For each idea, which side is stronger: arguments for, or arguments against? Why? Note down your answers below. Then discuss with a partner.

____

____

____

VOCABULARY EXTENSION

WORD WEB Business Words and Antonyms

Demand and *supply* are commonly used antonyms in the world of business. Below are other business words that have the opposite, or near opposite, meanings:

profit—loss
employer—employee
revenue—expenditure
shortage—surplus
lend—borrow
partner—competitor

A Choose the correct word to complete each sentence.

1. He can't pay for the house in cash, so he's going to have to **lend** / **borrow** some money from the bank.
2. Their marketing campaign was a huge success. **Demand** / **Supply** for their product tripled in just a month.
3. Many companies reinvest their **profits / losses** to help the business grow.
4. We expect our **expenditure** / **revenue** to decrease over the next year, so we've decided to reduce our **expenditure** / **revenue** slightly.
5. The lack of rain resulted in a **surplus** / **shortage** of rice and other crops in the region.

WORD FORMS *-ion* and *-ive*

Many nouns ending in *-ion* can be made into adjectives using the suffix *-ive*. The suffix *-ive* means *having the quality of*. For example, *competitive* means *having the quality of competition*. Here are some examples:

action — active
correction — corrective
destruction — destructive
competition — competitive
decision — decisive
instruction — instructive

B Complete each sentence with the correct noun or adjective from the box above.

1. The company is facing stiff ____________________ from its closest rival.
2. Her presentation on investment strategies was extremely ____________________.
3. The manufacture of biofuels can be very ____________________ to the environment if it is not carefully regulated.
4. The company was faced with a real dilemma, but its response was quick and ____________________.
5. During the 2008 financial crisis, many governments took prompt ____________________ to stabilize the financial markets.
6. The accident left him injured and in need of ____________________ surgery.

Video

A driverless bus in France

A Driverless Future

In recent years, numerous vehicle manufacturers and software companies have strived to create vehicles smart enough to operate autonomously. Huge progress has already been made, thanks to cities and towns like Trikala, Greece, that were willing to use their streets as testing grounds.

Critical Thinking | **A** **PREVIEW** Read the paragraph above. What do you think are some of the pros and cons of autonomous vehicles? Discuss with a partner.

B **MAIN IDEA** ▶ Watch the video. Which of the following statements better describes the video?

a. After testing autonomous buses, the city of Trikala has decided the vehicles are not yet suitable for public use.
b. Despite concern about their safety, the autonomous buses in the city of Trikala have proven to be safe.

C **DETAILS** ▶ Watch the video again. Answer the questions.

1. According to the mayor, why is Trikala a good place to test the autonomous buses?

____

2. In the event of an emergency, what safeguards are in place?

____

3. According to the CEO, was the public's concern about safety justified? Why or why not?

____

Critical Thinking | **D** **REFLECT** Work with a partner. Answer the questions.

1. Why did the mayor of Trikala compare the autonomous buses to the internet?
2. Think about your own town or city. Do you think it is a good place for testing autonomous vehicles? Why or why not?
3. What are some of the challenges of implementing an autonomous vehicle program?

Writing

EXPLORING WRITTEN ENGLISH

LANGUAGE FOR WRITING Writing Sentences with Initial Phrases

Initial phrases appear at the beginning of sentences. They can be used to avoid short sentences, vary sentence styles, show the relationship between ideas more clearly, and change the emphasis in a sentence. There are three types of initial phrases:

Verbal phrases:

Samsung was founded by Lee Byung-chul. It was originally a trading company.

***Founded by Lee Byung-chul**, Samsung was originally a trading company.*

(In this example, the initial phrase is used to avoid short sentences.)

Time phrases:

Ortega changed his store's name to Zara when he discovered that the name Zorba was taken.

***When he discovered that the name Zorba was taken**, Ortega changed his store's name to Zara.*

(In this example, the initial phrase is used to better show the relationship between ideas.)

Prepositional phrases:

Steve Jobs might not have succeeded in creating Apple without Steve Wozniak's help.

***Without Steve Wozniak's help**, Steve Jobs might not have succeeded in creating Apple.*

(In this example, the initial phrase is used to change the emphasis of a sentence.)

Remember to separate the initial phrase from the main clause using a comma.

See the Grammar Reference on page 249

A **NOTICE** Read the passage below. Note down the initial phrases in the chart. Then write whether they are prepositional, time, or verbal phrases.

Wilbur Wright was born in Ohio, U,S.A., in 1867. Four years later, his brother Orville was born. The two would eventually go on to become pioneers in aviation. Raised in a supportive environment, the Wright brothers were encouraged from a young age to pursue their intellectual interests. This made them both confident and curious. Despite never having attended college, the brothers grew up to be technically gifted. This allowed them to run a successful printing shop, and later a bicycle repair shop—the proceeds of which funded their aviation experiments. Working tirelessly, the pair eventually changed history. They became the first people ever to achieve heavier-than-air flight in a powered vehicle.

Initial phrase	Type of initial phrase

B **APPLY** Rewrite each sentence or combine the sentence pairs using initial verbal, prepositional, or time phrases. More than one answer may be possible.

1. Tesla released its first car, the Tesla Roadster, in 2008.

   ____

2. Japan's bullet train is safe and comfortable despite its extremely high speed.

   ____

3. The car was able to park itself autonomously. It relied on cameras and sensors.

   ____

4. The Concorde was the fastest passenger aircraft ever. It was developed in the 1960s.

   ____

WRITING SKILL Organizing a Comparative Essay

There are two main ways to organize a comparative essay:

Block method
Introduction + Thesis statement
Body paragraph 1: Subject A
Point 1
Point 2
Point 3
Body paragraph 2: Subject B
Point 1
Point 2
Point 3
Conclusion

Point-by-point method
Introduction + Thesis statement
Body paragraph 1: Point 1
Subject A
Subject B
Body paragraph 2: Point 2
Subject A
Subject B
Body paragraph 3: Point 3
Subject A
Subject B
Conclusion

With the **block method**, you discuss all the points of comparison about one subject, and then discuss those same points about the next subject. With the **point-by-point method**, you discuss each subject in terms of the points of comparison you've chosen.

C Look at the notes for a comparative essay on two companies. Use the notes to complete the outline on the next page for a block method comparative essay.

	Boeing	Airbus
Background	U.S. company founded in 1916. Specializes in commercial aircraft, but also military planes and space flight.	European company founded in 1970. Specializes in commercial aircraft, but produces military aircraft, too.
Automation	Automation is a useful tool, but pilot holds ultimate responsibility and makes the final decision.	Automation leads the way. Computers and sensors are capable of overriding pilot decisions.
Controls	More manual, customized controls. Pilots feel more engaged, but demands on them are higher.	More automated, standardized "fly-by-wire" controls. Reduces pilot workload but provides less sensory feedback.

Organization Method: Block

Introduction:

Boeing and Airbus are both highly successful aircraft manufacturers.

Thesis statement:

However, the two companies differ in terms of their attitudes toward automation and their pilot controls.

Body paragraph 1:

Topic sentence: ______________________________

Details: ______________________________

____

____

____

Body paragraph 2:

Topic sentence: ______________________________

Details: ______________________________

____

____

____

Conclusion:

While Boeing and Airbus may appear similar on the surface, differing attitudes regarding automation and pilot involvement separate the two companies.

D **VOCABULARY FOR WRITING** The following words and phrases can be useful for showing similarities and differences. Put each word in the correct category.

although	however	conversely	in the same way (that)
instead (of)	likewise	equally	on the other hand
similarly	unlike	whereas	the same is true for

Similarities	Differences

WRITING TASK

GOAL You are going to write a comparative essay on the following topic:

Compare two companies in the same industry. Consider different aspects such as their history, location, product types, and business practices.

A **BRAINSTORM** Think of major companies that you think are similar to each other. Consider different industries and note down examples below. Do some research and decide which pair of companies you think you'd have the most to write about.

Industry	Company 1	Company 2

B **COMPARE AND CONTRAST** Do additional research on the two companies you selected in Exercise A. Complete the Venn diagram with at least three similarities and/or differences between them.

Industry: ______________________

Company 1: _______________ **Company 2:** _______________

C **WRITE A THESIS STATEMENT** Decide on three aspects to focus on in your essay from your Venn diagram in Exercise B. Draft your thesis statement accordingly.

____

____

D **PLAN** Choose an organization method for your essay (block or point-by-point). Then use your information in Exercises B–C to complete an outline for your essay.

OUTLINE

Organization method: ______________________

Introduction:

____

____

Thesis statement: ____

____

____

Body paragraph 1:

Topic sentence: ____

____

Details: ____

____

____

Body paragraph 2:

Topic sentence: ____

____

Details: ____

____

____

Body paragraph 3: (for point-by-point essays only)

Topic sentence: ____

____

Details: ____

____

____

Conclusion:

____

____

E **FIRST DRAFT** Use the information in your outline to write a first draft of your essay. Remember to use initial phrases, and to vary the words you use to show similarities and differences.

F **REVISING PRACTICE** The essay below is similar to the one you are writing. Follow the steps to create a better second draft.

1. Add the sentences (a–c) in the most suitable spaces.
   a. There are advantages and disadvantages to each approach.
   b. While both companies specialize mainly in passenger aircraft and compete directly for clients, they are not exactly alike.
   c. If the aircraft deems a pilot's maneuver unsafe, it can override the pilot's decision.
2. Now fix the following problems (a–b) with the essay.
   a. Fix a problem with a comparison word in paragraph B.
   b. Fix a problem with a comparison word in paragraph C.

A The airplane manufacturing industry is worth over US$400 billion, and two companies consistently lead the way in the sector. Boeing is an American company that was founded in 1916, while its European counterpart Airbus was founded in 1970 to compete with Boeing. _____ They differ in terms of their attitudes toward automation, and in terms of how their airplane controls are designed to reflect these different attitudes.

B Both companies have very different attitudes toward automation. Airbus has long believed that automation should play a key role in piloting planes. However—as technology has progressed—Airbus's reliance on automation has increased so much that pilots today are actually limited by their planes' operating systems. _____ Whether this is good or bad is the subject of debate. Boeing believes that any final decision should rest in the hands of the pilot, not the plane. Likewise Boeing also exploits automation to a significant degree, it ultimately values human judgment over digital calculations—however sophisticated the chips and processors doing the math may be.

C Boeing's and Airbus's attitudes toward automation directly affect how their planes' controls are designed. While Boeing opts for a more traditional "yoke" (a steering wheel that can also be pulled and pushed to change altitude), Airbus prefers a simpler sidestick controller (similar to a video game joystick). _____ Boeing's more manual controls require greater pilot engagement, while Airbus's controls are simpler and more automated. Although, while Airbus's "fly-by-wire" system reduces pilot workload, many pilots actually prefer Boeing's controls as they allow more sensory feedback as the plane moves through the air.

D While these differences between Airbus and Boeing may seem striking, it is hard to tell the two companies apart in terms of the statistics that matter most. Both companies have similar safety records and fuel consumption rates, for example, and they're both similarly spacious and comfortable for passengers. Most importantly, both companies are steadfastly committed to innovation and development. As the industry continues to change and face new challenges, this can only be good for the healthy, ongoing competition that exists between these two firms, and that spurs them on to greater heights.

G REVISED DRAFT Now use the questions below to revise your essay.

- ☐ Does your introduction provide relevant background information on the topic?
- ☐ Does your thesis state the main points of comparison in the essay?
- ☐ Do you use the block method or the point-by-point method to organize your essay?
- ☐ Do your body paragraphs include enough details to fully explain your ideas?
- ☐ Do you use initial phrases correctly?
- ☐ Does your concluding paragraph include a final thought?

H EDITING PRACTICE Read the information below. Then find and correct mistakes with initial phrases in the sentences below (1–3).

In sentences with initial phrases, remember to use:
- a comma to separate the initial phrase from the main clause.
- a prepositional, time, or verbal phrase as the initial phrase.

1. In 1975 Steve Wozniak, and Steve Jobs built the first Apple computer.
2. It was founded in 1949, Adidas is now one of the world's leading sports brands.
3. Offering innovative tech products Samsung is one of the most successful businesses in Korea.

I FINAL DRAFT Follow these steps to write a final draft.

1. Check your revised draft for mistakes with initial phrases.
2. Now use the checklist on page 248 to write a final draft. Make any other necessary changes.
3. Work in pairs and read your partner's final essay. Give feedback on each other's writing.

A Boeing cockpit

An Airbus cockpit

Review

SELF-ASSESS **Consider the language and skills you learned in this unit.**

How well can you . . . ?	Very well	Pretty well	I need improvement
use the key vocabulary from this unit	☐	☐	☐
understand multiword phrases	☐	☐	☐
recognize and evaluate different viewpoints	☐	☐	☐
write sentences with initial phrases	☐	☐	☐
organize a comparative essay	☐	☐	☐

A **VOCABULARY** Do you remember the meanings of these words and phrases? Look back at the unit and review the ones you don't know.

advocate AW	alongside	aviation	campaign	capacity AW
catch on	committee	competitive	conversion AW	dilemma AW
disruption	elite AW	excessive	swap AW	urge

B **VOCABULARY EXTENSION** Complete these tasks with a partner.

1. Take turns making sentences using the words in the box.

profit	loss	shortage	surplus	demand	supply

2. Make sentences using both the *-ion* and *-ive* forms of two words from the Word Forms box on page 89.

C **READING SKILL** Look at the Unit 1 reading passage. Find one example of opposing viewpoints presented in the passage. Why do you think the author presents these opposing viewpoints, and which do you find more convincing? Discuss with a partner.

D **LANGUAGE FOR WRITING** Rewrite two sentences from this unit's reading passage using initial phrases.

SELF-ASSESS **Look back at the chart above. Did you assess your skills correctly? What skills or language do you still need help with?**

WORKING TOGETHER 5

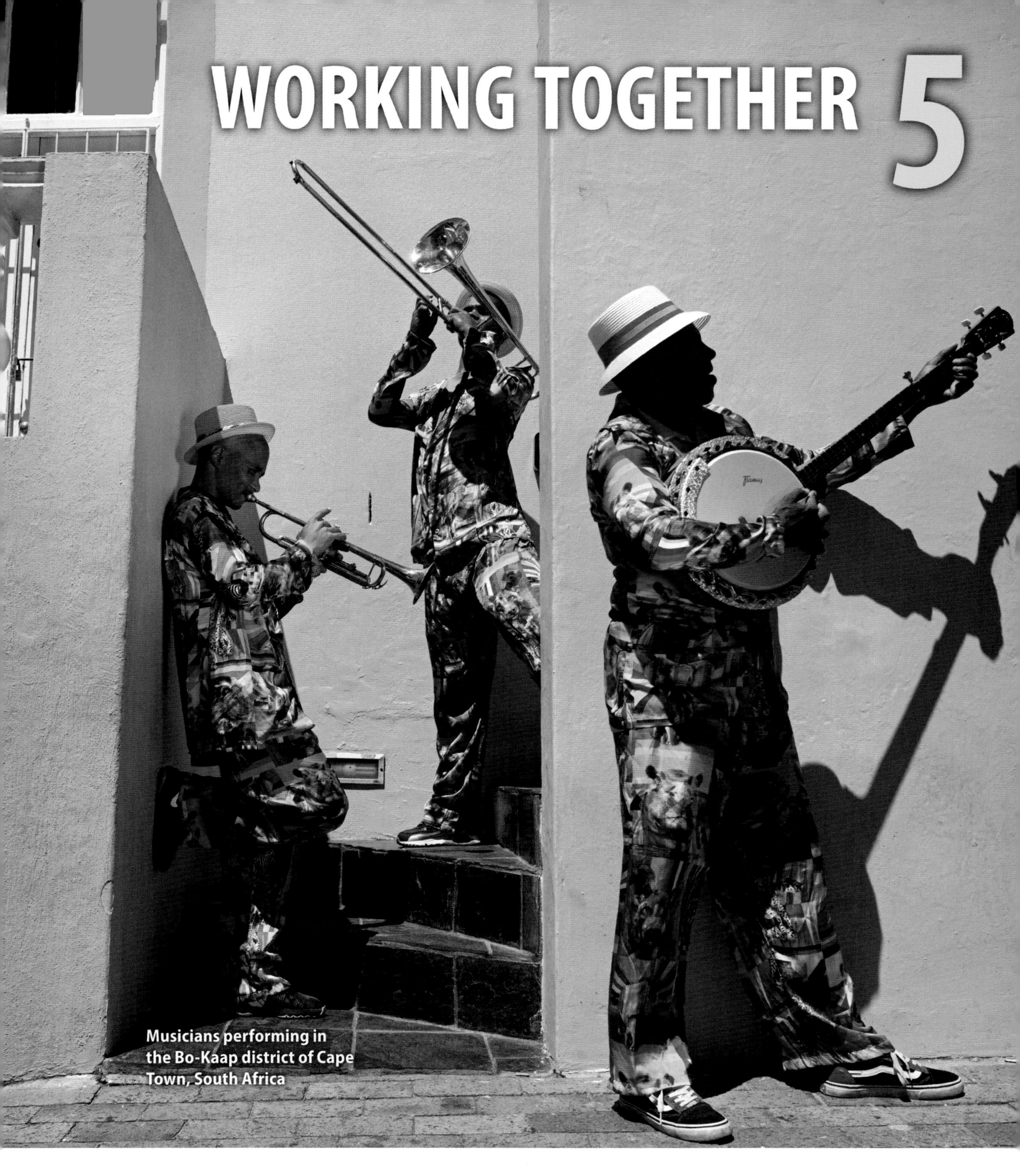

Musicians performing in the Bo-Kaap district of Cape Town, South Africa

IN THIS UNIT, YOU WILL:

- Read an article about swarm behavior
- Watch a video about ants cooperating
- Write a summary of an article about swarm behavior

THINK AND DISCUSS:

1. In the photo above, the South African band *Street Kings* performs against a colorful backdrop. How important is teamwork to a band like this? Why?
2. What are some activities you do that involve teamwork?

EXPLORE THE THEME

Look at the information on these pages and answer the questions.

1. In what ways do the people in the photo need to collaborate to complete their task?
2. Why do you think collaboration was key to the survival of early humans?
3. Have you ever used technology to collaborate? How?

Collaboration

For early humans, collaboration was a survival strategy. Today, it is a key feature of the complex organizational structures on which society is built. Collaboration has empowered us by allowing us to make use of each other's skills in order to advance ideas and solve complex problems.

But what drives us to collaborate? After studying the brain activity of people working together, anthropologist James K. Rilling found that the urge to cooperate may be innate. Human beings are a social species, seemingly hard-wired to communicate and work together.

In recent decades, the way we collaborate has changed dramatically. The internet allows people to work together remotely, around the clock and from any location. Crowdsourcing allows people, businesses, and even scientists to tap into global pools of data. Thanks to technology, we are collaborating now more than ever.

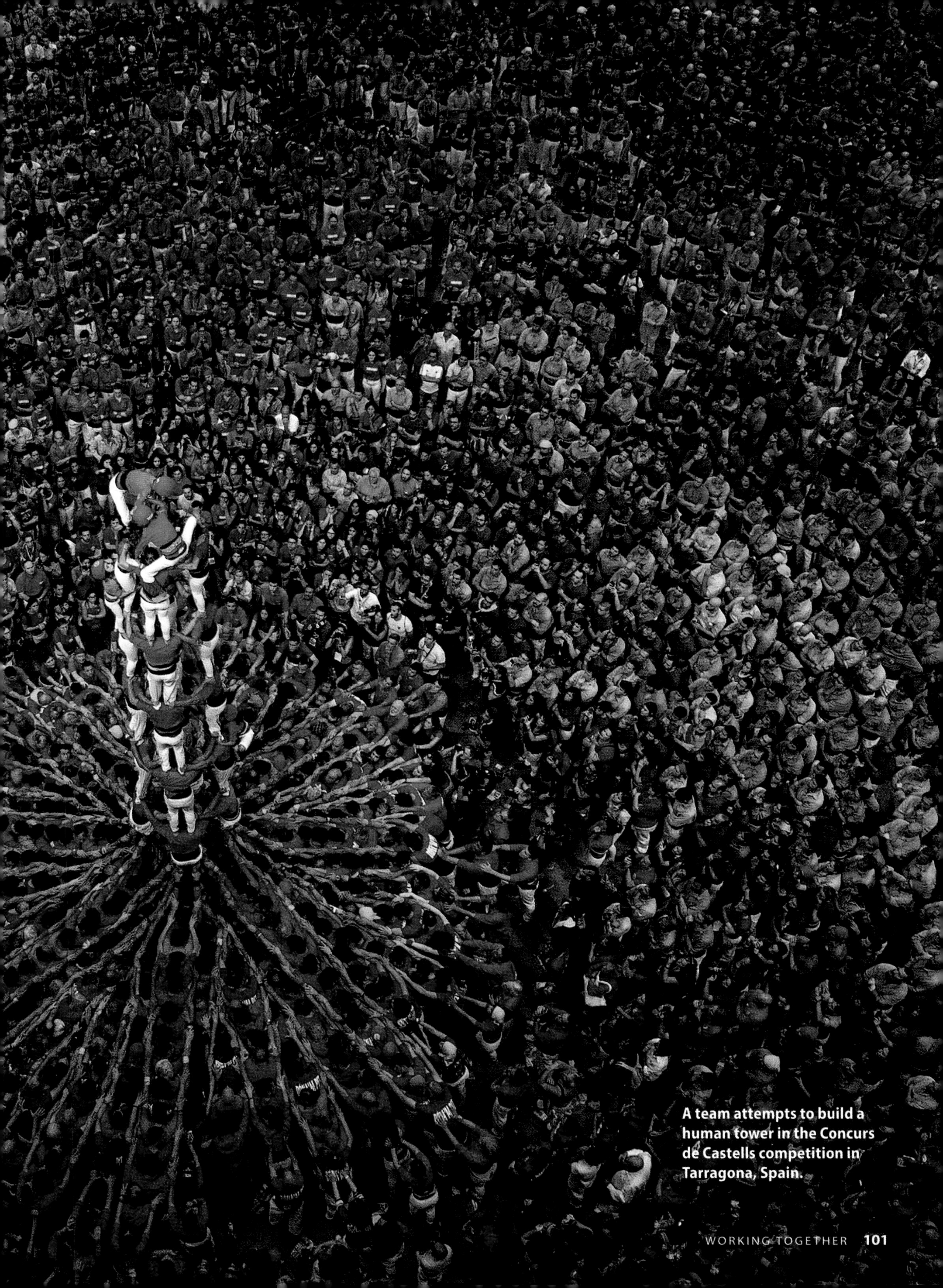

A team attempts to build a human tower in the Concurs de Castells competition in Tarragona, Spain.

Reading

PREPARING TO READ

A **BUILD VOCABULARY** The words in **blue** are used in the reading passage. Read the text below. Then write the correct form of each word next to its definition.

Scientists around the world are studying insect behavior in order to create tiny robots with the **capabilities** of these amazing creatures. Many insects, for example, are able to land on and take off from tiny surfaces. This could have many applications: military robots, for instance, could enter enemy territory without being seen, while emergency robots could access areas humans and other robots can't.

To better **imitate** insect flight, some engineers are developing ornithopters—small aircraft which get most of their lift from flapping wings. This technology offers several advantages: ornithopters can move in ways regular drones can't, plus they more **realistically** mimic birds and insects—a feature that could be useful to both the military and wildlife researchers.

Engineers are also exploring ways for their flying robots to master **synchronized** flight. This would allow the robots to operate in **swarms**, the way locusts and other insects do. While the applications for this aren't as obvious, it is hypothesized that in some situations, many small robots working together could collectively do much more than one large but **solitary** robot.

The **complexity** of insect and swarm behavior is not to be underestimated—it is the result of thousands of years of evolution—but if we can master it, the benefits would no doubt be immense.

1. ____________________ (v) to copy or mimic
2. ____________________ (n) a skill or quality
3. ____________________ (n) a large group of small animals (usually insects)
4. ____________________ (n) how complicated something is
5. ____________________ (adv) in a way that is believable
6. ____________________ (adj) single; lone
7. ____________________ (adj) happening at the same time in a well-orchestrated way

B **BUILD VOCABULARY** Complete the sentences below with the correct form of the words in **blue**. Use a dictionary to help you.

accomplish (v)	**anonymous** (adj)	**coordinate** (v)	**detect** (v)
phenomenon (n)	**shrewd** (adj)	**simulation** (n)	**uncertainty** (n)

1. We might both end up doing the same tasks if we don't ____________ our efforts.
2. In order to determine whether or not the robots would be able to handle a real emergency, the engineers first ran them through a series of ____________.
3. They could have ____________ their goal if they had worked more closely together as a team.
4. The researchers would not have noticed the gas leak if the sensors in the laboratory hadn't ____________ it.
5. You have to be careful when doing business with her. She's a really ____________ negotiator.
6. They're guilty of groupthink, a(n) ____________ that occurs when members of a group simply agree with each other without critically assessing their decisions or other alternatives.
7. Even though she donated the most money to the cause, she chose to remain ____________.
8. It was hard to make a sound decision at the time. There was a lot of ____________ surrounding the issue.

C **USE VOCABULARY** Discuss these questions with a partner.

1. Think of a team you're on. What are the strengths and **capabilities** of its various members? Do you feel the team is well balanced?
2. What are some of the **complexities** of working with others in teams?
3. What are some tasks that you could not have **accomplished** without the help of a team? Why couldn't you do the tasks alone?
4. What happens when you fail to **coordinate** with others properly on a project?

D **PREDICT** You are going to read about swarm behavior. Look at the photos and captions in the reading passage. Then read the first and last paragraphs (A and V). Discuss the questions below with a partner.

Critical Thinking

1. What animals might the passage discuss?
2. What aspects of their behavior might the passage discuss?
3. What human activities or inventions might the passage discuss?
4. What do you think is the main purpose of the article?

Check your answers as you read the passage.

The Smart Swarm

By Peter Miller

Starlings demonstrating swarm behavior over a lake in Wales

The study of swarms is providing insights that can help humans manage complex systems.

A How do the simple actions of individuals add up to the complex behavior of a group? How do hundreds of honeybees make a critical decision about their hive if many of them disagree? What enables a school of herring to **coordinate** its movements so precisely it can change direction in a flash—like a single, silvery organism? The answer has to do with a remarkable **phenomenon** I call the smart swarm.

B A smart swarm is a group of individuals who respond to one another and to their environment in ways that give them the power, as a group, to cope with **uncertainty**, **complexity**, and change. Take birds, for example. There's a small park near the White House in Washington, D.C., where I like to watch flocks of pigeons swirl over the traffic and trees. Sooner or later, the birds come to rest on ledges of buildings surrounding the park. Then something disrupts them, and they're off again in **synchronized** flight.

C The birds don't have a leader. No pigeon is telling the others what to do. Instead, they're each paying close attention to the pigeons next to them, each bird following simple rules as they wheel across the sky. These rules add up to a kind of swarm intelligence—one that has to do with precisely coordinating movement.

D Craig Reynolds, a computer graphics researcher, was curious about what these rules might be. So, in 1986, he created a deceptively simple steering program called boids. In this **simulation**, generic birdlike objects, or boids, were each given three instructions: (1) avoid crowding nearby boids, (2) fly in the average direction of nearby boids, and (3) stay close to nearby boids. The result, when set in motion on a computer screen, was a convincing simulation of flocking,[1] including lifelike and unpredictable movements.

E At the time, Reynolds was looking for ways to depict animals **realistically** in TV shows and movies. (*Batman Returns* in 1992 was the first movie to use his approach, portraying a swarm of bats and an army of penguins.) He later went on to work at Sony, doing research for games, such as for an algorithm[2] that simulated in real time as many as 15,000 interacting birds, fish, or people.

F By demonstrating the power of self-organizing models to mimic swarm behavior, Reynolds was also blazing the trail for robotics engineers. A team of robots that could coordinate its actions like a flock of birds could offer significant advantages over a **solitary** robot. Spread out over a large area, a group could function as a powerful mobile sensor net, gathering information about what's out there. If the group encountered something unexpected, it could adjust and respond quickly, even if the robots in the group weren't very sophisticated—just as ants are able to come up with various options by trial and error. If one member of the group were to break down, others could take its place. And, most important, control of the group could be decentralized, not dependent on a leader.

G "In biology, if you look at groups with large numbers, there are very few examples where you have a central agent," says Vijay Kumar, a professor of mechanical engineering at the University of Pennsylvania. "Everything is very distributed: They don't all talk to each

[1] When animals (usually birds) **flock**, they congregate and do things as a large group.
[2] An **algorithm** is a mathematical or logical rule which determines how a program or process operates.

other. They act on local information. And they're all **anonymous**. I don't care who moves the chair, as long as somebody moves the chair. To go from one robot to multiple robots, you need all three of those ideas."

H In the future, Kumar hopes to put a networked team of robotic vehicles in the field. One purpose might be as first responders. "Let's say there's a 911 call," he says. "The fire alarm goes off. You don't want humans to respond. You want machines to respond, to tell you what's happening. Before you send firemen into a burning building, why not send in a group of robots?"

I Taking this idea one step further, computer scientist Marco Dorigo's group in Brussels is leading a European effort to create a "swarmanoid," a group of cooperating robots with complementary abilities: "foot-bots" to transport things on the ground, "hand-bots" to climb walls and manipulate objects, and "eyebots" to fly around, providing information to the other units.

J The military is eager to acquire similar **capabilities**. In one experiment, researchers released a swarm of 66 pint-size robots into an empty office building at Fort A. P. Hill, a training center near Fredericksburg, Virginia. The mission: Find targets hidden in the building.

K Zipping down the main hallway, the 30-centimeter-long (one foot) red robots pivoted this way and that on their three wheels, resembling a group of large insects. Eight sonars[3] on each unit helped them avoid collisions with walls and other robots. As they spread out, entering one room after another, each robot searched for objects of interest with a small camera. When one robot encountered another, it used wireless network gear to exchange information. ("Hey, I've already explored that part of the building. Look somewhere else.")

[3] **Sonar** is equipment that can detect the position of objects using sound waves.

Swarm-bots work together using swarm theory.

A huge herd of wildebeest surge across the flooded Mara River in Serengeti National Park, Tanzania.

L In the back of one room, a robot spotted something suspicious: a pink ball in an open closet (the swarm had been trained to look for anything pink). The robot froze, sending an image to its human supervisor. Soon, several more robots arrived to form a perimeter around the pink intruder. Within half an hour, the mission had been **accomplished**—all six of the hidden objects had been found. The research team conducting the experiment declared the run a success. Then they started a new test.

M The demonstration was part of the Centibots project, an investigation to see if as many as a hundred robots could collaborate on a mission. If they could, teams of robots might someday be sent into a hostile village to flush out terrorists or locate prisoners; into an earthquake-damaged building to find victims; onto chemical-spill sites to examine hazardous waste; or along borders to watch for intruders. Military agencies such as DARPA (Defense Advanced Research Projects Agency) have funded a number of robotics programs using collaborative flocks of helicopters and fixed-wing aircraft, schools of torpedo-shaped underwater gliders, and herds of unmanned ground vehicles. But, at the time, this was the largest swarm of robots ever tested.

N "When we started Centibots, we were all thinking, this is a crazy idea, it's impossible to do," says Régis Vincent, a researcher at SRI International in Menlo Park, California. "Now we're looking to see if we can do it with a thousand robots."

O In nature, of course, animals travel in even larger numbers. That's because, as members of a big group, whether it's a flock, school, or herd, individuals increase their chances of **detecting** predators, finding food, locating a mate, or following a migration route. For these animals, coordinating their movements with one another can be a matter of life or death.

P "It's much harder for a predator to avoid being spotted by a thousand fish than it is to avoid being spotted by one," says Daniel Grünbaum, a biologist at the University of Washington. "News that a predator is approaching spreads quickly through a school because fish sense from their neighbors that something's going on."

Q When a predator strikes a school of fish, the group is capable of scattering in patterns that make it almost impossible to track any individual. It might explode in a flash, create a kind of moving bubble around the predator, or fracture into multiple blobs,[4] before coming back together and swimming away.

R That's the wonderful appeal of swarm intelligence. Whether we're talking about ants, bees, pigeons, or caribou, the ingredients of smart group behavior—decentralized control, response to local cues, simple rules of thumb—add up to a **shrewd** strategy to cope with complexity.

S "We don't even know yet what else we can do with this," says Eric Bonabeau, a complexity theorist and the chief scientist at Icosystem Corporation in Cambridge, Massachusetts. "We're not used to solving decentralized problems in a decentralized way. We can't control an emergent phenomenon like traffic by putting stop signs and lights everywhere. But the idea of shaping traffic as a self-organizing system, that's very exciting."

T The internet is already using a form of swarm intelligence. Consider the way Google uses group smarts to find what you're looking for. When you type in a search query, Google surveys billions of Web pages on its index servers[5] to identify the most relevant ones. One of the ways it ranks the search results is by the number of pages that link to them, counting links as votes (the most popular sites get weighted[6] votes since they're more likely to be reliable). The pages that receive more votes are listed higher in the search results. In this way, Google says, it "uses the collective intelligence of the Web to determine a page's importance."

U Wikipedia, a free collaborative encyclopedia, has also proved to be a big success, with millions of articles in more than 200 languages about everything under the sun, each of which can be contributed by anyone or edited by anyone. "It's now possible for huge numbers of people to think together in ways we never imagined a few decades ago," says Thomas Malone of MIT's Center for Collective Intelligence. "No single person knows everything that's needed to deal with problems we face as a society, such as health care or climate change, but collectively we know far more than we've been able to tap so far."

V Such thoughts underline an important truth about collective intelligence: crowds tend to be wise only if individual members act responsibly and make their own decisions. A group won't be smart if its members **imitate** one another, slavishly follow fads, or wait for someone to tell them what to do. When a group is being intelligent, whether it's made up of ants or attorneys, it relies on its members to do their own part. For those of us who sometimes wonder if it's really worth recycling that extra bottle to lighten our impact on the planet, the bottom line is that our actions matter, even if we don't see how.

Adapted from "Swarm Theory," by Peter Miller: National Geographic Magazine, July 2007

Peter Miller has worked as a reporter for *Life* magazine and as a senior editor at *National Geographic*. He is the author of the best-selling book *The Smart Swarm: How to Work Efficiently, Communicate Effectively, and Make Better Decisions Using the Secrets of Flocks, Schools, and Colonies.*

[4] A **blob** is an indistinct or shapeless form or object.
[5] A **server** is a program or device that does a task for other computers on a network, such as store information or run a program.
[6] If something is **weighted**, it is given more value because it is seen as more important.

UNDERSTANDING THE READING

A **UNDERSTAND MAIN IDEAS** Note answers to the questions below. Write the paragraph(s) that contain the answers (A–V).

1. What is a "smart swarm"? Explain it in your own words.

   ____

   ______________________________________ Paragraph(s) ______

2. What are the three key aspects of swarm intelligence?

   ____

   ______________________________________ Paragraph(s) ______

3. How does being part of a large group help animals?

   ____

   ______________________________________ Paragraph(s) ______

4. How do search engines and online encyclopedias make use of collective intelligence?

   ____

   ______________________________________ Paragraph(s) ______

B **UNDERSTAND PURPOSE** Match the paragraphs to their purpose.

1. ____ Paragraph B	a. show(s) how we already use swarm intelligence
2. ____ Paragraph G	b. describe(s) potential uses of smart swarm robots
3. ____ Paragraphs H–N	c. explain(s) why individual behavior matters
4. ____ Paragraphs O–Q	d. explain(s) why animals move in swarms
5. ____ Paragraphs T–U	e. list(s) three key features of smart swarms
6. ____ Paragraph V	f. give(s) a general definition of a smart swarm

C **INFER MEANING** Find and underline the following phrases in the reading passage. Use the context to identify their meanings. Then write the correct form of each phrase next to its definition.

Critical Thinking

add up to (paragraph A)	**set in motion** (paragraph D)	**blazing the trail** (paragraph F)
trial and error (paragraph F)	**flush out** (paragraph M)	**the bottom line** (paragraph V)

Review this Critical Thinking Skill in Unit 4

1. ____________________ to force a person or animal out of hiding
2. ____________________ the essential idea
3. ____________________ to initiate something
4. ____________________ to equal, or result in
5. ____________________ to be the first to do something
6. ____________________ trying different methods until something works

Review this Reading Skill in Unit 3

D **USE A CONCEPT MAP** Read paragraphs G–N of the reading passage again. Then complete the concept map using words from the passage.

Swarm members act [3] ______________________ ______________________.

Swarm members don't [2] ______________________ ______________________.

Have no [1] ______________________ ______________________.

Swarm members are [4] ______________________ ______________________.

SWARMS

Swarm tech applications

Could serve as [5] ______________________ ______________________, for example, to help firefighters do jobs that are dangerous.

Swarmanoid tech: groups of robots with [6] ______________________ ______________________

The [7] ______________________ is eager to acquire such capabilities.

Centibots project: a test to see if [8] ______________________ ______________________ ______________________ ______________________.

Possible future applications: [9] ______________________ ______________________ ______________________ ______________________.

CRITICAL THINKING Evaluating Sources

Writers often quote experts to support their main ideas. It is important to evaluate the source of each quote. When you read a quote, ask yourself: What are the credentials of the person being quoted? What is their background or affiliation? How is their experience or expertise relevant to the topic? Then ask yourself how the quotes support the writer's main ideas.

E **EVALUATE SOURCES** Find quotes by the following people in the reading passage. Write down their credentials, and summarize the claim they make briefly in a sentence.

Critical Thinking

1. Vijay Kumar (paragraph G)

   Credentials: ____________________

   Claim: ____________________

2. Daniel Grünbaum (paragraph P)

   Credentials: ____________________

   Claim: ____________________

3. Thomas Malone (paragraph U)

   Credentials: ____________________

   Claim: ____________________

F **EVALUATE SOURCES** Look at your information in Exercise E. Discuss the questions below with a partner.

Critical Thinking

1. How well do the people's credentials match what they are being quoted on?
2. What main ideas do the quotes support? Match the quotes (1–3) with the ideas (a–c).
   a. _____ Swarm behavior is a survival strategy.
   b. _____ Swarm intelligence has online applications.
   c. _____ Decentralization is a key aspect of swarm intelligence.

G **ANALYZE AND APPLY** Note answers to the questions below. Then discuss with a partner.

Critical Thinking

1. In what ways do humans exhibit swarm behavior in day-to-day life?

   ____

   ____

2. When is it a bad idea for humans to adopt swarm-like behavior?

   ____

   ____

DEVELOPING READING SKILLS

READING SKILL Understanding Complex Sentences

It is important for overall reading comprehension to be able to understand complex sentences. One way to do this is to break down complex sentences into smaller parts. Follow these steps:

1. Identify the main clause and any dependent clauses in the sentence.

main clause	*A team of robots ...*
dependent clause	*that could coordinate its actions like a flock of birds ...*
main clause	*could offer significant advantages over a solitary robot.*

2. Identify the subject, verb, and object in the main clause.

subject	*A team of robots ...*
verb	*could offer ...*
object	*significant advantages over a solitary robot.*

3. Look back at the dependent clause for any extra information to help you understand the full sentence.

A **UNDERSTAND COMPLEX SENTENCES** Use the steps above to break down the following complex sentences. Then answer the questions.

1. A team of robots that could coordinate its actions like a flock of birds could offer significant advantages over a solitary robot.
   a. How could the team of robots coordinate its actions? ______________________
   b. What could the team of robots offer? ______________________
2. There's a small park near the White House in Washington, D.C., where I like to watch flocks of pigeons swirl over the traffic and trees.
   a. What is near the White House? ______________________
   b. What does the writer like to do there? ______________________
3. He later went on to work at Sony, doing research for games, such as for an algorithm that simulated in real time as many as 15,000 interacting birds, fish, or people.
   a. What did he do at Sony? ______________________
   b. What did the algorithm do? ______________________
4. Whether we're talking about ants, bees, pigeons, or caribou, the ingredients of smart group behavior—decentralized control, response to local cues, simple rules of thumb—add up to a shrewd strategy to cope with complexity.
   a. What are the ingredients of smart group behavior? ______________________

   ____
   b. What is the purpose of smart group behavior? ______________________

B **UNDERSTAND COMPLEX SENTENCES** Scan paragraphs K, M, U, and V of the reading passage to find examples of complex sentences. Underline the subjects and circle the main verbs.

VOCABULARY EXTENSION

WORD LINK *co-, com-, col-*

The prefixes *co-*, *com-*, and *col-* usually mean *with* or *together*. For example, *cooperate* means to *work* (or *operate*) *together*.

A Match the words in **bold** (1–5) with the correct definitions (a–e).

1. _____ I was wearing the exact same T-shirt as another guy at the party. What a **coincidence**!
2. _____ To make pancakes, **combine** eggs, flour, milk, and butter. Then heat the mixture in a pan.
3. _____ Politicians and business leaders should **coordinate** to improve conditions for workers.
4. _____ There was heavy traffic yesterday following a **collision** between two vehicles.
5. _____ The best meals have flavors, textures, and colors that **complement** each other.

a. to put together to make a whole
b. to go well together
c. to organize and work together in a systematic way
d. a situation where two connected events occur at the same time by chance
e. a situation in which two or more objects crash into each other

WORD FORMS *-ate* and *-ion*

Many verbs ending in *-ate* can be made into nouns by deleting the *-e* and adding the suffix *-ion*. The suffix *-ion* means an act or process.

Here are some examples:

activate — activation
evaluate — evaluation
imitate — imitation
communicate — communication
collaborate — collaboration
manipulate — manipulation
coordinate — coordination
simulate — simulation

B Complete each sentence with a noun from the box above.

1. The researchers conducted a(n) ________________ of the robots' performance.
2. Playing the drums requires good ________________ of your hands and feet.
3. Many people are tired of his mind games and ________________.
4. This video game is basically a(n) ________________ of a military operation—it's very realistic!
5. You'll have to wait three more days for the ________________ of your new credit card.
6. That's not an actual Van Gogh painting—it's just a(n) ________________.

Video

Ant Teamwork

Ants are known for their strength, their industrious nature, and also their ability to operate seamlessly as a unit. Dr. Nigel Franks is interested to know how they do this. To find out, he conducts an experiment, mapping the behavior of individual ants within a nest.

Critical Thinking

A **PREVIEW** What types of group behavior have you seen ants display? Discuss with a partner.

B **MAIN IDEAS** ▶ Watch the video. Choose the correct option to complete each sentence.

1. The purpose of the experiment is to find out how ants ______.
   a. learn from each other b. make decisions
2. In the experiment, the ants need to ______ a new nest.
   a. locate b. build

C **DETAILS** ▶ Watch the video again. Note answers to the question below.

1. Why were microchips attached to the ants?
   ____
2. How do ants communicate their findings to each other?
   ____
3. What does Dr. Franks say tandem running is a unique example of?
   ____

Critical Thinking

D **COMPARE** Imagine a large group of people have to decide where to go for an event. How would their decision-making process compare with the ants' process? Discuss with a partner.

EXPLORING WRITTEN ENGLISH

LANGUAGE FOR WRITING Avoiding Plagiarism (I)—Paraphrasing

When writing a summary, it is important to paraphrase sentences from the original text. You can do this by replacing words with synonyms and changing sentence structures.

Synonyms:

Where possible, use synonyms for words that are in the original text.

*A ~~team~~ **group** of robots that could ~~coordinate its actions~~ **organize its behavior** like a flock of birds could ~~offer significant advantages over~~ **function better than** a ~~solitary~~ **single** robot.*

It's important to make sure the synonym you choose matches the context of your sentence. For example, *squad* and *bunch* are both synonyms for *team*, but *group* works better in the context above.

Sentence structure and parts of speech:

In addition to using synonyms, you should also change sentence structures and use different parts of speech. For example, the sentence above could be restructured accordingly:

A single robot might not function as well as a group of robots capable of organizing its behavior like a flock of birds.

See the Grammar Reference on page 250

A **APPLY** Choose the best synonym for each underlined word.

1. If any of the robots were to <u>break down</u>, others would take their place and the mission would continue uninterrupted.

   a. explain b. stop working c. destroy

2. When faced with an unfamiliar object, the robots would <u>freeze</u> and send an image to a human operator.

   a. stop b. suspend c. solidify

3. The military robots scanned the room for objects of <u>interest</u> using small cameras.

   a. curiosity b. appeal c. note

B **APPLY** Find synonyms for other words or phrases in the sentences in Exercise A. Then rewrite each sentence, changing the sentence structure and using different parts of speech.

1. ______________________________

   ____

2. ______________________________

   ____

3. ______________________________

   ____

C **REFLECT** Look back at the reading passage. Find three sentences with ideas you think are especially interesting. Then paraphrase each sentence. Use synonyms and different parts of speech, and change the sentence structure.

1. ____
____

2. ____
____

3. ____
____

WRITING SKILL Writing a Summary

Summary writing can be very useful. It can improve your own understanding of an article, demonstrate your understanding to someone else, or provide you with a condensed version of an article. Summaries are also useful for relaying the gist of a long message to someone quickly. When writing a summary, report—in your own words—only the most important information from a passage in the same order that it is originally given. A summary should be shorter than the original passage, and should not include any of your own opinions.

Follow these steps to summarize successfully.

1. Read the passage once. Underline the important information in the passage.
2. Without looking at the passage, write down the main ideas to include in your summary. Add any important details that you can remember.
3. Compare your notes against the passage to check your understanding. Correct any incorrect notes and add any important details that are missing.
4. Prepare an introductory statement. Remember that the introductory statement in a summary is not the same as the thesis statement in an essay. It is more like a restatement of the original author's main idea.
5. Compare your summary with the original passage. Make sure it expresses the same meaning as the original but uses synonyms and different sentence structures.

D Read the two summaries of paragraph B of *The Smart Swarm*. Then read the statements in the chart on the next page. For each statement, rate each summary on a scale of 1 (poor) to 10 (excellent). Then decide which summary you think is better and discuss with a partner.

A According to Peter Miller, smart swarms are groups of individuals that react to their surroundings and each other, and work together in order to make collective decisions. He explains that a group of birds is one example of a smart swarm. They fly to a location in a group, then fly away again in a coordinated manner.

B According to Peter Miller, a smart swarm is a group of individuals who respond to one another and to their environment in ways that give them the power, as a group, to cope with uncertainty, complexity, and change. He gives birds as an example of this. He watches flocks of pigeons in a park in Washington, D.C., and notices the way that they move together as a group. They fly over cars and trees together and land at the same time on the ledges of buildings around the park. Then something disturbs them, and they take off again in a synchronized manner.

	A	B
1. The summary expresses the same meaning as the original.		
2. The summary includes only important information.		
3. The summary replaces words in the original with synonyms.		
4. The summary uses different sentence structures from the original.		
5. The summary is shorter than the original.		

E Write a summary of the passage about insect-like robots on page 102. Keep your summary under 100 words.

____

____

____

____

____

____

____

____

____

____

____

F **VOCABULARY FOR WRITING** The words in the box can be used to introduce an author's ideas when writing a summary. Read the sentences below. Then choose the correct word to complete each sentence. Use a dictionary to help you.

The topic	Facts	Opinions	Requests	Questions
analyzes	reports	argues	urges	asks
explores	provides	claims	calls for	questions
examines	explains	believes	suggests	wonders
discusses	states	disputes	recommends	speculates

1. The writer **suggests** / **urges** his readers to take immediate action.
2. Kolbert **discusses** / **calls for** the causes of deforestation in great depth.
3. The author **argues** / **disputes** some of the ideas put forward by other historians.
4. She **questions** / **recommends** whether their actions have made any difference.
5. The writer **claims** / **provides** ample evidence to support her views on the topic.

WRITING TASK

GOAL You are going to write a summary on the following topic:
Write a summary of *The Smart Swarm*.

A **IDENTIFY MAIN IDEAS** Skim the reading passage on pages 104–108. Underline the information you think is most important.

B **ORGANIZE IDEAS** Look at the questions below. Without looking back at the reading passage, write notes in the chart. Then compare your notes with the information you underlined in Exercise A. Make any necessary corrections.

What is a smart swarm? How could humans make use of swarm intelligence?	
How does swarm intelligence help animals?	
How do humans already use swarm intelligence?	
What do individuals in human swarms have to do?	

C **WRITE AN INTRODUCTORY STATEMENT** Look at the four questions in the chart above that help outline *The Smart Swarm*. Write an introductory statement that sums up the overall main idea of the passage.

___

___

___

D **WRITE A CONCLUSION** Paraphrase Peter Miller's ideas for what he believes individuals in human swarms need to do.

___

___

___

E **PLAN** Use your information in Exercises A–D to complete an outline for your summary.

OUTLINE

Introductory statement: ______________________________

____

____

Body paragraph 1: What is a smart swarm?

Topic sentence: ______________________________

____

Details: ______________________________

____

____

Body paragraph 2: How does swarm intelligence help animals?

Topic sentence: ______________________________

____

Details: ______________________________

____

____

Body paragraph 3: How do humans already use swarm intelligence?

Topic sentence: ______________________________

____

Details: ______________________________

____

____

Notes for conclusion: ______________________________

____

____

F **FIRST DRAFT** Use the information in your outline to write a first draft of your summary. Remember to paraphrase the information in the original passage. Use synonyms, change sentence structures, and use different parts of speech as much as possible. In addition, use different words to introduce the author's ideas.

G **REVISING PRACTICE** The draft below is a summary that you can use as a model. It summarizes the reading passage "The Robot Revolution Has Arrived" from Unit 1. Follow the steps to create a better second draft.

1. Add the sentences (a–c) in the most suitable spaces.
   a. It is therefore vital that humans adapt and learn to accept having robots everywhere around us.
   b. However, with the aid of sensors and cameras, the robot was able to perform the task autonomously.
   c. They will instead simply take away tasks that are repetitive, freeing humans to do work that is more challenging and creative.

2. Now fix the following problems (a–c) with the summary.
   a. Paraphrase the underlined sentence in paragraph B.
   b. Paraphrase the underlined sentence in paragraph C.
   c. Paraphrase the underlined words in paragraph D.

A The reading passage "The Robot Revolution Has Arrived" describes how robots are becoming a common feature in many workplaces.

B The author starts by describing an excavator that was being operated by a robot to dig a large hole that would become the foundation for a wind turbine—a job usually done by humans. _____ The robot operating the excavator was small, adept, and mobile—very different from the large "mute and brute" robots usually used for repetitive, assembly-line work, which are often kept away from people for safety reasons. Once rare, devices like this—designed to work with people who have never met a robot—are moving steadily into daily life.

C This larger trend has been powered mainly by recent technological advances. Mechanical parts, for example, have gotten lighter, cheaper, and stronger. Devices are able to pack more computing power into smaller spaces. And better digital communications let them store robot "brains" in a computer elsewhere—or connect the minds of hundreds of robots, letting them share a collective intelligence, like bees in a beehive. As a result of these advances, robots have become common in many places of work such as supermarkets, farms, warehouses, and hospitals.

D The increased presence of robots in places of work raises some concerns. Many managers today prefer robots to human employees because they don't need paid vacations or medical insurance. As a result, many workers are concerned about their jobs. However, some managers feel that robots will not replace humans. _____ According to robotics experts, humans are still much better than robots at walking, performing delicate tasks, and handling a wide range of unexpected jobs, and this is not expected to change for a long time.

E According to the article, there is no doubt that machines and robots will become a significant part of our daily lives. _____

H **REVISED DRAFT** Now use the questions below to revise your summary.

- ☐ Does your summary begin with an introductory statement?
- ☐ Do you include only important details?
- ☐ Does information appear in the same order as the original passage?
- ☐ Do you use synonyms to replace words from the original passage?
- ☐ Do you use different sentence structures and parts of speech?
- ☐ Does your summary restate the author's original conclusion?

I **EDITING PRACTICE** Read the information below. Then find and correct one mistake with the underlined synonyms in each of the paraphrased sentences below.

When you use synonyms, remember to make sure your synonym:

- has the same meaning as the original word.
- fits the context of the sentence.

1. **Original:** What enables a school of herring to coordinate its movements so precisely it can change direction in a flash?

   Paraphrased: What supports a group of herring to coordinate its movements so accurately it can change direction in a flash?

2. **Original:** Zipping down the main hallway, the 30-centimeter-long red robots pivoted this way and that on their three wheels, resembling a group of large insects.

   Paraphrased: Speeding down the main hallway, the 30-centimeter-long red robots turned this way and that on their three wheels, approaching a group of large insects.

3. **Original:** When a predator strikes a school of fish, the group is capable of scattering in patterns that make it almost impossible to track any individual.

   Paraphrased: When a predator attacks a school of fish, the group is capable of throwing in patterns that make it almost impossible to follow any individual.

J **FINAL DRAFT** Follow these steps to write a final draft.

1. Check your revised draft for mistakes with paraphrasing.
2. Now use the checklist on page 248 to write a final draft. Make any other necessary changes.
3. Work in pairs and read your partner's final summary. Give feedback on each other's writing.

Review

SELF-ASSESS **Consider the language and skills you learned in this unit.**

How well can you . . . ?	Very well	Pretty well	I need improvement
use the key vocabulary from this unit	☐	☐	☐
evaluate sources	☐	☐	☐
understand complex sentences	☐	☐	☐
avoid plagiarism by paraphrasing	☐	☐	☐
write a summary	☐	☐	☐

A **VOCABULARY** Do you remember the meanings of these words? Look back at the unit and review the ones you don't know.

accomplish	anonymous	capability AW	complexity AW	coordinate AW
detect AW	imitate	phenomenon AW	realistically	shrewd
simulation AW	solitary	swarm	synchronized	uncertainty

B **VOCABULARY EXTENSION** Complete these tasks with a partner.

1. Think of words with *co-, col-, or com-*. Take turns making sentences with them.
2. Make sentences using the *-ion* form of these words. Take turns.

collaborate	evaluate	manipulate	simulate

C **READING SKILL** Work with a partner. Circle the subject of the main clause in each sentence below. Underline the verb of the main clause and the object if there is one.

1. When you type in a search query, Google surveys billions of Web pages on its index servers to identify the most relevant ones.
2. To better imitate insect flight, some engineers are developing ornithopters—small aircraft which get most of their lift from flapping wings.

D **LANGUAGE FOR WRITING** Work with a partner. Paraphrase the sentence.

By demonstrating the power of self-organizing models to mimic swarm behavior, Reynolds was also blazing the trail for robotics engineers.

SELF-ASSESS **Look back at the chart above. Did you assess your skills correctly? What skills or language do you still need help with?**

WHY LANGUAGE MATTERS 6

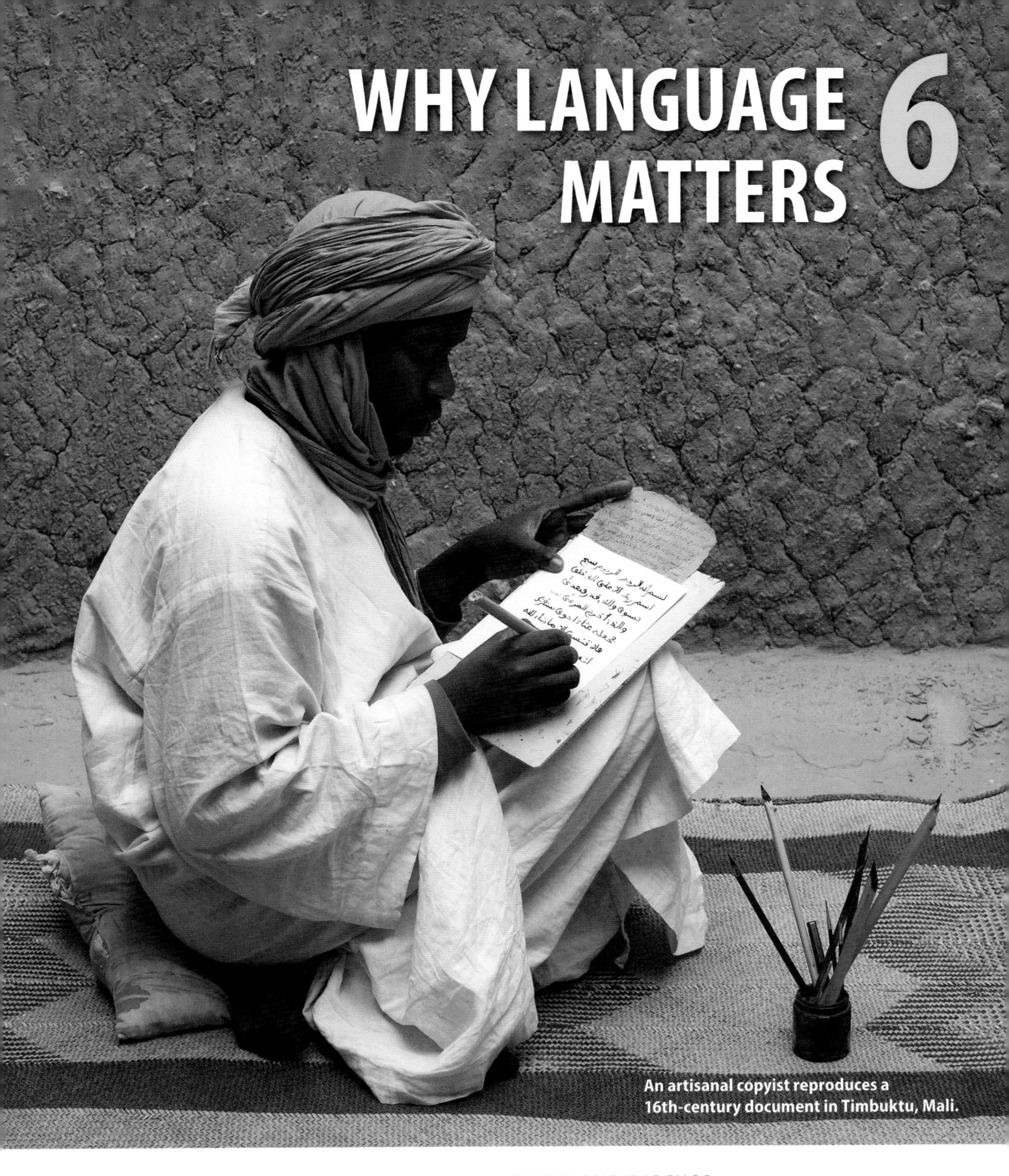

An artisanal copyist reproduces a 16th-century document in Timbuktu, Mali.

IN THIS UNIT, YOU WILL:

- Read an article about words around the world
- Watch a video about the discovery of a new language
- Write about how best to pick up a new language

THINK AND DISCUSS:

1. In the photo above, Boubacar Sadeck—one of Mali's last copyists—reproduces an old document using traditional techniques. Why do you think he does this?
2. What are some things that language could reveal about a culture?

EXPLORE THE THEME

Look at the information on these pages and answer the questions.

1. Which of the six words best describes the photograph?
2. Do you think you've experienced any of the feelings described by the six words? Give examples.
3. Do you know any other non-English words that can't be quickly or easily translated to English?

Our Words Are Our Reality

How do we make sense of the world, and everything within it? Without words, this would be impossible.

However, words can also be a constraint. Take English, a language of European heritage that has been shaped largely by the culture, practices, and needs of that region. Can its words really express all the thoughts, feelings, and realities of people around the world?

English has become much more of a global language in recent years, but—like any other language—it is only one small window through which we can interpret the world. There will always be thoughts and ideas for which its words are inadequate.

Words with No English Equivalent

While words and phrases like these can be defined in English, there aren't any convenient words or phrases that mean the same thing.

Gigil
(Tagalog)

A strong desire to squeeze or pinch something that's extremely cute.

Resfeber
(Swedish)

The mixture of anxiety and excitement one gets before a long journey.

Ya'aburnee
(Arabic)
An expression of hope that someone you care about will outlive you.

Aspaldiko
(Basque)
Joy that stems from meeting a long-lost friend.

Yoko meshi
(Japanese)
Stress triggered by having to speak a foreign language.

Saudade
(Portuguese)
A sad, hopeless longing for something that is impossible to obtain.

Reading

PREPARING TO READ

A **BUILD VOCABULARY** The words in **blue** are used in the reading passage. Read the text below. Then write the correct form of each word next to its definition.

While it would be easy to assume that most languages have a lot in common, the rules are a lot more different than we might assume. By applying a little bit of **scrutiny** to the English language, for example, we can identify many features that aren't the same in other languages.

The use of tense is an obvious example. English uses different verb forms to indicate when something happened, happens, or will happen. However, not all languages have those verb forms. In fact, many use just one verb form with different time expressions—such as yesterday, today, or next week—to provide context.

And what about pronouns? English uses gendered pronouns when referring to people in the third person. Again, this is a distinction that doesn't always exist in languages. In some languages, just one word is used for both *he* and *she*, or *her* and *him*. Other languages have pronouns that don't even have English **equivalents**. Such languages could, for example, have two forms of *we*: one that refers to me, my friends, and the person I'm speaking to; and another that includes me and my friends, but not the person being addressed. To speakers of these languages, the English version of *we* could be seen as a **limitation**.

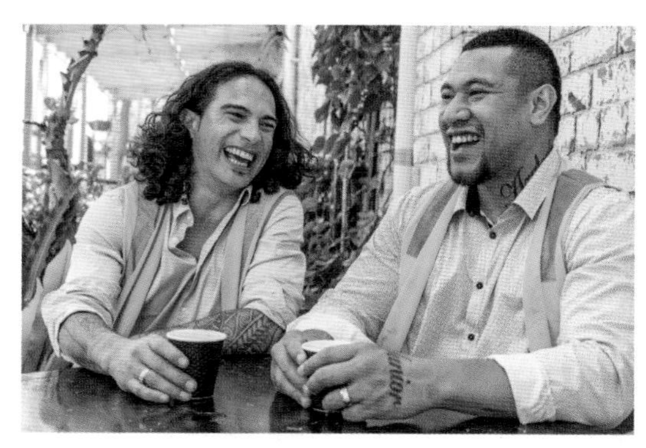

▲ **In Maori, *tāua* means *you and I*, *tātou* means *all of us*, and *mātou* means *I and them, but not you.***

Peer into the inner workings of any two **random** languages and you'll inevitably find many other differences like these—differences that could affect the way people string together thoughts and **conceive** new ideas. A new language is therefore not just a collection of new words: it's a new **paradigm** for interpreting life in general.

1. ______________________ (v) to look at something closely
2. ______________________ (adj) not planned; left to chance
3. ______________________ (n) a shortcoming, or a weakness
4. ______________________ (n) an equal, or a counterpart
5. ______________________ (v) to imagine or think of something
6. ______________________ (n) close inspection
7. ______________________ (n) a model or an example one uses to understand a concept

B **BUILD VOCABULARY** Complete the sentences below with the correct form of the words in **blue**. Use a dictionary to help you.

abstract (adj)	**coherent** (adj)	**dread** (n)	**glimpse** (n)
horizon (n)	**hospitality** (n)	**stereotype** (n)	**texture** (n)

1. Traveling can help you learn new things and expand your ______________.
2. The thought of speaking to people in a new language fills many language learners with ______________.
3. His movie explores several themes that are ______________ and difficult to define.
4. Her use of different languages and dialects in the script gave it a rich ______________.
5. You don't have to use impressive words in your presentation. You just have to be ______________.
6. Documentaries can only give you a(n) ______________ of what life is like in other countries.
7. I was grateful for the ______________ they showed me when I visited them last year.
8. They think teenagers are all lazy and irresponsible, but that's just a bad ______________.

C **USE VOCABULARY** Discuss these questions with a partner.

1. What are some **stereotypes** that exist about people from your country?
2. How do you show **hospitality** to others in your culture?
3. Do you think that learning a new language expands your **horizons**? If so, how?

D **SCAN** The reading passage expands on the topic of words with no English equivalent. Search the reading passage for non-English words and write them down in the chart below. Then, search for their meanings and write them in the chart, too.

Words with no English equivalent	English translation

E **SYNTHESIZE** Look at your answers to question 3 on page 124. Add the words you thought of and their meanings to the chart above.

Critical Thinking

Is Joy the Same in Every Language?

by Jen Rose Smith

The Arabic term *tarab* can be used to describe the intense emotions felt by this dervish dancer in Dubai, U.A.E.

"The lexicon[1] of a foreign language is like a map of a country you've never been to," says psychologist Tim Lomas, a lecturer at the University of East London.

A While travelers tend to think that seeing the world is central to understanding it, some language experts shift the **paradigm**: to them, it is actually words that shape our perspectives on the world. Studying words therefore offers a window into the human experience.

B To these researchers, dictionaries are like maps. They help define the topography[2] and **textures** of our world, and they can lead the way to discoveries. Next to traveling, learning new words—or an entire language—may be the most mind-expanding journey of all.

C As a word collector, Tim Lomas makes an excellent tour guide. He studies the words we use for our emotions, dreams, and desires—words that vary widely across the world's 7,117 spoken languages. His research constitutes a global glossary of feelings.

A WORLD OF EMOTIONS

D Languages from Aleut to Zulu contain unique terms for our internal lives, and Lomas has gathered thousands of them into an interactive lexicography. The searchable index of words is sorted by language and theme, and drawn from every part of the globe.

E His collection, featuring categories such as "revelry"[3] and "longing," brims with treasures: Roll your tongue around the German word *zielschmerz*, for example, to imagine the thrilling **dread** of finally chasing a long-held dream. Or crank up your stereo and channel the Arabic *tarab*, a state of enchantment[4] or ecstasy that only music can induce.

F Some such words are a journey in themselves. The Wolof term *teraanga* is a spirit of **hospitality**, generosity, and sharing that permeates life in Senegal, where travelers enjoy a warm welcome traditionally extended to guests.

G And Lomas's own lexicon is inspired, in part, by travel. More than two decades ago, a teenaged Lomas spent six months roaming around China—a trip that introduced him to far-ranging cultures and belief systems. "China had such detailed theories about the mind, well-being, and emotional states," he says. "I could definitely appreciate that lots of this fell outside my conceptual **horizon**."

H "There are real **limitations** if we only view our emotional lives through the prism of English," he says. It's a belief that he brings to his psychological research. If you want to understand the human mind, Lomas suggests, you have to look beyond your own culture.

---

[1] **Lexicon** refers to the entire collection of words in a language or field.
[2] **Topography** is a geological term that describes the features of an area of land.
[3] **Revelry** refers to celebration and having fun.
[4] A person feels **enchantment** when experiencing something extremely beautiful or magical.

ARE THERE UNTRANSLATABLE WORDS?

I You may recognize some of the words in Lomas's collection from the lists of "untranslatable" words that have taken the internet by storm in recent years. They include terms such as *hygge*, the Scandi-inflected pleasure of cozy comfort, and *sisu*, a kind of stoic[5] grit celebrated in Finland.

J Many language experts are skeptical of such lists. "Often, they hew suspiciously close to **stereotypes** about the culture in question," writes David Shariatmadari in his myth-busting linguistics[6] book *Don't Believe a Word: The Surprising Truth About Language.*

K The very idea of words being "untranslatable" doesn't stand up to much **scrutiny**, either, Shariatmadari explains. After all, such lists of words invariably go on to include perfectly good translations. Instead of "untranslatable," it's more accurate to say they lack a one-word, English-language **equivalent**.

L Here's the real surprise: This is the case not just for ultra-specific words like *hygge* and *sisu*. When it comes to feelings, one-to-one exact translations are less common than you might think. Even terms such as happiness, sadness, and anger—which seem basic to English speakers—are not universal and don't exist in every language.

M Take "happy," for instance. Flip through a Polish-English dictionary, and you'll find the term *szczęśliwy* offered as a direct translation. But the Polish word is actually different, said the late Polish poet Stanisław Barańczak, who translated emotion-rich works by authors including William Shakespeare and Emily Dickinson into his native language.

N While happiness can be casual, *szczęśliwy* is set aside for "rare states of profound bliss, or total satisfaction with serious things such as love, family, the meaning of life," Barańczak wrote in the book *Emotion and Cause: Linguistic Theory and Computational Implementation*. The emotional contours of *szczęśliwy* are different from that of happiness. What first appears to be an easy translation is anything but.

The Polish word *szczęśliwy* describes rare states of bliss that come from serious things, such as love and family.

WHY WORDS MATTER

O When learning a new language, students have been known to paste tiny vocabulary stickers all over the house, turning furniture into memory-jogging flash cards. But if words are just labels, why does it matter how we refer to emotions?

P Some researchers believe that words can subtly shape the way we see the world. One such researcher is neuroscientist[7] Kristen Lindquist at the University of North Carolina, who has found that the words we use play an important role in turning experiences into recognizable emotions. She described the process as a kind of categorization, like slipping an experience into a mental filing cabinet.

---

[5] A **stoic** person shows little or no feeling even through difficult or bad times.
[6] **Linguistics** is the study of how languages function.
[7] A **neuroscientist** studies how human brains work.

Q “The brain automatically and implicitly engages in categorization all the time,” Lindquist says. As an example, she describes the desktop display on her computer, which has a photo of a mountain on it. Tiny pixels of light beam out at her from the screen, and her brain uses categories acquired through experience—she’s seen plenty of mountains—to interpret the image. Without such categories, which rely on language, the display would be just a **random** smattering of color.

Language learners don’t just learn new words, but a new way to make sense of the world.

R “That’s the process by which any emotional experience is coming into being,” she says. “The concepts that we know, especially for categories such as emotion, which are really **abstract** categories, are supported in large part by the language that we speak.”

S Using a theory called psychological constructionism, Lindquist explains how an emotion, such as joy, might arise. First comes a constellation[8] of thoughts, sights, smells, and other experiences. Your brain uses existing categories, she says, to sort those incoming sensations into something you can make sense of.

T **Peer** inside each of those categories, and you’ll find impressive variety, Lindquist says. Feelings can be fuzzy, free-floating, and hard to define, but words help group them into something more **coherent**. “Language serves as the glue,” she says.

THE POWER OF LANGUAGE LEARNING

U Learning a new language might start to make that glue more flexible. “There are all sorts of differences in terms of how finely you break down your categories,” says Aneta Pavlenko, a linguist at the University of Oslo. Pavlenko argues that becoming bilingual or multilingual can restructure those categories, expanding the ways we **conceive** of emotions.

V “Maybe you see things as a single type of anger, but now you need to see them as three or four different varieties,” she says. The same goes for joy, delight, or even love.

W Pavlenko warns that simply picking up some flash cards won’t reshuffle your brain’s emotional categories. To do that, you need to put the new vocabulary to use, preferably in a situation where you’re sure to talk about feelings.

X But even if you’re not making cross-cultural small talk in Tagalog or Urdu, language study can still be a mind-expanding experience, says Lomas. While poring over a map isn’t the same as actually exploring the nooks and crannies of an unfamiliar landscape, it does hint at the shape of things—just as learning new words gives a **glimpse** of just how expansive the world of emotions can be.

Y “It’s trying to appreciate how people live and experience life,” Lomas says. “And I think words can do that.”

Adapted from “Is joy the same in every language?” by Jen Rose Smith: National Geographic, January 2021

Jen Rose Smith is a Vermont-based travel writer with a B.A. in linguistics from the University of California at Berkeley. She speaks French, Spanish, Portuguese, and Latin.

[8] A **constellation** is a collection of stars.

UNDERSTANDING THE READING

A **UNDERSTAND MAIN IDEAS** Match the paragraphs to their main ideas.

1. _____ Paragraphs A–B
2. _____ Paragraphs C–H
3. _____ Paragraphs I–K
4. _____ Paragraphs L–N
5. _____ Paragraphs O–T
6. _____ Paragraphs U–Y

a. To explore how humans think, Lomas put together a collection of words from different languages that describe emotions.

b. Even simple, everyday words often don't have one-to-one equivalents in other languages.

c. The words we know determine the way our brains classify and define objects and concepts.

d. Words from different languages give us insight into different countries and cultures.

e. Learning a new language allows us to form more precise descriptions of the world.

f. It is important not to read too much into lists of highly specific words with no English equivalent.

B **UNDERSTAND DETAILS** Read the statements. Choose **T** for true, **F** for false, or **NG** for not given.

1. Lomas's index focuses on words for emotions because such words are usually different across cultures. **T F NG**
2. In English, words for emotions tend to be less specific than in other languages. **T F NG**
3. *Szczęśliwy* describes a casual state of general happiness. **T F NG**
4. According to Lindquist, words are a way to categorize, and therefore define, abstract concepts. **T F NG**
5. Learning a new language helps us improve our proficiency in our first language. **T F NG**

Critical Thinking

C **INFER MEANING** Find and underline the following words and phrases in the reading passage. Use the context to identify their meanings. Then write the correct form of each word or phrase next to its definition.

permeates (paragraph F)	**skeptical** (paragraph J)	**invariably** (paragraph K)
smattering (paragraph Q)	**nooks and crannies** (paragraph X)	**expansive** (paragraph X)

1. ____________________ expressing a distrust of certain information
2. ____________________ small, hidden spaces
3. ____________________ wide in terms of size or scope
4. ____________________ to spread through something completely
5. ____________________ a small group of things randomly spread around
6. ____________________ always; without fail

CRITICAL THINKING Understanding Loaded Words

Writers often try to sound neutral when discussing a topic. However, they sometimes infuse their writing with subtle emotions in order to achieve their objectives. As a reader, it helps to spot such emotionally loaded language and understand the intentions behind it. For example, when describing the word *tarab*, the author uses language that is noticeably more descriptive: *"Or crank up your stereo and channel the Arabic* tarab, *a state of enchantment or ecstasy that only music can induce."* The phrase *crank up your stereo* is playful and informal, while the words *enchantment* and *ecstasy* are loaded with emotion. When an author chooses language like this, they want you to feel a certain way. It's important to try to infer why.

D **UNDERSTAND LOADED WORDS** Work with a partner. Read the three excerpts from the reading passage and note answers to the questions below.

Critical Thinking

"Roll your tongue around the German word *zielschmerz*, for example, to imagine the thrilling dread of finally chasing a long-held dream."

1. What informal phrase and descriptive adjectives does the author use?

____

____

2. How do you think the author wants you to feel about words like *zielschmerz*?

____

____

"Without such categories, which rely on language, the display would be just a random smattering of color."

3. The words "random smattering" are more emotionally loaded than the other words in the sentence. Why do you think the author uses them?

____

____

"First comes a constellation of thoughts, sights, smells, and other experiences. Your brain uses existing categories … to sort those incoming sensations into something you can make sense of."

4. What imagery does the word "constellation" evoke? Why do you think the author uses the word?

____

____

E **INTERPRET AND ANALYZE** Discuss the questions below with a partner.

Critical Thinking

1. In the reading passage, David Shariatmadari suggests that lists of "untranslateable" words often "hew suspiciously close to stereotypes… ." What does he mean by this?
2. How do the ideas described by Aneta Pavlenko in paragraphs U and V differ from what Shariatmadari warns about?

DEVELOPING READING SKILLS

READING SKILL Understanding Figurative Language

Abstract concepts can be difficult to explain. That's where figurative language can come in handy. It makes unfamiliar things more relatable by likening them to everyday experiences.

Similes

Similes use the words *as* or *like* to compare one thing to another. For example:

> *The lexicon of a foreign language is like a map of a country you've never been to.*
> *Learning a language can feel as difficult as climbing a mountain.*

Metaphors

Metaphors compare two things without using *like* or *as*. For example:

> *Some such words are a journey in themselves.*

Analogies

Analogies use simple processes to explain more complex ones. For example:

> *Kristen Lindquist … found that the words we use play an important role in turning experiences into recognizable emotions. She described the process as a kind of categorization, like slipping an experience into a mental filing cabinet.*

A **UNDERSTAND FIGURATIVE LANGUAGE** Read the quotes from the reading passage. Choose the simile.

a. … students have been known to paste tiny vocabulary stickers all over the house, turning furniture into memory-jogging flash cards.
b. To these researchers, dictionaries are like maps.
c. First comes a constellation of thoughts, sights, smells, and other experiences.

B **UNDERSTAND FIGURATIVE LANGUAGE** Read the two metaphors you didn't choose in Exercise A. Find them in the reading passage, and use the context to explain why you think the author used them.

1. ____

____

2. ____

____

C **UNDERSTAND FIGURATIVE LANGUAGE** Read the analogies below. What do you think they mean? Discuss with a partner.

1. "Feelings can be fuzzy, free-floating, and hard to define, but words help group them into something more coherent. 'Language serves as the glue,' she says." (from the reading passage)
2. "People are like stained glass windows. They sparkle and shine when the sun is out, but when the darkness sets in, their true beauty is revealed only if there is a light from within." (a quote by Elisabeth Kubler-Ross)
3. "Humor can be dissected, as a frog can, but the thing dies in the process and the innards are discouraging to any but the purely scientific mind." (a quote by Elwyn Brooks White)

VOCABULARY EXTENSION

WORD WEB Words for Looking at Things

There are many verbs we can use to describe the way people look at or observe things. Here are a few examples:

glimpse	*peer*	*scrutinize*	*gaze*
stare	*peek*	*glance*	*glare*

A Write the words from the box above in the correct column of the chart.

A brief or partial look at something	A long or careful look at something

B Choose the correct word to complete the sentences below.

1. I didn't want him to notice me, so I **gazed** / **glanced** quickly over my shoulder.
2. The police officer carefully **glimpsed** / **scrutinized** my driver's license.
3. You're not allowed to look, so close your eyes and don't **peek** / **peer**.
4. When he finally showed up an hour late, she **gazed** / **glared** at him furiously.

WORD PARTNERS Expressions with *horizon*

The word *horizon* literally refers to the line we see in the distance that separates the land or sea from the sky. However, it is often used figuratively to refer to the unknowable future, or the limits of one's knowledge. Here are a few expressions with the word *horizon*:

beyond the horizon	*broaden your horizons*
on the horizon	*a dark cloud on the horizon*

C Complete each sentence with words from the box above.

1. The news is worrying. I see ____________________ horizon.
2. The future is bright. We see plenty of opportunities ____________________ horizon.
3. With so many changes, I can't say what lies ____________________ horizon.
4. Reading is a great way to ____________________ horizons.

Video

National Geographic Explorer David Harrison interviews Abamu and Anthony Degio in an Indian village.

Discovering a Hidden Language

Around the world, language researchers are on a quest to document rare and disappearing languages. Sometimes, they discover languages that are completely new to them, like the Koro language, spoken by only a few people in Northeast India.

Critical Thinking

A **PREVIEW** Why do you think linguists believe that preserving rare and disappearing languages is important? Discuss with a partner.

B **MAIN IDEAS** ▶ Watch the video. Answer the questions below.

1. What was Harrison and Anderson's original reason for going to the village?

   ____

2. Why are Harrison and Anderson recording the Koro language?

   ____

3. Why does Harrison think recording the language is important?

   ____

C **DETAILS** ▶ Watch the video again. Choose **T** for true or **F** for false.

1. Harrison and his team were the first researchers to record Koro. **T** **F**
2. Koro belongs to a family of about 400 languages. **T** **F**
3. Most of the young people in the village speak Koro. **T** **F**
4. About 7,000 of the world's languages are endangered. **T** **F**

Critical Thinking

D **REFLECT** Work with a partner. Answer the questions.

1. In the video, Harrison says that "... if they switch to another language, much of [their] knowledge will simply be lost." Do you agree? Why or why not?
2. Do you think it is possible to prevent endangered languages like Koro from dying? Why or why not?

Writing

EXPLORING WRITTEN ENGLISH

LANGUAGE FOR WRITING Adding Information with Verbal Phrases

Verbal phrases begin with verbs, but function as different parts of speech (nouns or adjectives). They allow you to add extra information to sentences or combine two sentences that have the same subject. You can create verbal phrases using:

Participles (-*ing* or -*ed* verbs) that are used as adjectives:

She spoke slowly. She gave me directions to the train station.
Speaking slowly, she gave me directions to the train station.

To Kill a Mockingbird *was published in 1960. It was Harper Lee's first novel.*
Published in 1960, To Kill a Mockingbird *was Harper Lee's first novel.*

Gerunds (-*ing* verbs) used as nouns:

Zamora read literature. It gave her a deeper understanding of English.
Reading literature gave Zamora a deeper understanding of English.

Infinitives (*to* + base forms of verbs):

I wanted to learn Japanese quickly. I didn't allow myself to speak English for a month.
To learn Japanese quickly, I didn't allow myself to speak English for a month.

Verbal phrases can be used at the start, middle, or end of sentences. Notice how commas are used to set them apart from the rest of the sentence:

Jack apologized to his sister, feeling terrible about what he'd done.
Jack, feeling terrible about what he'd done, apologized to his sister.
Feeling terrible about what he'd done, Jack apologized to his sister.

A **NOTICE** Underline the verbal phrase in each excerpt. What type of verbal phrase is it? Write **P** for participle, **G** for gerund, or **I** for infinitive.

1. Wiping the tears from his face, he apologized to his sister. ________
2. She collapsed to the ground, exhausted from the long walk. ________
3. To celebrate their results, they went to a restaurant. ________
4. Lost in thought, her eyes looked straight ahead, unblinking. ________
5. Moving to the city taught me independence. ________

B **APPLY** Choose the correct word to complete each sentence.

1. **Memorized** / **Memorizing** vocabulary words can help you learn a new language.
2. **Felt** / **Feeling** a little unwell, he decided to take the day off.
3. He stopped talking, **interrupted** / **interrupting** by the noise in the other room.
4. **Excited** / **Exciting** to see her, the young boy ran quickly to his mother.
5. **To pay** / **Paying** for her new car, Selena got a second job.

C **APPLY** Combine the following pairs of sentences using the verbal phrases provided.

1. Many students rely solely on online self-study language programs. They miss out on opportunities to interact with others.

   ____

   missing out on ______________________________

2. Second-year language students have to study complex grammar. This can make them feel very frustrated.

   Studying ______________________________

   ____

3. Many teachers want to motivate their students. They make it a point to provide lots of positive feedback.

   To motivate ______________________________

   ____

D **REFLECT** Work with a partner. Write down tips for picking up a new language. Use verbal phrases in your tips.

1. *To pick up a new language, it's important that you speak it regularly.*

   ____

2. ______________________________

   ____

3. ______________________________

   ____

4. ______________________________

   ____

WRITING SKILL Writing Introductions and Conclusions

The first paragraph of an essay—the introductory paragraph—includes general information about the essay topic as well as the thesis statement. To grab the reader's attention, try starting your introduction with a hook such as a surprising statement, an interesting question, a quotation, or a brief story related to the topic.

The final, or concluding, paragraph of an essay should give the reader a sense of completeness. The conclusion usually includes a restatement of the thesis, a summary of the main supporting points made in the paper, and perhaps a final thought about the topic. The final thought can take the form of a provocative statement or question.

E Identify the features (a–e) in the following introduction and conclusion. Write the correct letter next to each feature. Discuss your answers with a partner.

a. summary of the main supporting points
b. interesting quote to introduce the topic
c. restatement of thesis
d. thesis statement
e. final thought

Essay topic:

The main benefit of learning a new language is the ability to communicate with speakers of that language. To what extent do you agree with this statement?

Introduction:

[Nelson Mandela said, "If you talk to a man in a language he understands, that goes to his head. If you talk to him in his own language, that goes to his heart." In other words, you can only communicate intimately with someone if you speak their language.] ☐ [However, while being able to communicate with speakers of other languages is a great benefit of language learning, I believe there are other equally important benefits: learning a new language helps us understand our own language better, improves our problem-solving skills and memory, and makes us better thinkers.] ☐

Conclusion:

[There are, therefore, several benefits to language learning that are just as important as being able to communicate with people who speak that language.] ☐ [Studying a second language improves our reading and listening skills in our own language. It improves our memories and our problem-solving capabilities. Finally, it can actually change our brain's shape in a way that helps us become better thinkers.] ☐ [It is arguable, too, that learning a new language fosters intercultural awareness and open-mindedness. It is perhaps good then that there are *several* compelling reasons why more of us should learn a new language.] ☐

F **VOCABULARY FOR WRITING** People frequently use phrases such as *I think*, *I believe*, and *In my opinion* to introduce their opinions. The phrases below can also be used to introduce personal and general opinions. Write each phrase in the correct column in the chart.

According to most people,	From my perspective,	In my experience,
It is generally accepted that	Many suggest/claim	Personally, I believe

Personal Opinions	General Opinions

WRITING TASK

GOAL You are going to write an opinion essay on the following topic:
What is the best way to learn a new language outside of school?

A **BRAINSTORM** Consider the methods of learning a second/foreign language below. How effective are they? Discuss the pros and cons of each method with a partner and take notes.

reading books	watching movies	traveling	language learning apps

Your own idea: ______________________

____

____

____

B **EVALUATE** Which method has the most pros and fewest cons? Choose your preferred method and list the three strongest reasons for it.

Method: ____

Reason 1: ____

Reason 2: ____

Reason 3: ____

Review this Writing Skill in Unit 1

C **WRITE A THESIS STATEMENT** Discuss the thesis statement below with a partner. What is the writer's position? What are the three supporting ideas? Then look at your information in Exercise B and prepare your own thesis statement for your essay.

For reading aloud to be truly beneficial to children, the stories must be interesting, relatable, and challenging.

____

____

____

D **PREPARE AN INTRODUCTION** Think about how to start your essay. You could use an anecdote, for example, a quote, or the results of a study. Write notes below.

____

____

____

E **PLAN** Use your information in Exercises B–D to complete an outline of your opinion essay. Make sure your topic sentences are about the supporting ideas in your thesis statement. Include examples of personal experiences where possible.

Review this Writing Skill in Unit 3

OUTLINE

Introduction:

____

____

____

Thesis statement: ______________________________

____

Body paragraph 1:

Topic sentence: ______________________________

Details: ______________________________

____

____

Body paragraph 2:

Topic sentence: ______________________________

Details: ______________________________

____

Body paragraph 3:

Topic sentence: ______________________________

Details: ______________________________

____

____

Conclusion:

Final thought: ______________________________

____

____

F **FIRST DRAFT** Use the information in your outline to write a first draft of your essay. Remember to include interesting information in your introduction, and use verbal phrases to explain your opinions. Conclude by restating your thesis, summarizing your supporting ideas, and including a final thought.

G **REVISING PRACTICE** The essay below is similar to the one you are writing. Follow the steps to create a better second draft.

1. Add the sentences (a–c) in the most suitable spaces.
   a. Giving young children a strong reading foundation can therefore only benefit them in the future.
   b. Finally, reading skills are developed further when children are challenged.
   c. Author Emilie Buchwald once said, "Children are made readers on the laps of their parents." I agree with her statement.
2. Now fix the following problems (a–c) with the essay.
   a. Fix an error with a verbal phrase in paragraph B.
   b. Delete an unrelated idea in paragraph C.
   c. Fix an error with a verbal phrase in paragraph D.

A _____ It is true that some children easily begin reading on their own because they were read to by their parents. However, I also believe that the choice of books is highly important. For reading aloud to be truly beneficial to children, the stories must be interesting, relatable, and challenging.

B Teaching children that reading can be fun, parents should select books that their children will find interesting. Children will pay attention to the stories their parents read to them when the events in them are fun. This will in turn help improve their reading comprehension skills. When the children later begin reading on their own, having books that they actually enjoy will encourage them to stay engaged and try to understand what they're reading.

C Children also find books that relate to their own lives engaging. Very young children struggle with abstract concepts, like those often explored in fantasy novels. One popular fantasy novel series, for instance, explores the differences between good and evil, loyalty and betrayal, courage and fear, and tradition and change. Stories about everyday experiences with relatable characters are much easier for children to understand. They also give children something to discuss, and they teach things that are practical and useful in everyday life.

D _____ Children need to encounter words they don't know in order to increase their vocabulary. Confused by these unfamiliar words children will naturally push themselves to try to understand. Parents would be shrewd not to explain what they mean. Instead, they should encourage their children to re-read the surrounding sentences and guess the words' meanings.

E Reading aloud to children is important, but so is selecting the right books. Interesting, relatable, and challenging stories build in children a strong desire to read. This aids in the acquisition of reading skills, which in the age of the internet and social media are more important than ever. _____

H **REVISED DRAFT** Now use the questions below to revise your essay.

- ☐ Does your introduction provide relevant background information on the topic?
- ☐ Does your thesis state the main points of the essay?
- ☐ Do your body paragraphs include enough details to fully explain your ideas?
- ☐ Do you use verbal phrases correctly?
- ☐ Do all your sentences relate to the main idea?
- ☐ Does your concluding paragraph have a summary statement and a final thought?

I **EDITING PRACTICE** Read the information below. Find and correct one mistake with verbal phrases in each sentence (1–6). Then match each sentence with the type of mistake it contains.

When you use verbal phrases, remember:

- that verbal phrases modify nouns, pronouns, or whole clauses.
- to separate verbal phrases from clauses with commas.
- you don't need a comma if an infinitive verbal phrase comes at the end of a sentence.

Types of mistakes:

a. missing noun or pronoun b. unnecessary comma c. missing comma

1. _____ Taking classes every night, learned a lot quickly.
2. _____ You can take private lessons, to learn a new language.
3. _____ Living in a bilingual household I learned Spanish easily.
4. _____ To improve your pronunciation you have to practice.
5. _____ Watching TV in English, learned a lot of natural language.
6. _____ Using flashcards, is a great way to learn new words.

J **FINAL DRAFT** Follow these steps to write a final draft.

1. Check your revised draft for mistakes with verbal phrases.
2. Now use the checklist on page 248 to write a final draft. Make any other necessary changes.
3. Work in pairs and read your partner's final essay. Give feedback on each other's writing.

Review

SELF-ASSESS **Consider the language and skills you learned in this unit.**

How well can you . . . ?	Very well	Pretty well	I need improvement
use the key vocabulary from this unit	☐	☐	☐
understand loaded words	☐	☐	☐
understand figurative language	☐	☐	☐
add information with verbal phrases	☐	☐	☐
write introductions and conclusions	☐	☐	☐

A **VOCABULARY** Do you remember the meanings of these words? Look back at the unit and review the ones you don't know.

abstract AW	coherent AW	conceive AW	dread	equivalent AW
glimpse	horizon AW	hospitality	limitation	paradigm AW
peer	random AW	scrutiny	stereotype AW	texture

B **VOCABULARY EXTENSION** Complete these tasks with a partner.

1. Make sentences using four words for looking at things from the Word Web box on page 135.
2. Make two sentences using expressions with the word *horizon*.

C **READING SKILL** Work with a partner. Use figurative language to describe the following.

1. a simile to describe what your native language sounds like
2. a metaphor to describe what learning a new language is like
3. an analogy to describe a concept of your own choosing

D **LANGUAGE FOR WRITING** Work with a partner. Combine the sentences using verbal phrases.

1. He wanted to improve his Korean. He started watching a lot of Korean dramas.
2. I was looking for a challenge. I decided to learn Arabic.
3. I learned Japanese. It helped me understand Japanese culture much better.

SELF-ASSESS **Look back at the chart above. Did you assess your skills correctly? What skills or language do you still need help with?**

RESOURCES AND DEVELOPMENT

Modern skyscrapers tower over more traditional low-rise buildings in Frankfurt, Germany.

IN THIS UNIT, YOU WILL:

- Read an article about Africa's geography
- Watch a video about two unique Cameroonian exports
- Write about how a country is affected by its history and geography

THINK AND DISCUSS:

1. The photo above shows modern high-rise buildings in Frankfurt, Germany. Do you think such development is good for places like this? Why or why not?
2. Which part of the city above would you enjoy living in more? What about visiting or working in? Why?

EXPLORE THE THEME

Look at the information on these pages and answer the questions.

1. What are some factors that have led to population growth?
2. Which parts of the world have the most people?
3. Is the population in your country rising? Why or why not?

8 Billion People

High-density residential blocks in Hong Kong, China

In 2023, the world's human population reached 8 billion. It was 7 billion just 12 years prior. So why the sharp increase?

The rapid rise is in no small part due to economic development. Increased standards of living have resulted in better health care, cleaner water, and improvements in sanitation. Fertilizers and irrigation have boosted crop yields, allowing us to sustain larger populations. And greater access to healthcare means more children are born healthy.

Our population is projected to grow even more over the next few decades, but how will countries cope with the strain this will place on resources and infrastructure? Economic development brings great benefits, but left unchecked, it could also be the cause of many new problems.

World Population by Region

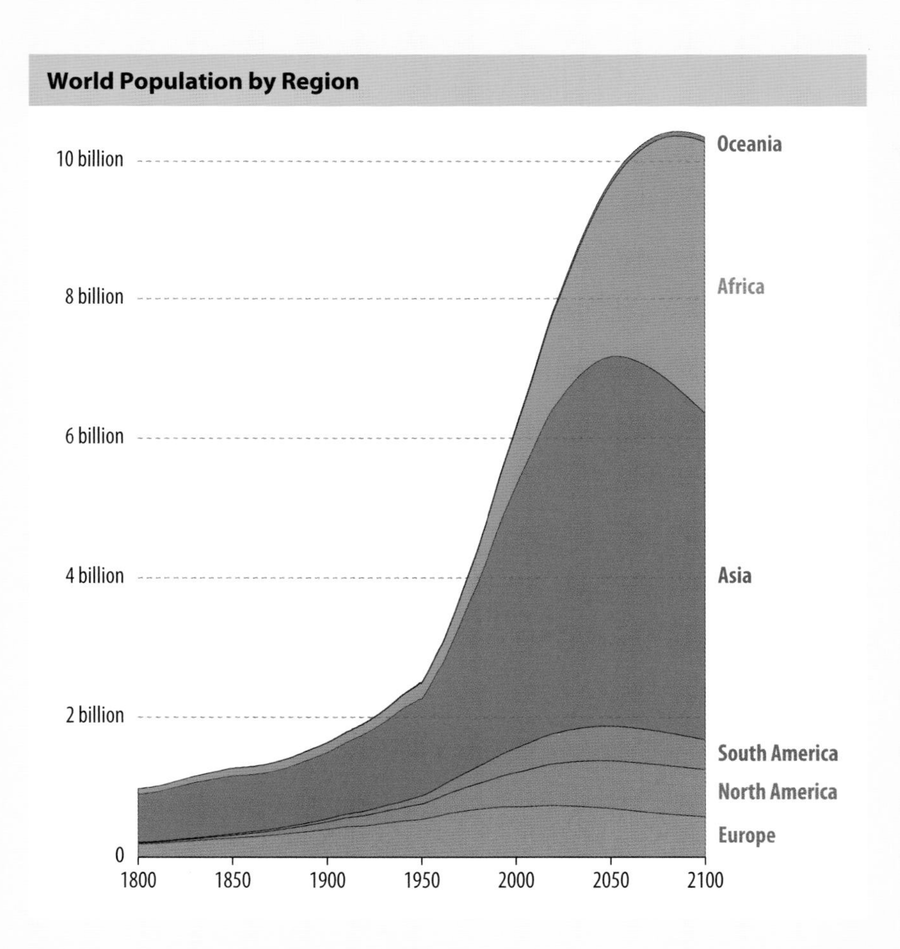

Reading

PREPARING TO READ

A **BUILD VOCABULARY** The words in **blue** are used in the reading passage. Match each word to its definition. Use a dictionary to help you.

1. ____ **adaptation** (n) a. to look similar to something else
2. ____ **arise** (v) b. the people employed in an organization or place
3. ____ **distinct** (adj) c. bad luck
4. ____ **dominant** (adj) d. to start to develop or exist
5. ____ **misfortune** (n) e. the act of changing in order to survive in a particular environment
6. ____ **resemble** (v) f. more powerful than other groups
7. ____ **workforce** (n) g. noticeable or different

B **BUILD VOCABULARY** Complete the sentences below with the correct form of the words in **blue**. Use a dictionary to help you.

associate (v)	**burden** (n)	**corruption** (n)	**mining** (n)
radically (adv)	**sole** (adj)	**thrive** (v)	**undergo** (v)

1. The country ____________ a transformation in the 1970s, after it signed the trade deal.
2. They grew up there, so they ____________ that place with their youth.
3. After she announced the bad news, the mood in the room changed ____________.
4. There are a lot of minerals in the ground, so ____________ is a big industry here.
5. Creating more jobs for the unemployed is the ____________ purpose of this proposal.
6. Her ambition is to work hard and ____________ in the city.
7. The cost of housing is a huge ____________ for people living in the city.
8. If we want to reduce crime, we need to fix ____________ in the police force.

C **USE VOCABULARY** Discuss these questions with a partner.

1. What are some changes your country has **undergone** in the last 20 years?
2. What do people usually **associate** your country or region with?

Critical Thinking

D **PREDICT** Read the first two paragraphs of the reading passage. How do you think Africa's shape affects life on the continent? Discuss with a partner.

DEVELOPING READING SKILLS

READING SKILL Annotating a Text

Annotating—or marking up—a text while you read it helps you to stay focused on what you are reading. It also helps you remember and find important information later. Here are some ways to annotate a text:

- Highlight important ideas. Use one color for main ideas and another for supporting information.
- Circle new vocabulary to check later.
- Underline and put a question mark next to parts you don't understand, to re-read later.
- Break the text into sections by sub-topic and label each section in the margins.

Here is an example of a paragraph with annotations:

> For people in developing nations, solar-powered devices can offer several distinct advantages. The availability of low-cost solar lamps, for example, means longer working hours and better security at night. One organization in Uganda—Solar Sister—is using solar power to turn local women into solar entrepreneurs. It employs them to sell its solar-powered products. The women don't require qualifications or experience to start because Solar Sister provides them with training. Furthermore, Solar Sister empowers these women to start businesses of their own by providing them with products to sell at no initial financial cost. ?

In the paragraph above, a reader has highlighted the main idea in pink and supporting ideas in blue. An unfamiliar word, *entrepreneurs,* is circled. A question mark indicates that the student is unsure about the last underlined sentence and plans to re-read it.

A **ANNOTATE A TEXT** The paragraphs below are from the reading passage. Annotate them using the methods in the Reading Skill box above.

Ask someone to tell you quickly what they associate with Africa and the answers you'll get will probably range from "cradle of humankind" and "big animals" to "poverty" and "tribalism." How did one continent come to embody such extremes?

Geography and history go a long way toward providing the explanations. Geographically, Africa resembles a bulging sandwich. The sole continent to span both the north and south temperate zones, it has a thick tropical core lying between one thin temperate zone in the north and another in the south. That simple geographic reality explains a great deal about Africa today.

B **DISCUSS** Work with a partner. Compare your annotations. Are there any other ways you could annotate these paragraphs? Discuss your ideas.

C **ANNOTATE A TEXT** Read the entire reading passage. Annotate as you read.

THE SHAPE OF AFRICA

By Jared Diamond

The hope for Africa's future lies with its abundant human and natural resources.

A Ask someone to tell you quickly what they **associate** with Africa and the answers you'll get will probably range from "cradle of humankind" and "big animals" to "poverty" and "tribalism." How did one continent come to embody such extremes?

B Geography and history go a long way toward providing the explanations. Geographically, Africa **resembles** a bulging sandwich. The **sole** continent to span both the north and south temperate zones,[1] it has a thick tropical core lying between one thin temperate zone in the north and another in the south. That simple geographic reality explains a great deal about Africa today.

C As to its human history, this is the place where—some seven million years ago—the evolutionary lines of apes and protohumans[2] diverged. It remained the only continent our ancestors inhabited until around two million years ago, when Homo erectus expanded out of Africa into Europe and Asia. Over the next 1.5 million years, the populations of those three continents followed such different evolutionary courses that they became **distinct** species. Europe's became the Neanderthals, Asia's remained Homo erectus, but Africa's evolved into our own species, Homo sapiens. Sometime between 100,000 and 50,000 years ago, our African ancestors **underwent** some further profound change. Whether it was the development of complex speech or something else, such as a change in brain wiring, we aren't sure. Whatever it was, it transformed those early Homo sapiens into what paleoanthropologists[3] call "behaviorally modern" Homo sapiens. Those people, probably with brains similar to our own, expanded again into Europe and Asia. Once there, they exterminated or replaced or interbred with Neanderthals and Asia's hominins[4] and became the **dominant** human species throughout the world.

D In effect, Africans enjoyed not just one but three huge head starts over humans on other continents. That makes Africa's economic struggles today, compared with the successes of other continents, particularly puzzling. It's the opposite of what one would expect from the runner first off the block. Here again, geography and history give us answers.

E It turns out that the rules of the competitive race among the world's humans changed **radically** about 10,000 years ago, with the origins of agriculture. The domestication of wild plants and animals meant our ancestors could grow their own food instead of having to hunt or gather it in the wild. That allowed people to settle in permanent villages, to increase their populations, and to feed specialists—inventors, soldiers, and kings—who did not produce food. With domestication came other advances, including the first metal tools, writing, and state societies.

[1] **Temperate zones** are areas between the tropics and the polar circle.
[2] A **protohuman** is an early ancestor of modern humans.
[3] **Paleoanthropologists** are scientists who study human fossils.
[4] **Hominins** are the early forms of humans that descended from primates.

Africa's unique geography makes agriculture in much of the continent challenging.

F The problem is that only a tiny minority of wild plants and animals lend themselves to domestication, and those few are concentrated in about half a dozen parts of the world. As every schoolchild learns, the world's earliest and most productive farming arose in the Fertile Crescent of southwestern Asia, where wheat, barley, sheep, cattle, and goats were domesticated. While those plants and animals spread east and west in Eurasia, in Africa they were stopped by the continent's north-south orientation. Crops and livestock tend to spread much more slowly from north to south than from east to west because different latitudes require **adaptation** to different climates, seasonalities, day lengths, and diseases. Africa's own native plant species—sorghum, oil palm, coffee, millets, and yams—weren't domesticated until thousands of years after Asia and Europe had agriculture. And Africa's geography kept oil palm, yams, and other crops of equatorial Africa from spreading into southern Africa's temperate zone. While South Africa today boasts[5] the continent's richest agricultural lands, the crops grown there are mostly northern temperate crops, such as wheat and grapes, brought directly on ships by European colonists. Those same crops never succeeded in spreading south through the thick tropical core of Africa.

G The domesticated sheep and cattle of Fertile Crescent origins took about 5,000 years to spread from the Mediterranean down to the southern tip of Africa. The continent's own native animals—with the exception of guinea fowl and possibly donkeys and one breed of cattle—proved impossible to domesticate. History might have turned out differently if African armies, fed by barnyard-giraffe meat and backed by waves of cavalry[6] mounted on huge rhinos, had swept into Europe to

---

[5] To **boast** something is to possess a feature that is a source of pride.
[6] A **cavalry** is a group of soldiers who ride horses.

overrun its mutton-fed soldiers mounted on puny horses. That this didn't happen was no fault of the Africans; it was because of the kinds of wild animals available to them.

H Ironically, the long human presence in Africa is probably the reason the continent's species of big animals survive today. African animals coevolved with humans for millions of years, as human hunting prowess gradually progressed from the basic skills of our early ancestors. That gave the animals time to learn a healthy fear of man and, with it, a healthy avoidance of human hunters. In contrast, North and South America and Australia were settled by humans only within the last tens of thousands of years. To the **misfortune** of the big animals of those continents, the first humans they encountered were already fully modern people, with modern brains and hunting skills. Most of those animals—woolly mammoths, saber-toothed cats, and, in Australia, marsupials[7] as big as rhinoceroses—disappeared soon after humans arrived. Entire species may have been exterminated before they had time to learn to be wary of hunters.

I Unfortunately, the long human presence in Africa also encouraged something else to **thrive**—diseases. The continent has a well-deserved reputation for having spawned some of our nastiest ones: malaria, yellow fever, East African sleeping sickness, and AIDS. These and many other human illnesses arose when microbes causing disease in animals crossed species lines to evolve into a human disease. For a microbe already adapted to one species, to adapt to another can be difficult and require a lot of evolutionary time. Much more time has been available in Africa, cradle of humankind, than in any other part of the planet. That's half the answer to Africa's disease **burden**; the other half is that the animal species most closely related to humans—those whose microbes required the least adaptation to jump species—are the African great apes and monkeys.

[7] **Marsupials** are animals such as kangaroos. Female marsupials carry their babies in pouches on their bellies.

Like this oryx antelope, much of Africa's wildlife can't easily be domesticated.

J Africa continues to be shaped in other ways by its long history and its geography. Of mainland Africa's ten richest countries, eight lie partly or entirely within its temperate zones: Egypt, Libya, Tunisia, and Algeria in the north; and Angola, South Africa, Botswana, and Namibia in the south. Gabon and Equatorial Guinea are Africa's only tropical countries to make the list. In addition, nearly a third of the countries of mainland Africa (15 out of 47) are landlocked, and the only African river navigable from the ocean for long distances inland is the Nile. Since waterways provide the cheapest way to transport cumbersome[8] goods, geography again thwarts Africa's progress.

K All these factors can lead to the question: "Is the continent, or at least its big tropical core, doomed eternally to wars, poverty, and devastating diseases?" I'd answer, "Absolutely not." On my own visits to Africa, I've been struck by how harmoniously ethnic groups live together in many countries—far better than they do in many other parts of the globe. Tensions **arise** in Africa, as they do elsewhere, when people see no other way out of poverty except to fight their neighbors for dwindling resources. But many areas of Africa have an abundance of resources: The rivers of central Africa are great generators of hydroelectric power; the big animals are a major source of ecotourism revenue in eastern and southern Africa; and the forests in the

[8] If something is **cumbersome**, it is large and heavy and therefore difficult to carry or handle.

wetter regions, if managed and logged sustainably, would be renewable and lucrative[9] sources of income.

L As for Africa's health problems, they can be greatly alleviated with the right planning and funding. Within the past half century, several formerly poor countries in Asia recognized that tropical diseases were a major drain on their economies. By investing in public health measures, they have successfully curbed those diseases, and the increased health of their people has led to far healthier economies. Within Africa itself, some international **mining** and oil companies have been funding successful public health programs throughout their concession areas[10] because they realized that protecting the health of their workers was an excellent business investment for them.

M What's the best case for Africa's future? If the continent can overcome its health problems and the **corruption** that plagues many of its governments and institutions, then it could take advantage of today's globalized, technological world in much the same way that China and India are now doing. Technology could give Africa the connections that its geography, particularly its rivers, long denied it. Nearly half of all African countries are English speaking—an advantage in trade relations—and an educated, English-speaking **workforce** could well attract service jobs to many African countries.

N If Africa is to head into a bright future, outside investment will continue to be needed, at least for a time. The cost of perpetual aid to or military intervention in Africa is thousands of times more expensive than solving its health problems and supporting local development, thereby heading off[11] conflicts. The entire world will be healthier and safer if Africa's nations increasingly take their places as peaceful and prospering members of the world community.

Adapted from "The Shape of Africa," by Jared Diamond: National Geographic Magazine, September 2005

Jared Diamond is an American ecologist, geographer, and anthropologist. His book *Guns, Germs, and Steel: The Fates of Human Societies* won the Pulitzer Prize.

A vibrant, thriving community in Kinshasa, Democratic Republic of the Congo

[9] A **lucrative** activity, job, or business is one that's very profitable.
[10] A **concession area** is a place where someone is given the right to sell a product or run a business.
[11] If you **head off** an event, you prevent it from happening.

UNDERSTANDING THE READING

A **UNDERSTAND MAIN IDEAS** Match paragraphs B–H to their main ideas.

1. _____ Paragraph B
2. _____ Paragraph C
3. _____ Paragraph D
4. _____ Paragraph E
5. _____ Paragraph F
6. _____ Paragraph G
7. _____ Paragraph H

a. African animals are resilient because they evolved alongside humans.
b. Humans have been in Africa for a very long time.
c. Africa's geographical orientation restricted the spread of agriculture.
d. Despite Africa's long human history, much of the continent has not thrived.
e. Africa's geography explains the extremes that exist on the continent.
f. The development of agriculture impacts a culture.
g. Most of the animals in Africa were unsuitable for domestication.

Review Paraphrasing in Unit 5

B **UNDERSTAND MAIN IDEAS** Write the main ideas of the paragraphs below.

1. Paragraph I: The long human presence in Africa led to ______________________________
____
2. Paragraph K: Africa has hope because ______________________________
____
3. Paragraph L: ______________________________
____
4. Paragraph M: ______________________________
____

Critical Thinking

C **UNDERSTAND CHRONOLOGY** Look again at paragraph C. Put the events (a–f) in the correct order in the timeline.

a. "Behaviorally modern" Homo sapiens appears in Africa.
b. Protohumans remain as Homo erectus in Asia, but evolve into Neanderthals in Europe and Homo sapiens in Africa.
c. Apes and protohumans split.
d. Homo erectus moves to Europe and Asia.
e. Homo sapiens becomes the dominant species as other forms of humans die out.
f. Homo sapiens moves into Europe and Asia.

☐ ☐ ☐ ☐ ☐ ☐

Seven million years ago — Approx. 100–50 thousand years ago

D **INFER MEANING** Find and underline the following words and phrases in the reading passage. Use the context to identify their meanings. Then match each word or phrase to its definition (a–h).

Critical Thinking

1. ____ **go a long way toward** (paragraph B)
2. ____ **head starts** (paragraph D)
3. ____ **lend themselves to** (paragraph F)
4. ____ **spawned** (paragraph I)
5. ____ **landlocked** (paragraph J)
6. ____ **struck** (paragraph K)
7. ____ **a (major) drain on** (paragraph L)
8. ____ **plagues** (paragraph M)

a. a heavy use of something such as resources
b. caused to happen
c. without access to the ocean or sea
d. contribute greatly to
e. advantages in a competition
f. continually causes problems
g. surprised or greatly affected
h. are suitable for, or adapt easily to

E **UNDERSTAND DETAILS** Note answers to the questions below. Then discuss with a partner.

1. What were some effects of the development of agriculture?

____

____

2. What blocked the spread of agriculture in Africa, and why?

____

____

3. Why is the proximity to great apes and monkeys a problem in Africa?

____

____

4. How does the lack of access to waterways affect many African countries?

____

____

F **UNDERSTAND DETAILS** Read paragraphs M–N of the reading passage and complete the summary. Use no more than two words from the reading passage for each answer.

For Africa to thrive, it has to overcome its [1]__________ and stamp out [2]__________. Then, it can make use of [3]__________ to tap into global markets. A significant advantage Africa enjoys is that a substantial portion of its workforce is educated and [4]__________. This could help African countries attract many [5]__________. While [6]__________ will still be necessary at least for a while, the continent will have to stop relying on foreign aid and military intervention. It will need to eventually solve its health issues and fund its own [7]__________.

CRITICAL THINKING Analyzing Point of View

It is often necessary to identify a writer's attitude toward the topic to evaluate their content effectively. Look for clues in how the writer uses language. Point of view can be indicated indirectly through word choices—for example, the use of words and expressions with positive or negative connotations.

Critical Thinking

G **ANALYZE POINT OF VIEW** Read the statements below. How strongly do you think the author would agree or disagree with each one? Rate each statement from 1 (strongly disagree) to 5 (strongly agree). Note down words or phrases from the passage that helped you understand the author's point of view. Discuss your ideas with a partner.

1. Many large animal species remain in Africa today because humans have lived there for so long. (paragraph H)

   1 **2** **3** **4** **5**

   key words/phrases: ______________________________

   ____

2. Africa is "doomed eternally to wars, poverty, and devastating diseases." (paragraph K)

   1 **2** **3** **4** **5**

   key words/phrases: ______________________________

   ____

3. In Africa, many ethnic groups live together happily. (paragraph K)

   1 **2** **3** **4** **5**

   key words/phrases: ______________________________

   ____

4. Many areas of Africa have adequate natural resources. (paragraph K)

   1 **2** **3** **4** **5**

   key words/phrases: ______________________________

   ____

5. It will take a lot of work to ensure that Africa has a bright future. (paragraph M)

   1 **2** **3** **4** **5**

   key words/phrases: ______________________________

   ____

Critical Thinking

H **EVALUATE** Look at the statements in Exercise G. Do you feel differently about them from the author? Why or why not? Discuss with a partner.

VOCABULARY EXTENSION

WORD PARTNERS Adjective + *economy*

Here are some adjectives that collocate with the noun *economy*:

booming economy | *developing economy* | *global economy*
service-based economy | *weak economy*

A Complete each sentence with the correct form of an expression from the box above.

1. Tourism and retail are major elements of ____________________.
2. Unemployment is expected to rise because of the ____________________.
3. In 2009, many countries faced significant drops in their GDPs, causing the ____________________ to suffer.
4. Many companies are experiencing sharp growth thanks to the ____________________.
5. Countries with slower growth and lower levels of personal income are regarded as ____________________.

WORD PARTNERS *distinct* + Noun

The adjective *distinct* can mean two different things: distinguishable or noticeable. Here are some nouns that collocate with the adjective *distinct:*

distinct advantage | *distinct possibility* | *distinct groups*
distinct difference | *distinct pattern* | *distinct smell*

B Complete the paragraph with words from the box above.

Immigration is a complex issue. Many people welcome it, while others want to limit or control it. But what do economists think? Most experts agree: immigration is—in general—a good thing. First, countries with large immigrant populations have a distinct [1]_______________ in terms of entrepreneurship and innovation. Furthermore, global trade and living standards increase with immigration. Still, many worry about its adverse effects and see a distinct [2]_______________ between legal and illegal immigration. Globally, immigration is on the rise, and there is a distinct [3]_______________ that more countries will start implementing policies to slow it down. However, we should always remember that many nations are already home to large, distinct [4]_______________ whose ancestors chose to leave their lands a long time ago in search of brighter futures elsewhere. Immigration has gone on for centuries, and will continue for centuries more. To expect it to suddenly stop would probably be naive.

Video

Honey and Pepper

Around the world, there are certain foods that can only emerge from specific regions because of the unique properties of those places. Such foods are often assigned geographical indications, or G.I. labels, by the European Commission. These labels protect regional foods by preventing similar foods grown elsewhere from using their names.

Critical Thinking

A **PREVIEW** Read the paragraph above. Can you think of any regional foods or drinks that are protected? In what ways are they protected? Discuss with a partner.

B **MAIN IDEA** ▶ Watch the video. What is it mainly about?

a. two Cameroonian food products that hope to receive G.I. labels in the future
b. why it is often harder for African food products to receive G.I. labels
c. two Cameroonian food products that have already received G.I. labels

C **DETAILS** ▶ Watch the video again. Complete the Venn diagram. Write the letters a–e.

a. It sells for up to 35 dollars per 100 grams.
b. Its unique properties come from volcanic soil.
c. Its unique properties come from a plant that grows in the area.
d. Its price rose after receiving the G.I. label.
e. It is popular with chefs in Europe.

Oku White Honey **Penja Pepper**

Critical Thinking

D **INFER** Why do you think obtaining a G.I. label often leads to a rise in the price of a product? Discuss with a partner.

Writing

EXPLORING WRITTEN ENGLISH

LANGUAGE FOR WRITING Avoiding Plagiarism (II)—Referring to Sources

Review Paraphrasing in Unit 5

When using other people's ideas in your writing, you can either quote them directly or paraphrase. Try to paraphrase as much as possible, but use direct quotations when the original words are particularly effective. Here are some ways to refer to sources:

According to Diamond, *"The long human presence in Africa is probably the reason the continent's species of big animals survive today."*

As Diamond says, *"The long human presence in Africa is probably the reason the continent's species of big animals survive today."*

Diamond says that *"the long human presence in Africa is probably the reason the continent's species of big animals survive today."*

Diamond says that *the fact that humans have been in Africa for a very long time probably explains why many large animal species still exist on the continent today.*

In academic writing, it is common to use *that* after reporting verbs. When using *that*, make sure the quote fits grammatically into the sentence.

Vary your style by using different reporting verbs. For example: *says, states, claims, believes, explains, points out, suggests, reports, concludes, argues.*

Choose a reporting verb that matches your intention. For example: if you are using a study to make a point, you might say, "X concludes that ..."; if you wish to contradict someone's idea, you might say, "X argues that ..."; and if you are reporting someone's opinion, you might say, "X thinks/believes/feels that ...".

A **NOTICE** Read the sentence below that refers to an argument made by Jared Diamond in the reading passage. Then answer the questions.

As Jared Diamond says, "Unfortunately, the long human presence in Africa also encouraged something else to thrive—diseases."

1. Which two words from the box below can be used to replace the word *says*?

feels	informs	suggests	states	tells

2. What other words could replace the word *says*? Note some ideas below. Then compare your answers with a partner.

___

___

___

B **APPLY** Answer the questions below by quoting information from the reading passage.

1. Directly quote author Jared Diamond: What may have happened to the large animals that disappeared in Australia and North and South America? (paragraph H)

   ____

   ____

2. Paraphrase Diamond's opinion: How well do people get along with each other in Africa? (paragraph K)

   ____

   ____

3. Use a reporting verb: What is the main point Diamond makes in paragraph L?

   ____

   ____

4. Use a reporting verb: What is the main point Diamond makes in paragraph M?

   ____

   ____

WRITING SKILL Doing Research Online

When doing research online, it helps to be able to evaluate sources quickly and effectively. Use these tips to help you:

- Limit search results by using precise key words within quotation marks.
- Scan your search results to quickly eliminate sites that are irrelevant.
- Avoid using encyclopedia sites as your main source. Use original sources instead. The references at the end of encyclopedia articles can be a good place to find original sources.
- Be alert to signs that a site and its contents may be unreliable. Ask yourself: Is the site trustworthy? Is the information accurate? Is it current?

While researching, it helps to take notes. In your notes, consider including the following:

- Useful information: you could label information you wish to paraphrase with a P and information you wish to quote directly with a Q.
- Information about your sources: e.g., the names of the people you're quoting, the publications you're quoting from, and the URLs of articles you're using.

C Work with a partner. Read the following research questions (1–3). For each question, answer the following: What key words could you use for an online search? What types of websites would give you the best information?

1. What are some ways to improve agricultural production in Africa?
2. What languages are most spoken in Africa?
3. What can landlocked nations in Africa do to boost trade?

D Research a country or region that interests you. Take notes on the following points.

1. Background: What is the country or region like today?
2. Geography: What are two or three features affecting its current situation?
3. History: What two or three events shaped its current situation?

Country or Region:	
Background	**Source Information**
Geography	**Source Information**
History	**Source Information**

E Look at your notes in Exercise D. Write P next to the points you would like to paraphrase, and Q next to the points you would like to quote directly.

F **VOCABULARY FOR WRITING** The following words can be useful when writing about geography and history. Find the words in the reading passage and use the context to guess their meanings. Then write each word next to its definition.

span (paragraph B)	**temperate** (paragraph B)	**tropical** (paragraph B)
concentrated (paragraph F)	**native** (paragraph F)	**mainland** (paragraph J)

1. ________________ naturally occurring in a particular place
2. ________________ to extend over a large area or length of time
3. ________________ located in one place; not spread out
4. ________________ having a climate that is never very hot or cold
5. ________________ located near the Earth's Equator
6. ________________ related to the main part of a country or continent, excluding its islands

WRITING TASK

GOAL You are going to write an opinion essay on the following topic:
Explain how a country or region has been affected by its geography and history.

A **SELECT YOUR IDEAS** Look at your answers in Exercise D on page 163. Choose the three geographical or historical factors that most affect how the country or region is today.

1. ______________________________
2. ______________________________
3. ______________________________

B **ORGANIZE YOUR IDEAS** Use your answers in Exercise A to to complete the chart below.

Country or Region:	
Factor 1	**How it affects the country/region**
Factor 2	**How it affects the country/region**
Factor 3	**How it affects the country/region**

C **WRITE A THESIS STATEMENT** Use your answers in Exercise B to prepare a thesis statement for your essay. Mention the three geographical and historical factors you identified.

____
____
____

D **PLAN** Use your information in Exercises B–C to complete an outline for your essay.

OUTLINE

Introduction:

____

____

Thesis statement: ______________________________

____

____

____

Body paragraph 1:

Topic sentence: ______________________________

____

Explanation and examples: ______________________________

____

____

Body paragraph 2:

Topic sentence: ______________________________

____

Explanation and examples: ______________________________

____

____

Body paragraph 3:

Topic sentence: ______________________________

____

Explanation and examples: ______________________________

____

____

Conclusion:

____

____

Review Writing Introductions and Conclusions in Unit 6

E **FIRST DRAFT** Use the information in your outline to write a first draft of your essay. Remember to paraphrase information unless you are quoting directly from a source, and to use different reporting verbs to vary your sentences.

F **REVISING PRACTICE** The essay below is similar to the one you are writing. Follow the steps to create a better second draft.

1. Add the sentences (a–c) in the most suitable spaces.
   a. As with many countries, Singapore has been shaped by its geography and history.
   b. Its geographical location, lack of natural resources, and recent immigration history have all played a significant part in shaping this small nation.
   c. As a result, the Port of Singapore is one of the busiest ports in the world.

2. Now fix the following problems (a–b) with the essay.
   a. Fix a problem with referring to a source in paragraph C.
   b. Fix a problem with referring to a source in paragraph D.

A Singapore is a small island-nation in Southeast Asia. Most of its population is concentrated on the mainland, a diamond-shaped island 49 kilometers wide and 25 kilometers long. Singapore is a financial powerhouse, a center for international trade, and a leader in scientific research and innovation. How did Singapore become the country it is today? _____

B Thanks to its geographical location, trade has become a pillar of Singapore's economy. The country's position at the south of Malaysia makes it a key stop-off point for ships traveling between Asia and Europe. _____ Singapore's strategic position has helped the small country become one of the largest importers and exporters worldwide today.

C Singapore's lack of natural resources has also forced the country to be innovative. Take, for example, the country's lack of fresh water. Singapore receives over 90 inches of rainfall a year, but has little land to retain that water. It has therefore had to import drinking water from nearby countries. However, the country has also built cutting-edge facilities that transform wastewater into drinking water, and that remove salt from seawater. According to Singapore's Public Utilities Board (PUB) current and planned plants will meet up to 55 percent of the country's fresh water needs by 2060.

D Singapore's recent immigration history has also contributed to its strong economy. For many years, Singapore's birthrate has been in decline. The country has therefore had to have liberal immigration policies. In 2010, about 40 percent of its population was born outside Singapore. While there was opposition to this, many experts believed that immigration was necessary for Singapore to remain competitive. In a Forbes magazine interview, investor and Singapore resident Jim Rogers argued that, if Singapore didn't get enough labor through immigration, its economy would suffer. According to Rogers, "Every country in history that has a backlash against foreigners is going to go into decline."

E _____ Since gaining independence in 1965, it has grown from a poor trading port to one of the wealthiest states in the world. Despite its size, Singapore's location, innovativeness, and policies make it the global landmark it is today.

G **REVISED DRAFT** Now use the questions below to revise your essay.

- ☐ Does your introduction provide relevant background information on the topic?
- ☐ Does your thesis state the main points of the essay?
- ☐ Do your body paragraphs include enough details to explain your ideas?
- ☐ Does your information come from a variety of reliable and trustworthy sources?
- ☐ Do you quote material and refer to sources correctly?
- ☐ Do all your sentences relate to the main idea?

H **EDITING PRACTICE** Read the information below. Then find and correct one mistake with quotes or paraphrases in each sentence (1–4).

When you refer to sources, remember:

- When quoting directly, use quotation marks (and a comma if necessary) to separate a person's exact words from the rest of the sentence.
- Use a comma after a phrase that includes *According to*.
- Do not use a comma when using the word *that* with a reporting verb.
- Make sure that sentences referring to sources are grammatical. For example, do not use *that* with "As X says that ..."
- In American English, commas and periods should go inside the end quotation marks. For example:

✓ *"With time running out," says Alexander, "tough priorities must be set."*

✗ *"With time running out", says Alexander, "tough priorities must be set".*

1. "Whether we like it or not", says Magle, "we live with wildlife."
2. According to Green hope is an embedded theme in her collections.
3. As Vijay Kumar says that, "They act on local information."
4. Diamond asks, What's the best case for Africa's future?"

I **FINAL DRAFT** Follow these steps to write a final draft.

1. Check your revised draft for mistakes with referring to sources.
2. Now use the checklist on page 248 to write a final draft. Make any other necessary changes.
3. Work in pairs and read your partner's final essay. Give feedback on each other's writing.

Review

SELF-ASSESS **Consider the language and skills you learned in this unit.**

How well can you . . . ?	Very well	Pretty well	I need improvement
use the key vocabulary from this unit	☐	☐	☐
annotate a text	☐	☐	☐
analyze point of view	☐	☐	☐
avoid plagiarism by referring to sources	☐	☐	☐
do research online	☐	☐	☐

A **VOCABULARY** Do you remember the meanings of these words? Look back at the unit and review the ones you don't know.

adaptation AW	arise	associate	burden	corruption AW
distinct AW	dominant AW	mining	misfortune	radically AW
resemble AW	sole AW	thrive	undergo	workforce

B **VOCABULARY EXTENSION** Complete these tasks with a partner.

1. Think of expressions with the word *economy*. Take turns making sentences with them.
2. Choose a word from the box below and make a sentence with *distinct*. Take turns.

advantage	possibility	groups	difference	pattern	smell

C **READING SKILL** List four ways to annotate a text. Which ones do you use? Tell a partner.

1. ______________________
2. ______________________
3. ______________________
4. ______________________

D **LANGUAGE FOR WRITING** Choose a quote from the reading passage. Write two sentences, referring to the quote in two different ways.

SELF-ASSESS **Look back at the chart above. Did you assess your skills correctly? What skills or language do you still need help with?**

LIVING LONGER 8

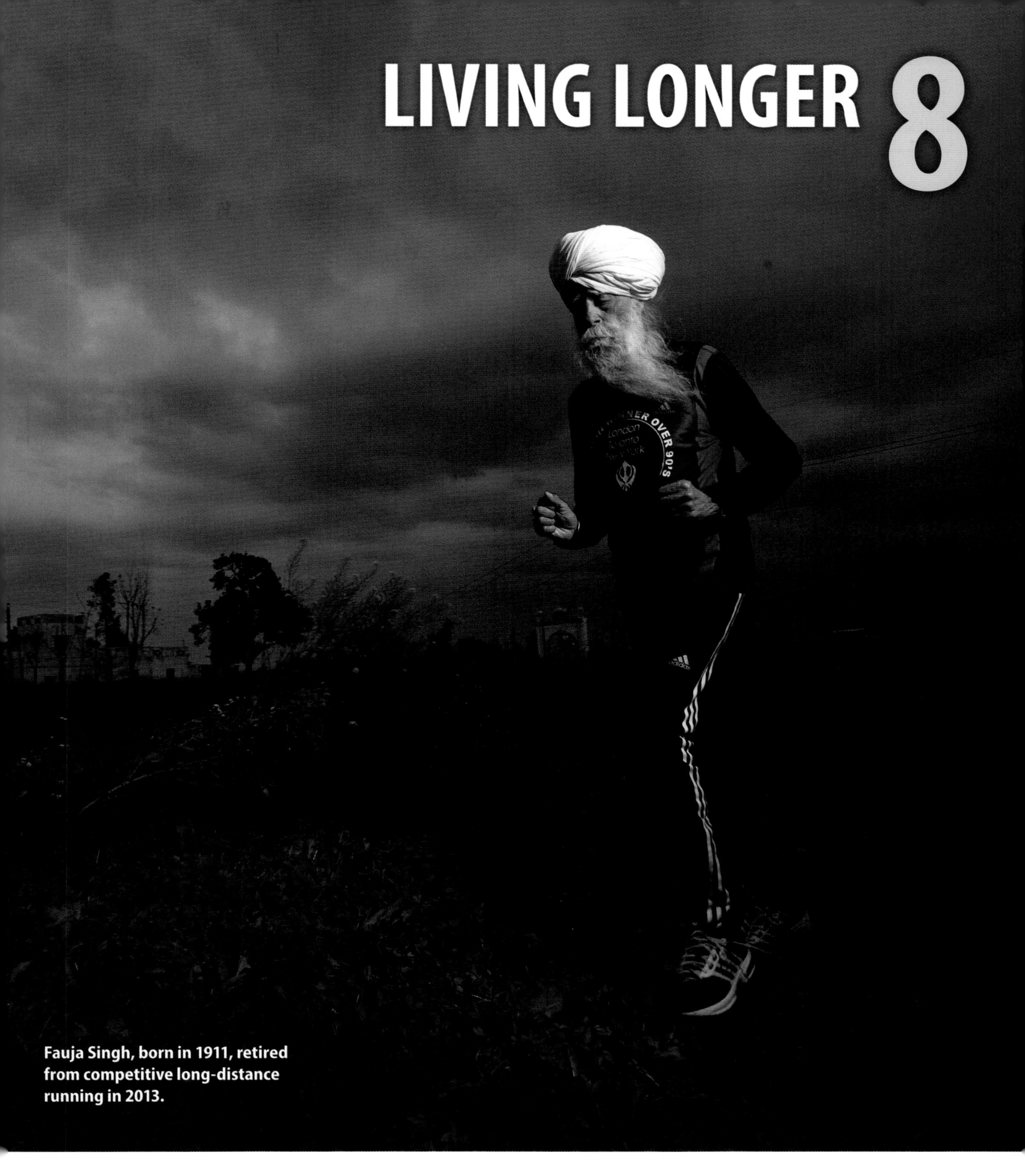

Fauja Singh, born in 1911, retired from competitive long-distance running in 2013.

IN THIS UNIT, YOU WILL:

- Read an article about centenarians
- Watch a video about a town where people live longer than usual
- Write about whether it is worth investing in longevity

THINK AND DISCUSS:

1. At the age of 100, Fauja Singh became the oldest person believed to have completed a marathon. What factors do you think contributed to his good health?
2. How long do you think you would like to live? Why?

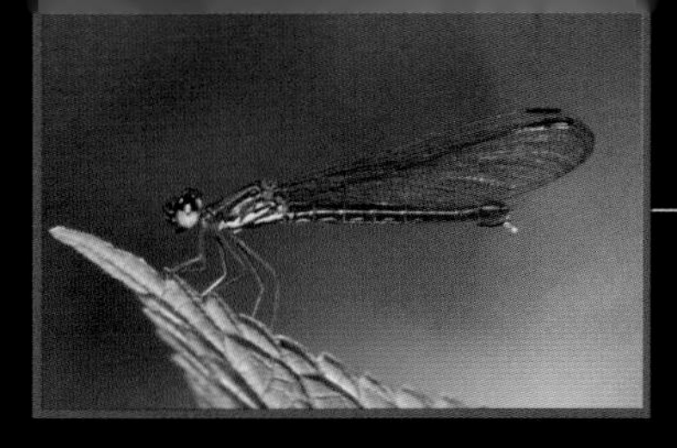

Mayfly
Hours–1 week

Common Octopus
1–2 years

Bengal Tiger
10 years

Immortal jellyfish
Forever?

EXPLORE THE THEME

Look at the information on these pages and answer the questions.

1. What factors do you think contribute to longevity in the animal kingdom?
2. Why do you think human females live longer on average than males?
3. What are some events that a 200-year-old bowhead whale would have lived through?

Life Spans

In the animal kingdom, life expectancy varies from just a few hours to over 200 years.

Mayfly

Some mayflies live for just a few hours. Once mature, they have roughly three hours to reproduce before they die.

Dog
13 years

Cat
15 years

Lion
20 years

Chimpanzee
45 years

Life Expectancy *in the* Animal Kingdom

Human (male)
68 years

Human (female)
72 years

Bowhead Whale
200 years

Quahog Clam
225 years

Bowhead Whale
Scientists believe that bowhead whales can live for over 200 years, making them the longest-living mammal on Earth.

Quahog Clam
With an average life span of around 225 years, the quahog clam is the world's longest-living animal. One quahog, discovered in 2006, was thought to be an incredible 507 years old.

Immortal Jellyfish
While nobody knows how long these animals live in the wild, the immortal jellyfish—which can age backwards—could theoretically live forever.

Reading

PREPARING TO READ

A **BUILD VOCABULARY** The words in **blue** are used in the reading passage. Read the text below. Then write the correct form of each word next to its definition.

Science has shown us that what we eat affects our **life spans**. But when it comes to food, most of us fixate on quantity. People often diet unsustainably, skipping too many meals or eating much less than they should. Unfortunately, such harsh dietary **restrictions** often end up having an adverse effect on our weight and, by extension, our health and **longevity**.

The human body is equipped with biological **mechanisms** that send signals to the brain whenever it needs food. "Overhunger," however, tells our brains that there is a food shortage and that we need to eat as much as possible. **Ultimately**, we end up eating excessively—much more than we would have over the next few meals.

For most of us, it is better to simply listen to our bodies and eat when we're hungry. However, the trick is knowing what to eat and when to stop. Generally, we want to minimize our consumption of fatty foods and simple carbohydrates, like those found in white bread. Instead, we should eat more proteins, fruit, and vegetables. It is worth noting, though, that there is no perfect **ratio** of food groups: what's healthy depends largely on lifestyle and **genetic** makeup. So try documenting what you eat and learning what works for you.

Finally, don't just listen to your body when you are hungry. Recognize when you don't actually need to eat, and stop once you've had enough.

1. ______________ (n) something that limits what we can do
2. ______________ (adj) biologically determined through genes or heredity
3. ______________ (n) the amount of time that something is alive for
4. ______________ (n) the ability to live for a long time
5. ______________ (adv) in the end
6. ______________ (n) a set of numbers that describes how things are related proportionally
7. ______________ (n) a system, or a well-established process

B **BUILD VOCABULARY** Complete the sentences with the correct form of the words in **blue**. Use a dictionary to help you.

component (n)	**contradictory** (adj)	**dismiss** (v)	**historically** (adv)
implication (n)	**outcome** (n)	**outnumber** (v)	**reconstruct** (v)

1. He's not clear about his own position. He makes ______________ statements throughout his research paper.
2. We don't have all the information, but we've tried our best to ______________ events using what we know.

3. They're probably going to lose because the other team ________________ them three to one.

4. Their job performance has been unsatisfactory, so the company has little choice but to ________________ them.

5. That may be the case today, but ________________, that hasn't always been true.

6. The discovery may not seem like a big deal to most, but its ________________ are profound.

7. The experiment led to ________________ that were highly unexpected.

8. Diet is just one of many ________________ of a healthy lifestyle.

C **USE VOCABULARY** Discuss these questions with a partner.

1. Have you ever come across health tips that are **contradictory**? Give examples.
2. What are some traits that are **genetic**?
3. What are some **implications** of longer **life spans**?

D **PREDICT** Note answers to the questions below. Then discuss with a partner.

Critical Thinking

1. What are some factors that can affect a person's life expectancy?

____

2. What do you think are the biggest factors that affect life expectancy?

____

E **SKIM** Skim the reading passage. Are any of your ideas in Exercise D mentioned? What other factors are mentioned that can affect a person's life expectancy?

A farmers' market in Riga, Latvia

DEVELOPING READING SKILLS

READING SKILL Asking Questions as You Read

As you read, note questions you have, and try to predict their answers. This can help you stay engaged and give you a deeper understanding of the text. For example, after reading paragraph A of the reading passage, you might ask, "Why are Passarino and Berardelli going to Molochio?" You might then predict that they want to talk to a centenarian. This is later confirmed in paragraph B.

Most importantly, asking questions can help you identify gaps or assumptions in the passage. For example, in paragraph C, Salvatore Caruso attributes his longevity to eating mostly figs and beans while growing up, and hardly ever any red meat. You might ask yourself upon reading this, "Is there any scientific basis for this?"

After you read, it's possible for some of your questions to remain unanswered. This could be because the writer has made assumptions or left out some information. It could also be that your question is not very relevant. Reassess your questions, and decide if they are questions that really need to be answered.

A **ASK QUESTIONS AS YOU READ** Read paragraphs A–H of the reading passage. As you read, note down questions you have in the chart. As you continue reading, note down if your questions are answered later in the passage, and if so, how.

Paragraph	Questions raised	Were they answered? If so, how?

B **ANALYZE** Work with a partner. Look at your questions in Exercise A.

1. Which of your unanswered questions were you able to infer answers for?
2. Did any of your questions reveal gaps or assumptions in the passage?
3. Were any of your unanswered questions not very relevant or important?

C **ASK QUESTIONS AS YOU READ** As you read the rest of the reading passage, note down questions you have. Check if they are answered in the paragraphs that follow.

Beyond 100

by Stephen S. Hall

A man from the province of Ogliastra in Italy—an area known for the longevity of its people—prepares food for his friends.

Our genes harbor many secrets to a long and healthy life. And now scientists are beginning to uncover them.

A On a crisp January morning, with snow topping the distant Aspromonte mountains and oranges ripening on the nearby trees, Giuseppe Passarino guided his silver minivan up a curving mountain road into the hinterlands of Calabria, mainland Italy's southernmost region. As the road climbed through fruit and olive groves, Passarino—a geneticist at the University of Calabria—chatted with his colleague Maurizio Berardelli, a geriatrician.[1] They were headed for the small village of Molochio, which had the distinction of numbering four centenarians[2]— and four 99-year-olds—among its 2,000 inhabitants.

B Soon after, they found Salvatore Caruso warming his 106-year-old bones in front of a roaring fire in his home on the outskirts of the town. Known in local dialect as "U' Raggiuneri, the Accountant," Caruso was calmly reading an article about the end of the world in an Italian version of a supermarket tabloid.[3] A framed copy of his birth record, dated November 2, 1905, stood on the fireplace mantle.

C Caruso told the researchers he was in good health, and his memory seemed prodigiously intact. He recalled the death of his father in 1913, when Salvatore was a schoolboy; how his mother and brother had nearly died during the great influenza pandemic of 1918–19; and how he'd been **dismissed** from his army unit in 1925 after accidentally falling and breaking his leg in two places. When Berardelli leaned forward and asked Caruso how he had achieved his remarkable **longevity**, the centenarian said with an impish smile, "No bacco, no tabacco, no venere—No drinking, no smoking, no women." He added that he'd eaten mostly figs and beans while growing up and hardly ever any red meat.

D Passarino and Berardelli heard much the same story from 103-year-old Domenico Romeo—who described his diet as "poco, ma tutto—a little bit, but of everything"—and 104-year-old Maria Rosa Caruso, who, despite failing health, regaled[4] her visitors with a lively version of a song about the local patron saint.[5]

E On the ride back to the laboratory in Cosenza, Berardelli remarked, "They often say they prefer to eat only fruit and vegetables."

F "They preferred fruit and vegetables," Passarino said drily, "because that's all they had."

G Although eating sparingly may have been less a choice than an involuntary circumstance of poverty in places like early 20th-century Calabria, decades of research have suggested that a severely restricted diet is connected to a long **life span**. Lately, however, this theory has fallen on hard scientific times. Several recent studies have undermined the link between longevity and caloric **restriction**.

H In any case, Passarino was more interested in the centenarians themselves than in what they had eaten during their lifetimes. In a field **historically** marred[6]

[1] A **geriatrician** is a doctor who specializes in old age.
[2] A **centenarian** is someone aged 100 or older.
[3] A **tabloid** is a newspaper that that is considered less serious than regular newspapers.
[4] If you **regale** people with songs or stories, you entertain them.
[5] A **patron saint** is a person from the past who is regarded as holy, and who is considered a protector or helper of a place or group of people.
[6] If something is **marred**, it is spoiled or damaged.

A 98-year-old man with his wife in Ikaria, Greece, where one in three people live past 90

by exaggerated claims, scientists studying longevity have begun using powerful genomic technologies, basic molecular research, and—most importantly—data on small, genetically isolated communities of people to gain increased insight into the maladies[7] of old age. In regions around the world, studies are turning up molecules and chemical pathways that may **ultimately** help everyone reach an advanced age in good, or even vibrant, health.

I In Calabria, the hunt for hidden molecules and **mechanisms** that confer longevity on people like Salvatore Caruso begins in places like the *Ufficio Anagrafe Stato Civile* (Civil Registry Office) in the medieval village of Luzzi. The office windows here offer stunning views of snow-covered mountains to the north, but to a population geneticist the truly breathtaking sights are hidden inside the tall file cabinets ringing the room, and on shelf after shelf of precious ledgers numbered by year—starting in 1866. Despite its well-earned reputation for chaos and disorganization, the Italian government—shortly after the unification of the country in 1861—ordered local officials to record the birth, marriage, and death of every citizen in each commune, or township.

J Since 1994, scientists at the University of Calabria have combed through these records in every one of Calabria's 409 *comuni* to compile an extraordinary survey. Coupling family histories with simple physiological[8] measurements of frailty and the latest genomic technologies, they set out to address fundamental questions about longevity. How much of it is determined by genetics? How much by the environment? And how do these factors interact to promote longevity—or, conversely, to hasten the aging process? To answer all those questions, scientists must start with rock-solid demographic[9] data.

K "Here is the book from 1905," explained Marco Giordano, one of Giuseppe Passarino's young colleagues, opening a tall green ledger. He pointed to a record, in careful cursive, of the birth of Francesco D'Amato on March 3, 1905. "He died in 2007," Giordano noted, describing D'Amato as the central figure of an extensive genealogical tree. "We can **reconstruct** the pedigrees[10] of families from these records."

L Cross-checking the ledger entries against meticulously detailed registry cards (pink for women, white for men)

[7] A **malady** is a disease or health problem.
[8] If something is **physiological**, it has to do with how the body functions.
[9] **Demographic** information is information about different groups of people in a particular society.
[10] Someone's **pedigree** is his or her background or ancestry.

going back to the 19th century, Giordano—along with researchers Alberto Montesanto and Cinzia Martino—has reconstructed extensive family trees of 202 nonagenarians[11] and centenarians in Calabria. The records document not only siblings of people who lived to 100, but also the spouses of siblings, which has allowed Passarino's group to do a kind of historical experiment on longevity. "We compared the ages of D'Amato's brothers and sisters to the ages of their spouses," Giordano explained. "So they had the same environment. They ate the same food. They used the same medicines. They came from the same culture. But they did not have the same genes." In a 2011 paper, the Calabrian researchers reported a surprising conclusion: Although the parents and siblings of people who lived to at least 90 also lived longer than the general population—a finding in line with earlier research—the **genetic** factors involved seemed to benefit males more than females.

M The Calabrian results on gender offer yet another hint that the genetic twists and turns that confer longevity may be unusually complex. Major European studies had previously reported that women are much likelier to live to 100, **outnumbering** male centenarians by a **ratio** of four or five to one, with the **implication** that some of the reasons are genetic. But by teasing out details from family trees, the Calabrian researchers discovered an intriguing paradox: The genetic **component** of longevity appears to be stronger in males—but women may take better advantage of external factors such as diet and medical care than men do.

N In the dimly lit, chilly hallway outside Passarino's university office stand several freezers full of tubes containing centenarian blood. The DNA from this blood and other tissue samples has revealed additional information about the Calabrian group. For example, people who live into their 90s and beyond tend to possess a particular version, or allele, of a gene important to taste and digestion. This allele not only gives people a taste for bitter foods like broccoli and field greens, which are typically rich in compounds that promote cellular health, but also allows cells in the intestine to extract nutrients more efficiently from food as it's being digested.

O Passarino has also found in his centenarians a revved-up[12] version of a gene for what is called an uncoupling protein. The protein plays a central role in metabolism—the way a person consumes energy and regulates body heat—which in turn affects the rate of aging.

P "We have dissected five or six pathways that most influence longevity," says Passarino. "Most of them involve the response to stress, the metabolism of nutrients, or metabolism in general—the storage and use of energy." His group is currently examining how environmental influences—everything from childhood diet to how long a person attends school—might modify the activity of genes in a way that either promotes or curtails longevity.

Q Around the world, studies are being done to determine the causes of longevity and health in old age. If nothing else, the plethora of new studies indicates that longevity researchers are pushing the scientific conversation to a new level. In October 2011, the Archon Genomics X Prize launched a race among research teams to sequence the DNA of a hundred centenarians (dubbing the contest "100 over 100").

[11] A **nonagenarian** is someone who is 90 to 99 years old.
[12] If something is **revved up**, it is more active or intense than usual.

THE COST OF CARE

Are the funds used by countries on healthcare well spent? One way to find out is to compare per-person healthcare costs against longevity.

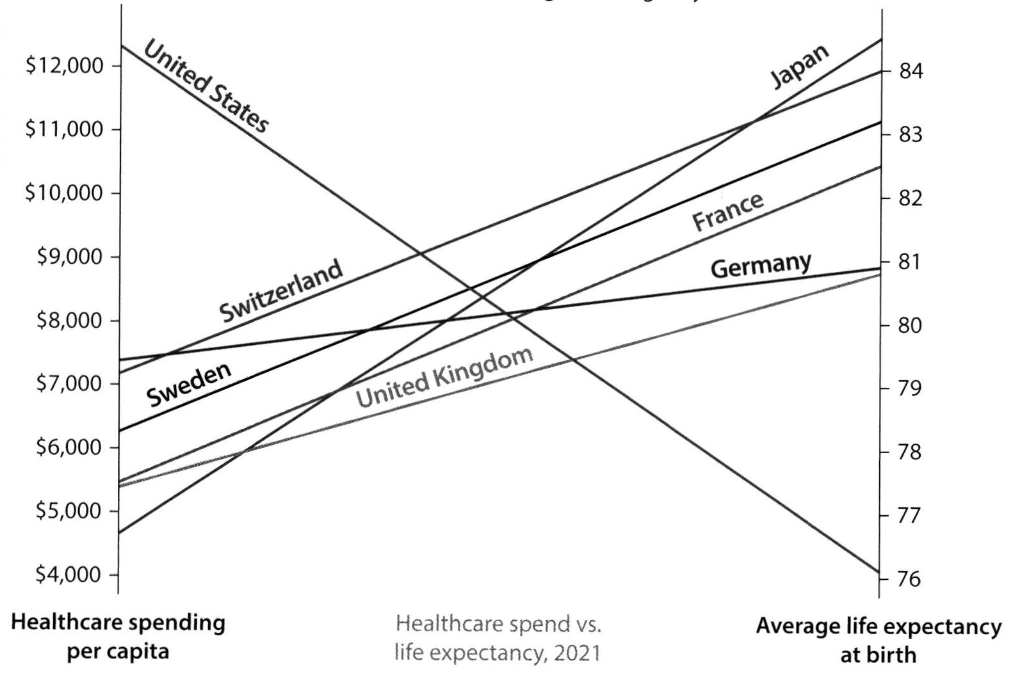

United States
Japan
Switzerland
France
Germany
Sweden
United Kingdom

$12,000
$11,000
$10,000
$9,000
$8,000
$7,000
$6,000
$5,000
$4,000

84
83
82
81
80
79
78
77
76

Healthcare spending per capita

Healthcare spend vs. life expectancy, 2021

Average life expectancy at birth

R But genes alone are unlikely to explain all the secrets of longevity, and experts see a cautionary tale[13] in recent results concerning caloric restriction. Experiments on 41 different genetic models of mice, for example, have shown that restricting food intake produces **outcomes** that are wildly **contradictory**. About half the mouse species lived longer, but just as many lived less time on a restricted diet than they would have on a normal diet. And last August, a long-running National Institute on Aging experiment on primates concluded that monkeys kept on a restricted-calorie diet for 25 years showed no longevity advantage. Passarino made the point while driving back to his laboratory after visiting the centenarians in Molochio. "It's not that there are good genes and bad genes," he said. "It's certain genes at certain times. And in the end, genes probably account for only 25 percent of longevity. It's the environment, too, but that doesn't explain all of it either. And don't forget chance."

S Which brought to mind Salvatore Caruso of Molochio, 107 years old and still going strong. Because he broke his leg 88 years ago, he was unfit to serve in the Italian Army when his entire unit was recalled during World War II. "They were all sent to the Russian front," he said, "and not a single one of them came back." It's another reminder that although molecules and mechanisms yet unfathomed[14] may someday lead to drugs that help us reach a ripe and healthy old age, a little luck doesn't hurt either.

Adapted from "On Beyond 100," by Stephen S. Hall: National Geographic Magazine, May 2013

Award-winning writer Stephen S. Hall has written extensively about science and society for nearly 30 years. His work has appeared in numerous publications including *The New York Times Magazine*.

---

[13] A **cautionary tale** is a story or situation that can serve as a warning to people.

[14] If something is **unfathomed**, it has not been understood or explained, usually because it is strange or complicated.

UNDERSTANDING THE READING

A **UNDERSTAND MAIN IDEAS** Check (✓) the answers to the questions below. More than one answer may be possible.

1. Why is Calabria a good place to study longevity?
   - ☐ a. It has the best genetic research labs in Europe.
   - ☐ b. Many universities with good science departments are located there.
   - ☐ c. It has an unusual number of people over 90 and even over 100.
   - ☐ d. Many of the communities keep excellent family records.
2. What are some of the main points scientists have learned about longevity?

   In general, . . .
   - ☐ a. eating less increases longevity.
   - ☐ b. genetics contribute more to longevity in men than women.
   - ☐ c. women live longer because they look after themselves better.
   - ☐ d. how our bodies respond to stress and different foods affects our longevity.
   - ☐ e. our genes are the most significant factor affecting our longevity.

B **UNDERSTAND DETAILS** Work with a partner. Find information in the reading passage to answer these questions.

1. Why did the researchers compare centenarians with their spouses and siblings?

   ____

   ____
2. What resources did the researchers use to make family trees of people in Calabria?

   ____

   ____

An 89-year-old fisherman from Okinawa Island, Japan, shows off his muscles. ▶

3. What are two ways that people's genetic backgrounds can affect longevity?

____

____

4. What evidence shows that caloric restriction may not lead to greater longevity?

____

____

C **UNDERSTAND SUPPORTING EXAMPLES** Complete the chart with information about factors that affect life span. If the information is not included in the reading passage, leave the space blank.

	Genetics	External Factors	Chance
Salvatore Caruso			
Men in general			
Women in general			

D **INFER MEANING** Find and underline the following words in the reading passage. Use the context to identify their meanings. Then match each word to its definition.

Critical Thinking

prodigiously (paragraph C) **impish** (paragraph C) **sparingly** (paragraph G)
breathtaking (paragraph I) **chaos** (paragraph I) **meticulously** (paragraph L)
paradox (paragraph M)

1. ______________ a state of disorder and confusion
2. ______________ in a way that is extremely impressive or remarkable
3. ______________ mischievous or naughty
4. ______________ infrequently or in small quantities
5. ______________ very carefully, with great attention to detail
6. ______________ extremely beautiful or amazing
7. ______________ a situation or theory in which two ideas that that seem to contradict each other coexist

CRITICAL THINKING Interpreting Visual Data

When you interpret visual data, look for patterns or correlations (links) between different data sets. Consider the implications of these correlations, and also of the lack of any clear correlation. Lastly, look for anomalies, or exceptions that stand out. Do they tell you anything significant?

Critical Thinking

E **INTERPRET VISUAL DATA** Look at the chart about healthcare on the last page of the reading passage and note answers to the questions below.

1. Can you spot a pattern in the dataset? What does the pattern, or lack of pattern, tell you?

___

___

___

2. Can you spot any anomalies in the dataset? Which two countries stand out the most, and why?

___

___

___

Critical Thinking

F **INTERPRET VISUAL DATA** Look at the chart again and answer the questions below.

1. Which sentence correctly describes the correlation between life expectancy and healthcare spending?
   a. In general, life expectancy tends to rise as spending on healthcare increases.
   b. There is no clear relationship between a country's healthcare spending and its population's life expectancy.
2. Which of the following is NOT a fair inference to make based on the chart?
   a. Some countries make better use of the money they spend on healthcare than others.
   b. There are probably factors that contribute more significantly to longevity than healthcare spending.
   c. Japan's longevity is largely due to the unique diets of the people there.

Critical Thinking

G **INTERPRET VISUAL DATA** Work with a partner. Write one or two sentences about what you think the main takeaway from the chart is.

___

___

___

Critical Thinking

H **REFLECT** Would you like to live to be a centenarian? Why or why not? Discuss with a partner.

VOCABULARY EXTENSION

WORD PARTNERS Words and Phrases with *life*

There are many words and phrases with *life*, such as *life span*. Here are some other examples:

life expectancy:	how long living things are expected to live
life story:	the history of someone's life
private life:	a person's life outside of work or school
lifetime:	the period during which someone was or will be alive
lifelong:	lasting all of one's life
life-threatening:	extremely dangerous, to the point that lives are at risk
real-life:	not imaginary or theoretical

A Complete each sentence using the correct form of a word or phrase from the box above.

1. For some elderly people, getting the flu can be ________________.
2. Many famous people avoid talking about their ________________. They want to keep the focus away from their families.
3. In 2022, actress Julie Andrews received an award for a ________________ of achievement in the film industry.
4. She may be quiet and reserved, but she's been through a lot, and her ________________ is fascinating.
5. My grandfather had a ________________ interest in photography, starting from when he was just a child.

WORD FORMS *out-*

The prefix *out-* is extremely versatile. Here are three of its functions:

- to turn certain verbs into nouns (e.g., *outcome, outlook, output*)
- to state that one thing exceeds another thing (e.g., *outnumber, outperform, outgrow*)
- to show an outward position or trajectory (e.g., *outdoor, outbreak*)

B Complete each sentence using the correct form of a word from the box above.

1. He can't wear those shoes anymore. He's ________________ them.
2. She doesn't think we'll succeed. She has a rather negative ________________.
3. He didn't get the job even though he ________________ all the other applicants.
4. If the infected patients leave the hospital, they might trigger a(n) ________________.
5. She's an extremely efficient worker. I'm so impressed by her ________________.
6. I don't enjoy ________________ activities when it's cold or rainy.

Video

Longevity Village

Bama County in China boasts the highest percentage of centenarians in the country. However, increased tourism is threatening the factors that contribute most to its residents' longevity. Locals are forced to grapple with conflicting interests as their ways of life slowly change.

Critical Thinking

A **PREVIEW** Look at the photo and paragraph above. How do you think tourism will affect a place like Bama County? Discuss with a partner.

B **MAIN IDEAS** ▶ Watch the video. What do the locals say about tourism in Bama County? Check (✓) the two correct answers.

☐ a. Tourists are not welcome in their communities.
☐ b. Tourists often litter and pollute the area.
☐ c. Tourism revenue will help them live healthier lives.
☐ d. Tourism will ultimately do more harm than good.

C **DETAILS** ▶ Watch the video again. Complete the sentences with words from the video.

1. A plan is underway to turn the village into a place for ecological ______________.
2. Currently, the lifestyle there is ______________, unlike in the hot, overpopulated city.
3. One villager believes tourism income will help them live better lives and enjoy ______________.
4. There are plans to build a new eco ______________ in the village.

Critical Thinking

D **SYNTHESIZE** What do the centenarians of Calabria have in common with the centenarians in Bama County? Discuss with a partner.

Critical Thinking

E **EVALUATE** Do you think the benefits of tourism in Bama County outweigh the disadvantages? Why or why not?

Writing

EXPLORING WRITTEN ENGLISH

WRITING SKILL Planning an Argumentative Research Paper

In essays, writers often present their views without referring to sources. Research papers are different: the writer must first state their position, and then defend it using research and evidence from sources like journals, books, or websites.

There are several steps involved in planning an argumentative research paper.

Choose a topic
The topic for your research paper may be given to you, but if you are free to choose your own topic, pick one you can research and take a position on.

Research different perspectives
Note down the arguments frequently put forward on all sides of the topic. Remain neutral. Note down information about your sources, too.

Look for evidence
Note down the evidence supporting each of the arguments you uncovered in your research.

Brainstorm
Consider other possible perspectives. Research these new angles. If no information is available, evaluate your ideas carefully and expand on them yourself if possible.

Draft a thesis statement
Look at the evidence and decide what position you'd like to take. Draft a thesis statement. Include your opinion and your main supporting ideas.

Prepare an outline
Consider how best to convince your readers: Which supporting idea do you want to share first, second, and so on? Draft a basic outline, then expand on it with information from your research notes.

Review this Writing Skill in Unit 7

A Check (✓) the four statements that would be most suitable as topics for an argumentative research paper. Share your reasons with a partner. How would you rewrite the other four statements to make them more suitable?

- ☐ 1. Cigarette advertisements are no longer permitted in some countries.
- ☐ 2. Fast food advertisements on television are harmful.
- ☐ 3. There would be fewer auto accidents if the legal driving age were changed to 21.
- ☐ 4. The legal driving age is different all over the world.
- ☐ 5. Cigarette smoking around children should be made illegal.
- ☐ 6. In the past, tobacco was used medicinally.
- ☐ 7. Approximately 30% of fatal traffic accidents involve motorcycles.
- ☐ 8. Cars and motorcycles should have separate lanes to better protect motorcyclists.

B Check (✓) the three pieces of evidence that best support the following thesis statement: "Cigarette smoking around children should be made illegal."

☐ 1. Smoking is common in countries around the world.

☐ 2. Some cigarette advertisements target children.

☐ 3. According to James Garbarino of Cornell University, "More young children are killed by parental smoking than by all unintentional injuries combined."

☐ 4. A recent study shows that the children of smokers are more likely to become smokers than the children of parents who don't smoke.

☐ 5. A recent German study showed that teenagers who are exposed to tobacco ads are more likely to start smoking than teens who don't see these ads.

☐ 6. According to recent figures, the total number of smokers in the world is approximately 1.3 billion.

☐ 7. According to the World Health Organization, about 1.3 million nonsmokers die from secondhand smoke every year.

C What other arguments might support the thesis in Exercise B? Discuss with a partner.

____

____

LANGUAGE FOR WRITING Explaining the Significance of Evidence

As a writer, you need to show your readers why a piece of evidence is important. After you have provided the evidence, explain how it supports your argument. You can introduce your explanation using phrases like these:

This research shows that ...	*As this evidence shows, ...*
The implication of this is ...	*The evidence suggests that ...*
This supports the idea that ...	*Studies have reported that ...*

For example:

In a recent German study, teenagers who were exposed to tobacco ads were more likely to start smoking than teens who didn't see these ads. ***This research shows that*** *tobacco advertisements have a negative effect on teenagers. They result in an increase in teen smoking, which will in turn lead to an increase in tobacco-related medical problems such as lung cancer and strokes.*

College students participate in an anti-smoking campaign in Liaocheng, China.

D **NOTICE** The sentences below are from the reading passage. Complete them using the words used in the passage. Then work with a partner. Can you complete the sentences using other words from the box?

implication	report	show	suggest	support

1. … decades of research have ____________ that a severely restricted diet is connected to a long life span. (paragraph G)
2. Major European studies had previously ____________ that women are much likelier to live to 100, … with the ____________ that some of the reasons are genetic. (paragraph M)
3. Experiments on 41 different genetic models of mice … have ____________ that restricting food intake produces outcomes that are wildly contradictory. (paragraph R)

E **APPLY** Explain the significance of each piece of evidence below. How does the evidence support the thesis statement "Cigarette smoking around children should be made illegal"?

1. According to James Garbarino of Cornell University, "More young children are killed by parental smoking than by all unintentional injuries combined."

   ____

   ____

   ____

2. According to the World Health Organization, 1.3 million nonsmokers die from secondhand smoke every year.

   ____

   ____

   ____

3. A recent study shows that the children of smokers are more likely to become smokers than the children of parents who don't smoke.

   ____

   ____

   ____

F **VOCABULARY FOR WRITING** The words in **bold** below can be useful when explaining the relevance of evidence to support a position on a topic. Choose the correct word to complete each sentence.

1. New research **undermines** / **indicates** the ideas they previously had about aging.
2. The study **proves** / **reveals** new information about the extent of climate change.
3. The experiment **concludes** / **demonstrates** how common cognitive biases are.
4. Their findings **confirmed** / **validated** that their theories were correct.
5. The results completely **challenged** / **disproved** his theories about longevity.

WRITING TASK

GOAL You are going to write an argumentative research paper on the following topic:

Governments should not invest so much in helping people live beyond 100 years, as an aging population will cause problems for society.

To what extent do you agree?

Review this Writing Skill in Unit 7

A **RESEARCH** Do research, and note down in the chart the main arguments for and against the motion, as well as evidence for each argument. Include information about your sources, such as who they are, what organizations they represent, and where their information was found.

Arguments supporting the motion	Arguments against the motion

B **BRAINSTORM** What are your own opinions on the topic? Look for evidence for or against your ideas. If you can't find any, evaluate and expand on them yourself if possible. If you think your ideas are valid, add them to the chart above.

C **WRITE A THESIS STATEMENT** Look at both sides of the argument. Choose the side you agree with more and the three best arguments supporting your position from the chart in Exercise A. Then draft a thesis statement.

____

____

____

D **PLAN** Use your information in Exercises A–C to complete the outline for your essay on the next page. Note that it is often a good idea to present your strongest argument last.

OUTLINE

Introduction:

____

____

Thesis statement: ______________________________

____

____

Body paragraph 1: (first argument supporting your thesis)

Topic sentence: ________________________________

____

Explanation and examples: ________________________

____

____

Body paragraph 2: (second argument supporting your thesis)

Topic sentence: ________________________________

____

Explanation and examples: ________________________

____

____

Body paragraph 3: (third argument supporting your thesis)

Topic sentence: ________________________________

____

Explanation and examples: ________________________

____

____

Conclusion:

____

____

____

E **FIRST DRAFT** Use the information in your outline to write a first draft of your essay. Remember to mention your research sources, and to use appropriate words and expressions for explaining the significance of the evidence you present.

F **REVISING PRACTICE** The essay below is similar to the one you are writing. It argues the point that smoking around children should be banned. Add the missing information (a–f) to create a better second draft.

a. Research shows that secondhand smoke endangers nonsmokers' lives.
b. Perhaps most importantly, it would protect those who can't protect themselves.
c. New laws banning smoking around children must therefore be created for three reasons:
d. By making smoking around children illegal, lives would be saved in both the short term and the long term.
e. According to the WHO, while secondhand smoke can cause serious heart and lung conditions to develop in adults, it can lead to sudden death in infants.
f. Exposure to smoking is also known to encourage children to take up smoking later in life.

A When Europeans began smoking tobacco, people were not aware of its dangers. In fact, according to the article "Tobacco: From Miracle Cure to Toxin," doctors often prescribed it as a medicine. But in the early 20th century, attitudes toward smoking began to change. These days, there are laws in most countries discouraging its use, particularly among children. However, there are far fewer laws protecting children from secondhand smoke. _____ Secondhand smoke is deadly; children can't protect themselves from secondhand smoke; and finally, children exposed to smoking are more likely to become smokers themselves.

B _____ The World Health Organization (WHO) states that 1.3 million nonsmokers die from secondhand smoke every year, and approximately 65,000 of these are children. As James Garbarino of Cornell University states, "More children are killed by parental smoking than by all unintentional injuries combined." According to the WHO, an alarming 40 percent of children worldwide have at least one smoking parent. Enacting laws that prohibit parents from smoking around children would therefore dramatically limit children's exposure to the dangerous toxins found in cigarette smoke, which have been found to affect young children differently than adults. _____

C While it is true that secondhand smoke endangers both children and adults, it is more important to have laws that protect children specifically. Adults who don't want to be around secondhand smoke can usually just walk away, but children don't always have that option. This is especially so for children whose parents frequently smoke in the house. While it is true that laws prohibiting the smoking of cigarettes around children at home might not be be easy to enforce, such laws would no doubt raise awareness of the issue and compel many parents to stop smoking when at home with their children.

D _____ According to an article in *Medical News Today*, children of smokers were "more than two times as likely to begin smoking cigarettes on a daily basis between the ages of 13 and 21 than were children whose parents didn't use tobacco," greatly increasing their chances of an eventual early death. While secondhand smoke is responsible for about a million deaths annually, smoking kills over six million people a year. These statistics combined demonstrate how dangerous smoking around children can be. _____

E Cigarette smoking is so popular that it will probably never completely disappear, even though people are aware of the dangers. But more needs to be done to protect the people who do not wish to be exposed to the dangers of cigarette smoke—particularly children. Making it illegal to smoke around children is a good start because it would result in fewer children dying or eventually becoming smokers themselves. _____

G **REVISED DRAFT** Now use the questions below to revise your essay.

- ☐ Does your introduction give background on the topic?
- ☐ Does your thesis statement state your position and supporting ideas?
- ☐ Do you provide evidence in your body paragraphs?
- ☐ Do you explain the significance of the evidence you present?
- ☐ Does your concluding paragraph contain a summary statement and a final thought?

H **EDITING PRACTICE** Read the information below. Then correct one error with explaining the significance of evidence in each sentence (1–3).

When explaining the significance of evidence, remember:

- Use the word *that* when necessary.
- Do not use a comma after *that*.
- Treat the word *evidence* as a singular noun.

1. The research shows that, people raised by nonsmokers are less likely to become smokers themselves.
2. The evidence suggest that there is a link between secondhand smoke and lung cancer.
3. The findings show, secondhand smoke is deadly and needs to be taken seriously.

I **FINAL DRAFT** Follow these steps to write a final draft.

1. Check your revised draft for mistakes with words and expressions for explaining the significance of evidence.
2. Now use the checklist on page 248 to write a final draft. Make any other necessary changes.
3. Work in pairs and read your partner's final essay. Give feedback on each other's writing.

Review

SELF-ASSESS **Consider the language and skills you learned in this unit.**

How well can you . . . ?	Very well	Pretty well	I need improvement
use the key vocabulary from this unit	☐	☐	☐
ask questions as you read	☐	☐	☐
interpret visual data	☐	☐	☐
plan an argumentative research paper	☐	☐	☐
explain the significance of evidence	☐	☐	☐

A **VOCABULARY** Do you remember the meanings of these words? Look back at the unit and review the ones you don't know.

component AW	contradictory AW	dismiss	genetic AW	historically AW
implication AW	life span	longevity	mechanism AW	outcome AW
outnumber	ratio AW	reconstruct AW	restriction AW	ultimately AW

B **VOCABULARY EXTENSION** Complete these tasks with a partner.

1. What words and phrases do you remember with *life*? Take turns making sentences with them.
2. What words do you remember with the prefix *out-*? Take turns making sentences with them.

C **READING SKILL** Read the Unit 1 reading passage again. As you read, note down any questions you have, and whether they were subsequently answered in the passage. Then discuss your questions and the answers with a partner.

D **LANGUAGE FOR WRITING** Work with a partner. Explain how the research findings below support the arguments for and against increasing the average human life span.

1. Retirees have higher levels of life satisfaction than younger people.
2. By 2030, one in six people worldwide will be over the age of 60.

SELF-ASSESS **Look back at the chart above. Did you assess your skills correctly? What skills or language do you still need help with?**

TRUTH AND DECEPTION 9

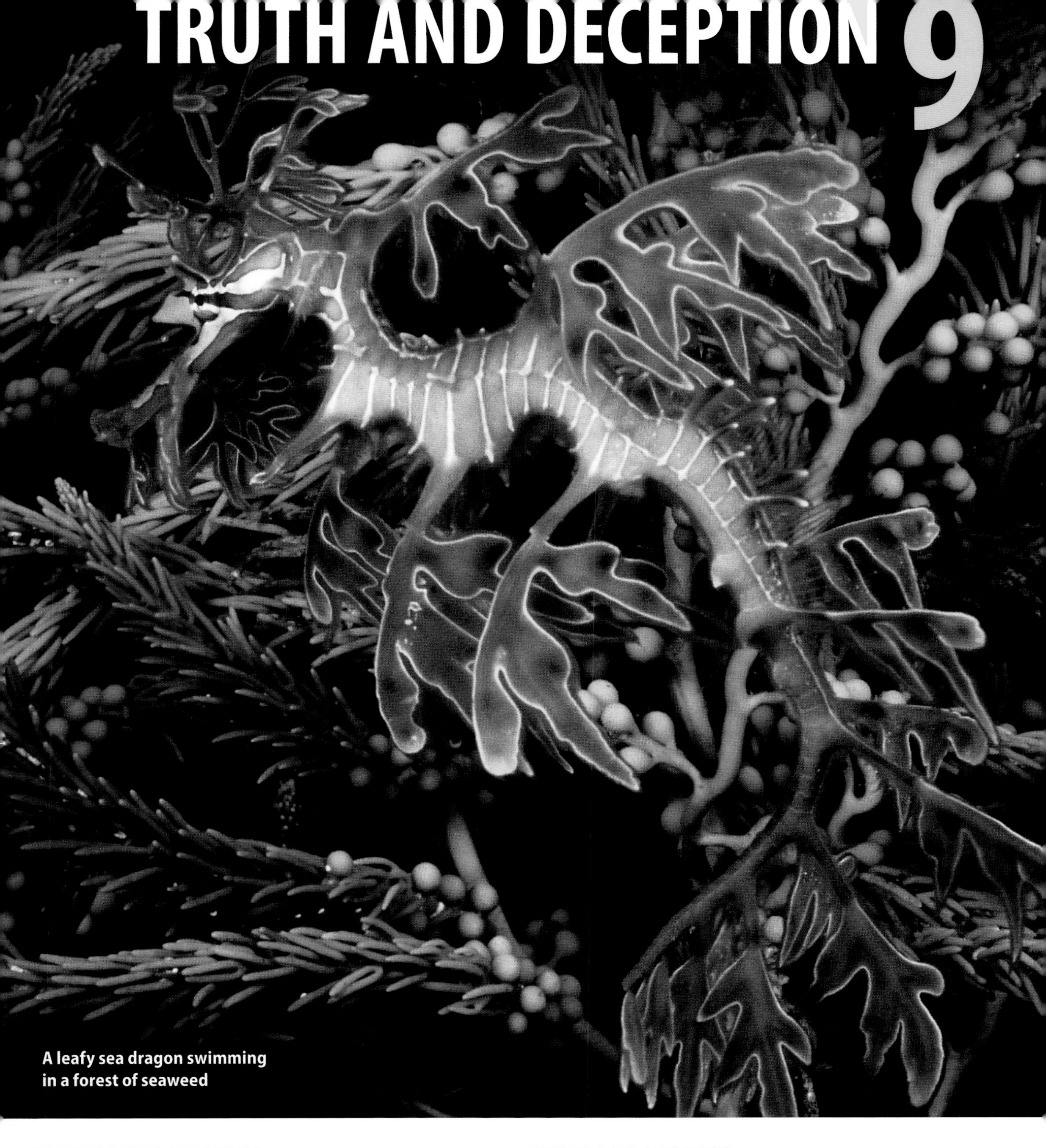

A leafy sea dragon swimming in a forest of seaweed

IN THIS UNIT, YOU WILL:

- Read an article about dishonesty
- Watch a video about children and lying
- Write a research summary of a study

THINK AND DISCUSS:

1. The photo above shows a leafy sea dragon off the coast of Spencer Gulf in South Australia. How does the animal use deception to its advantage?
2. Is lying or dishonesty always wrong? In what situations would it be OK to lie?

Look at the information on these pages and answer the questions.

1. Why did Holmes and Nixon lie? Pick reasons from the chart.
2. Which reasons for lying in the chart are well intentioned?
3. What are some reasons you have lied in the past?

The Best Policy?

In 2016, behavioral scientist Timothy Levine conducted a survey to find out why people lie. He asked approximately 500 participants from five countries to describe a time that they lied or were lied to.

Levine identified four main reasons why people mislead others: to protect oneself; to promote oneself; to impact others—that is, to protect them or to harm them; and for reasons that are not clear. The infographic on the right breaks down these four main categories into more specific reasons for lying, such as to cover up a mistake, or to gain financial benefits.

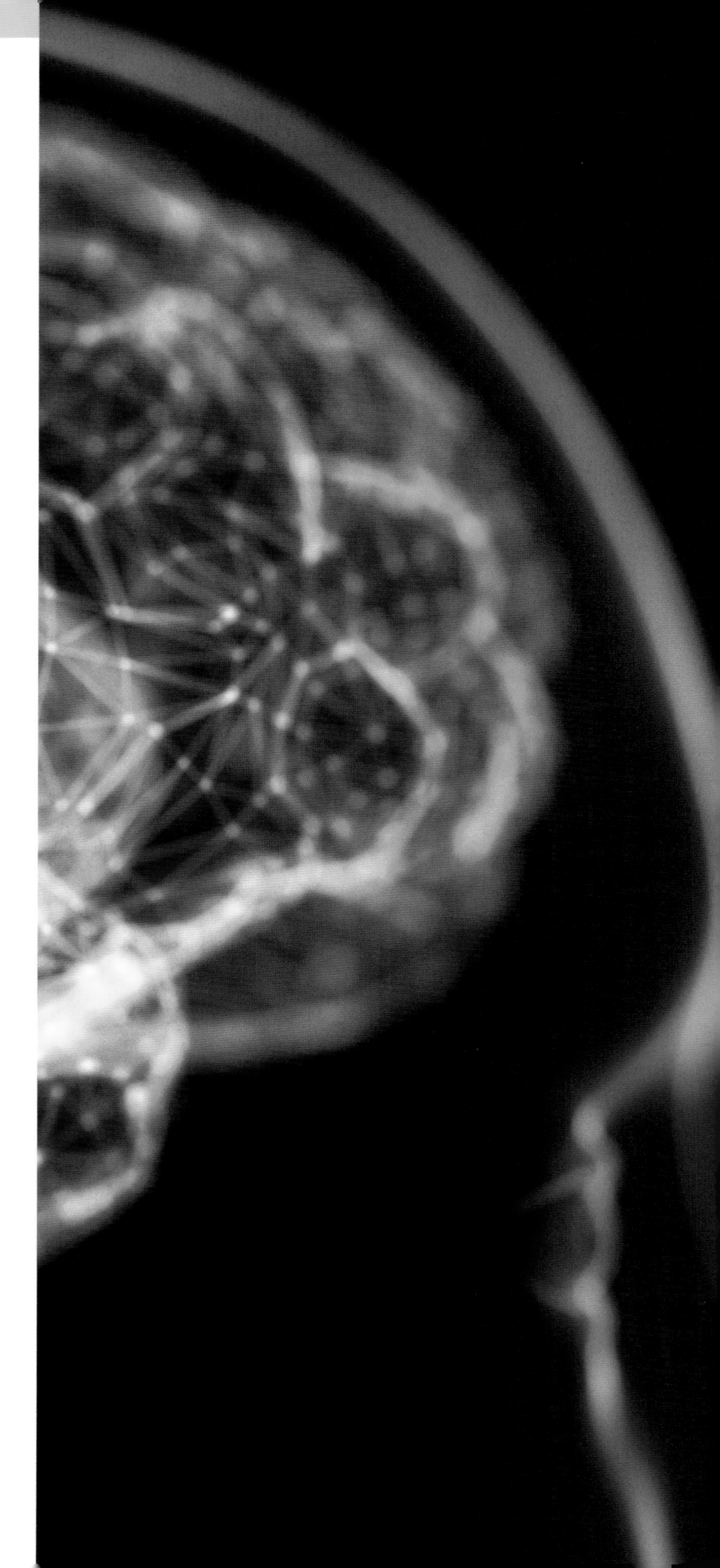

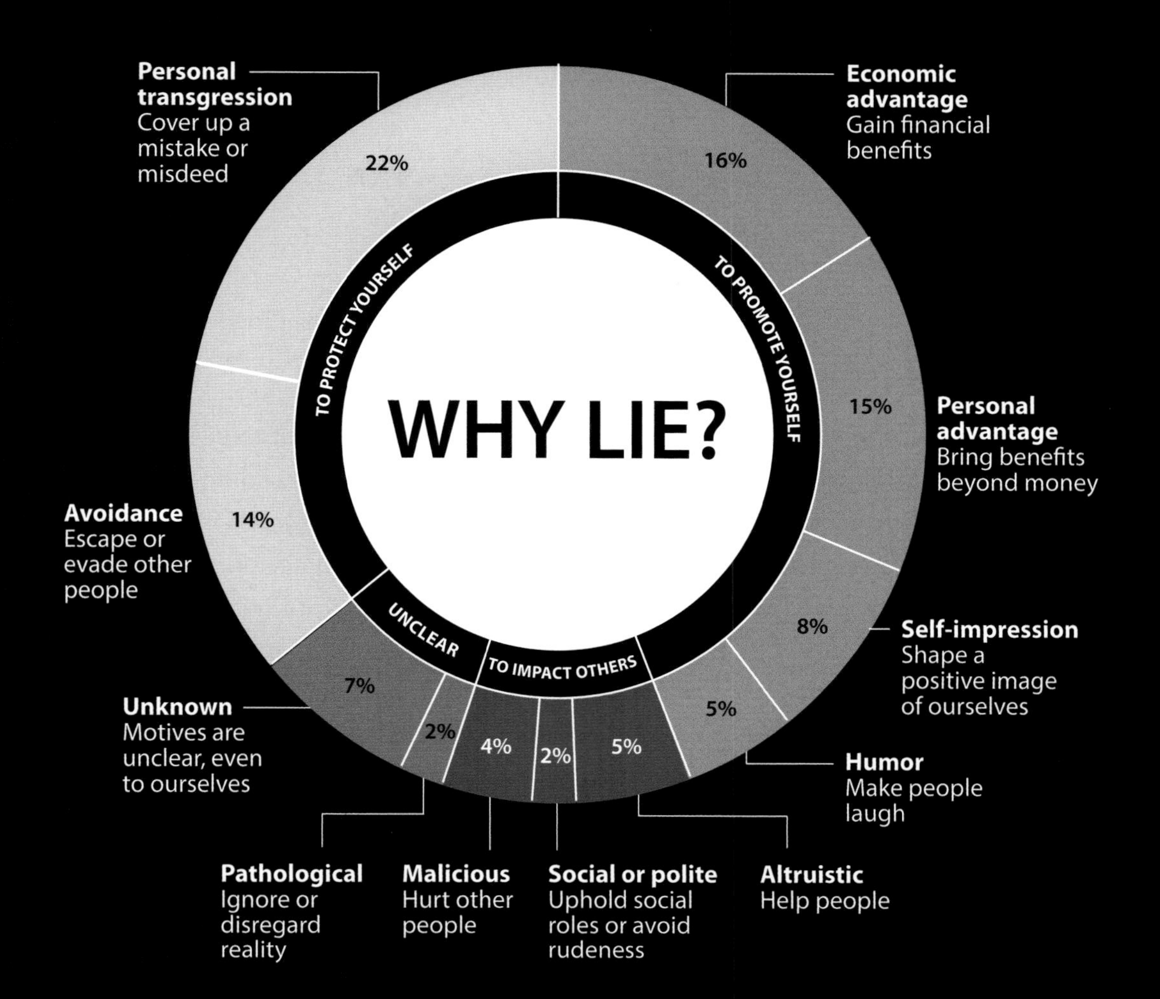

FAMOUS LIES

Elizabeth Holmes

In 2003, 19-year-old American Elizabeth Holmes dropped out of Stanford University in California, U.S.A., to start Theranos, a biotech company that quickly rose to prominence because of a breakthrough medical test kit it was developing. Holmes was able to secure billions in investment in her product, becoming a multi-billionaire herself in the process. However, upon closer scrutiny, it was discovered that she had greatly exaggerated the effectiveness of her product. She was eventually charged with fraud and sentenced to over 11 years in prison.

Richard Nixon

In 1972, five men broke into the Watergate building in Washington, D. C. Their mission: to help President Richard Nixon win his reelection campaign by illegally photographing documents and recording phone conversations. The individuals were caught and later revealed Nixon's role in orchestrating the break-in. However, when pressed, Nixon publicly denied his involvement, declaring, "I am not a crook." His cover-up ultimately failed. Humiliated, Nixon was left with little choice but to do what no other U.S. President had done: resign from office.

Reading

PREPARING TO READ

A **BUILD VOCABULARY** The words in **blue** are used in the reading passage. Read the sentences below. Then write the correct form of each word or phrase next to its definition.

Don't let his words fool you—he's quite capable of being **deceptive**.
Kang Lee, a **prominent** psychologist, has researched lying in children extensively.
One can only **speculate** why habitual liars choose to lie even when there's no real benefit.
Young children have a **tendency** to lie to avoid getting into trouble.
The politicians were not able to **cover up** their lies and corruption.
It may be **reassuring** to learn that lying is a perfectly normal part of a child's behavior.
Most marriage experts say that honesty is the **foundation** of a healthy relationship.

1. ______________ (adj) important, well-known, or obvious
2. ______________ (phr) to try to hide bad behavior or wrongdoings
3. ______________ (n) the basic principle upon which something is developed or built
4. ______________ (adj) misleading; giving a false impression
5. ______________ (adj) comforting; offering a measure of relief
6. ______________ (v) to guess or hypothesize
7. ______________ (n) an inclination to do something often

B **BUILD VOCABULARY** Complete the sentences below with the correct form of the words and phrases in **blue**. Use a dictionary to help you.

fundamental (adj)	**impede** (v)	**implicit** (adj)	**lessen** (v)
prone to (adj)	**systematically** (adv)	**twist** (n)	**universally** (adv)

1. Their progress was ______________ by the bad weather.
2. She's careless and ______________ making mistakes.
3. We thought we could solve the problem without a plan, but soon realized we needed to approach it more ______________.
4. Teamwork and trust were ______________ to the success of the project.
5. She told a few white lies to ______________ the impact of the bad news.
6. She smiled as she spoke, but her words contained a(n) ______________ threat.
7. Nobody expected the clever ______________ at the end of the story.
8. The idea is now ______________ accepted in the scientific community.

C **USE VOCABULARY** Note answers to the questions below. Then discuss with a partner.

1. Are people in certain professions more **prone to** lying than others? Why do you think so?

   ____

   ____

2. What are some ways in which people **cover up** lies?

   ____

   ____

3. What are some **deceptive** claims or messages you've encountered?

   ____

   ____

4. Do you know of any **prominent** people who have been caught lying? Give examples.

   ____

   ____

D **PREDICT** Work with a partner. Make a list of things that people often lie about. Note your ideas below.

Critical Thinking

____

____

Check your ideas as you read the passage. Were any mentioned? What other ideas are mentioned in the passage?

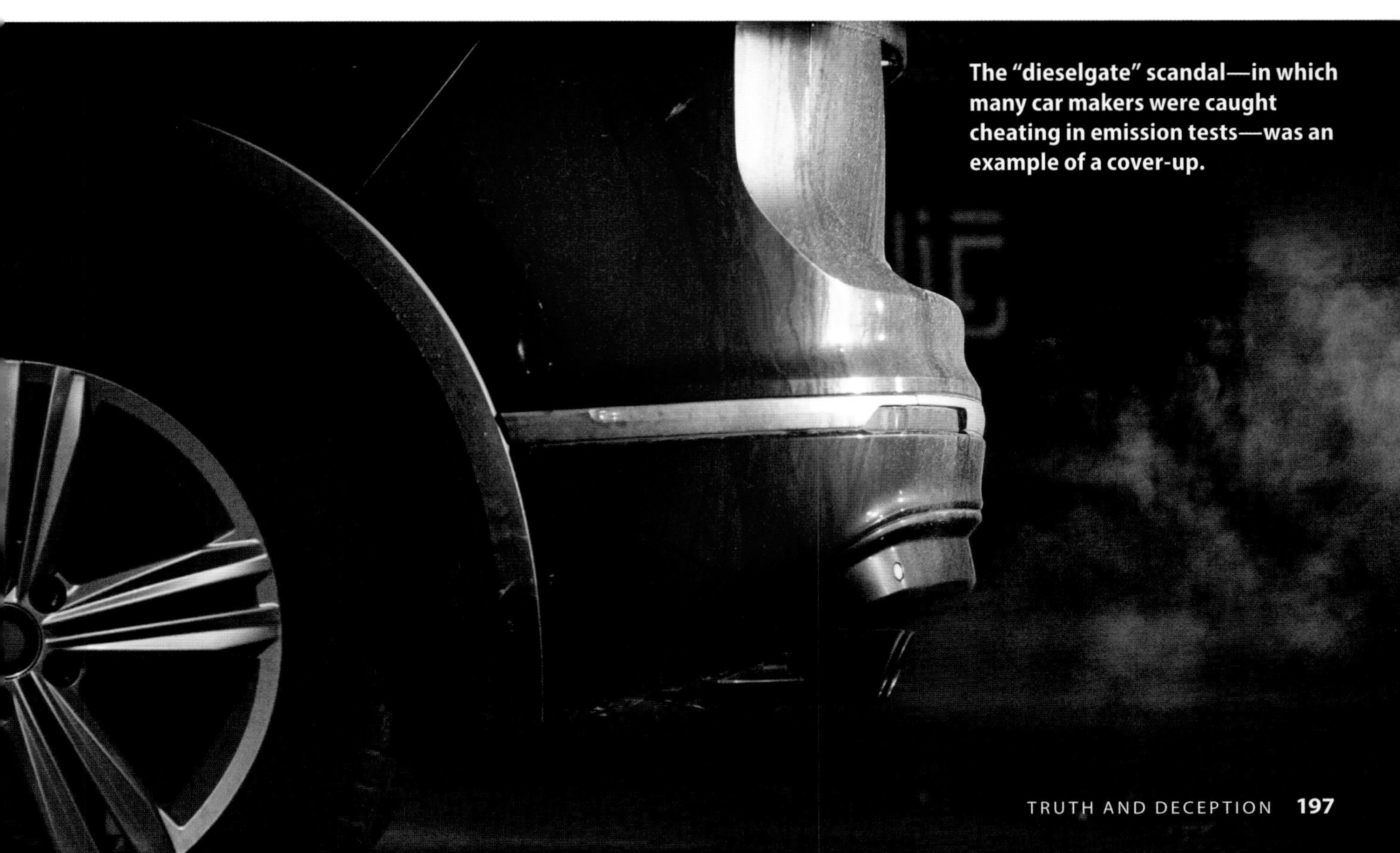

The "dieselgate" scandal—in which many car makers were caught cheating in emission tests—was an example of a cover-up.

WHY WE LIE

by Yudhijit Bhattacharjee

Honesty may be the best policy, but scheming and dishonesty may be part of what makes us human.

A The history of humankind is filled with skilled and practiced liars. Many are criminals who spin lies and weave **deceptive** tales to gain unjust rewards. Some are politicians who lie to gain power, or to cling to it. Sometimes people lie to boost their image, while others lie to **cover up** bad behavior. Even the academic science community—a world largely devoted to the pursuit of truth—has been shown to contain a number of deceivers. But the lies of impostors, swindlers, and boasting politicians are just a sample of the untruths that have characterized human behavior for thousands of years.

B Lying, it turns out, is something that most of us are very skilled at. We lie with ease, in ways big and small, to strangers, co-workers, friends, and loved ones. Our capacity for lying is as **fundamental** to us as our need to trust others. Being deceitful is part of our nature, so much so that we might say that to lie is human.

C Our natural **tendency** to lie was first **systematically** documented by Bella DePaulo, a social psychologist at the University of California, Santa Barbara. Two decades ago, DePaulo and her colleagues asked 147 adults to note down every instance they lied or tried to mislead someone during one week. The researchers found that the subjects lied on average one or two times a day. Most of these untruths were harmless, intended to hide one's failings or to protect the feelings of others. Some lies were excuses—one person blamed their failure to take out the garbage on not knowing where it needed to go. Yet other lies—such as a claim of being a diplomat's son—were told to present a false image. While these were minor transgressions, DePaulo and other colleagues observed [in a later study] that most people have, at some point, told one or more "serious lies": hiding an affair from a husband or wife, for example, or making false claims on a college application.

D That human beings should **universally** possess a talent for deceiving one another shouldn't surprise us. Researchers **speculate** that lying as a behavior arose not long after the emergence of language. The ability to manipulate others without using physical force may have helped us compete for resources—something similar to the evolution of deceptive strategies like camouflage[1] in the animal kingdom. "Lying is so easy compared to other ways of gaining power," notes ethicist[2] Sissela Bok of Harvard University, one of the most **prominent** thinkers on the subject. "It's much easier to lie in order to get somebody's money or wealth than to hit them over the head or rob a bank."

E As dishonesty has come to be recognized as a fundamental human trait, social science researchers and neuroscientists have sought to understand the nature and roots of the behavior. How and when do we learn to lie? What are the psychological **foundations** of dishonesty? And why do we believe lies so easily?

[1] **Camouflage** is the way in which some animals are colored and shaped so that they cannot easily be seen in their surroundings.
[2] An **ethicist** is someone who studies questions about what is morally right and wrong.

F Lying is something of a developmental milestone—like learning to walk and talk. Parents often find their children's lies troubling, as they signal the beginning of a loss of innocence.[3] However, Kang Lee, a psychologist at the University of Toronto, sees the emergence of the behavior in toddlers as a **reassuring** sign that their cognitive growth is on track.

G To study lying in children, Lee and his colleagues use a simple experiment. They ask kids to guess the identity of hidden toys, based only on an audio clue. For the first few toys, the clue is obvious—a bark for a dog, a meow for a cat—and the children answer easily. Then they play a sound that has nothing to do with the toy. "So you play Beethoven, but the toy's a car," Lee explains. The experimenter leaves the room pretending to take a phone call—a lie for the sake of science—and asks the child not to peek[4] at the toy. Returning, the experimenter asks the child for the answer, then follows up with the question: "Did you peek?"

H Using hidden cameras, Lee and his researchers have discovered that the majority of children can't resist peeking. The percentage of children who peek and then lie about it depends on their age. Among two-year-olds who peek, only about one third lie about it. Among three-year-olds, half lie. And by age eight, approximately 80 percent claim they didn't peek.

I Kids also get better at lying as they get older. When asked to guess the identity of the toy that they have secretly looked at, three- and four-year-olds typically give the right answer straightaway—they don't realize that this reveals that they cheated. At seven or eight, kids learn to deliberately give a wrong answer at first, or they try to make their answer seem like a reasoned guess.

J Five- and six-year-old kids fall in between. In one study, Lee used a Barney The Dinosaur toy. One five-year-old girl denied that she had looked at the toy, which was hidden under a cloth. Then she told Lee she wanted to feel it before guessing. "So she puts her hand underneath the cloth, closes her eyes, and says, 'Ah, I know: it's Barney,'" Lee recalls. "I ask, 'Why?' She says, 'Because it feels purple.'"

[3] **Innocence** is the state of being morally pure and incapable of immoral behavior.
[4] If you **peek** at something, you have a quick look at it, often secretly.

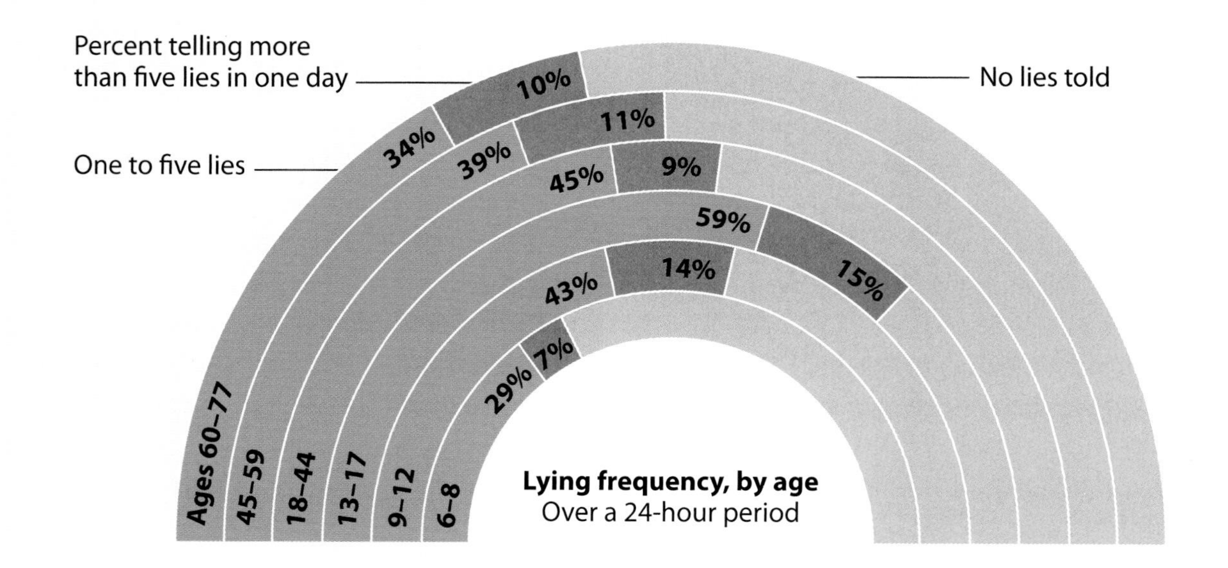

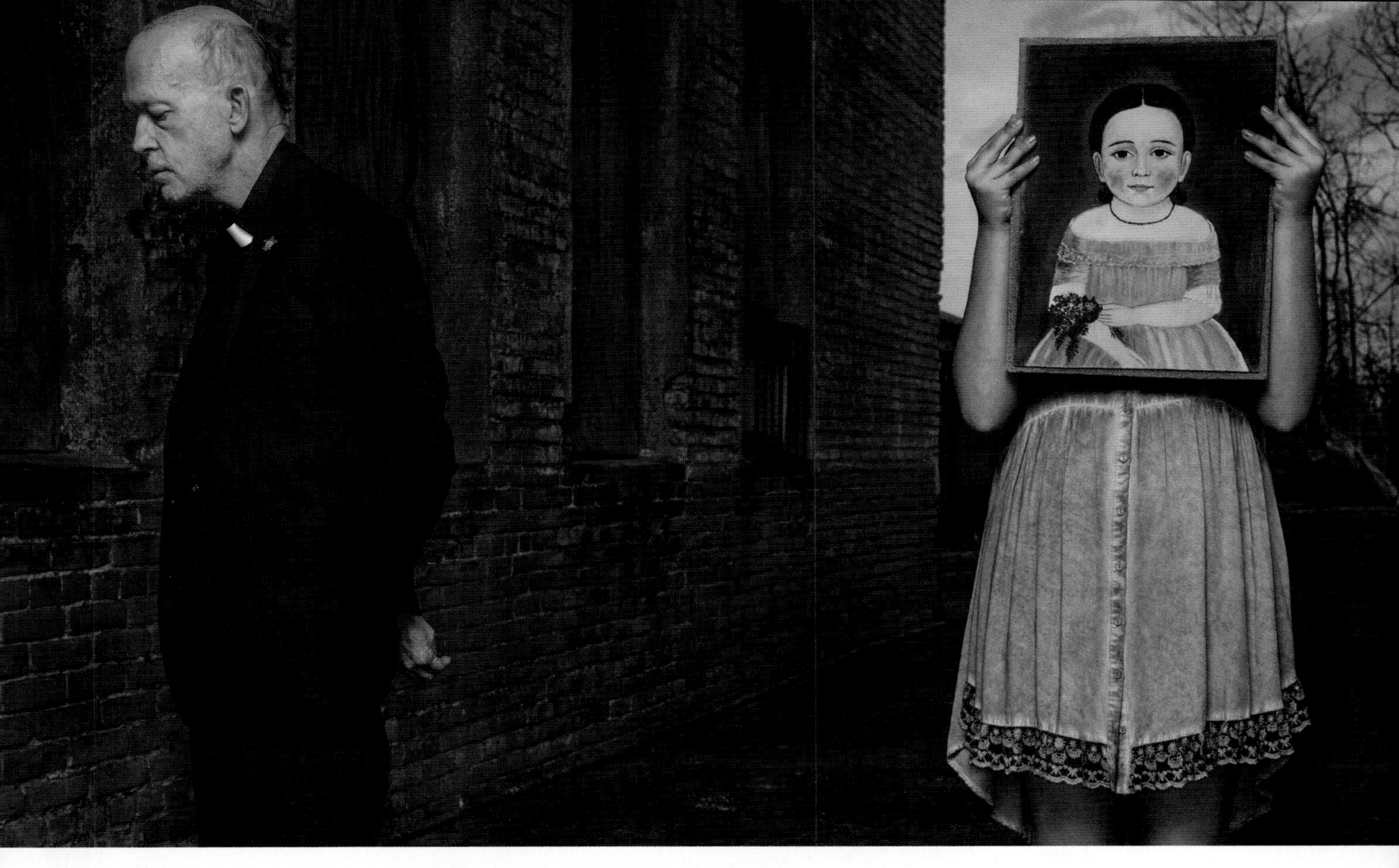

▲ ***Lying for self-aggrandizement:*** **Mark Landis spent nearly three decades forging the works of famous painters. While he did profit substantially from this, he was also motivated by the admiration his imitations received.**

K What drives this increase in lying sophistication[5] is the development of a child's ability to put himself or herself in someone else's shoes. Known as "theory of mind," this is the facility we acquire for understanding the beliefs, intentions, and knowledge of others. Also fundamental to lying is the brain's executive function: the abilities required for planning, making decisions, and self-control. This explains why the two-year-olds who lied and lied well in Lee's experiments performed better on tests of theory of mind and executive function than those who didn't.

L As we grow older, much of the knowledge we use to navigate the world comes from what others tell us. Without the **implicit** trust that we place in human communication, we would be paralyzed[6] as individuals and cease to have social relationships. "We get so much from believing, and there's relatively little harm when we occasionally get duped," says Tim Levine, a psychologist at the University of Alabama.

M Being programmed to trust makes us naturally gullible.[7] "If you say to someone, 'I am a pilot,' they are not sitting there thinking: 'Maybe he's not a pilot. Why would he say he's a pilot?' They don't think that way," says Frank Abagnale, Jr. Now a security consultant, Abagnale's cons[8] as a young man—including forging checks and pretending

[5] If something has a high level of **sophistication**, it is more advanced or complex than other things.
[6] If you are **paralyzed**, you are unable to act or function properly.
[7] If someone is **gullible**, they can be tricked easily.
[8] Short for *confidence trick*, a **con** is a trick in which someone deceives you with the intention of gaining money.

to be an airline pilot—inspired the 2002 movie *Catch Me If You Can*. "This is why scams work," he says. "When the phone rings and the caller ID says it's the Internal Revenue Service,[9] people automatically believe it is the IRS. They don't realize that someone could manipulate the caller ID."

N Robert Feldman, a psychologist at the University of Massachusetts, calls that "the liar's advantage." "People are not expecting lies, people are not searching for lies," he says, "and a lot of the time, people want to hear what they are hearing." We put up little resistance[10] to the deceptions that please or comfort us—such as false praise or the promise of impossibly high investment returns. And when we deal with people who have wealth, power, and status, the lies appear to be even easier to swallow.

[9] In the United States, the **Internal Revenue Service (IRS)** is the government authority that collects taxes.
[10] To **put up resistance** to something means to refuse to accept it and to try to prevent it.

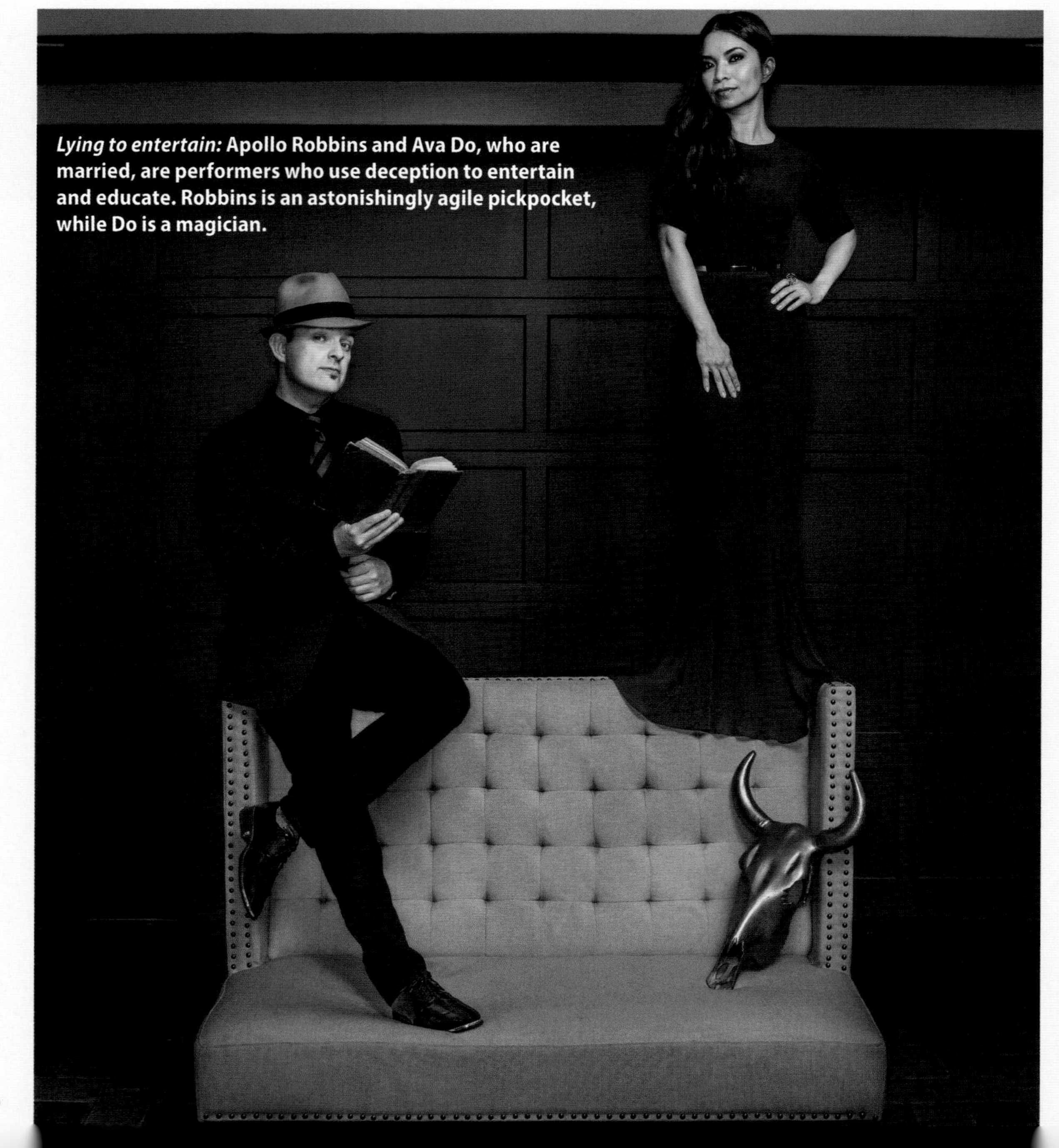

Lying to entertain: **Apollo Robbins and Ava Do, who are married, are performers who use deception to entertain and educate. Robbins is an astonishingly agile pickpocket, while Do is a magician.**

O Researchers are now learning that we are **prone to** believe some lies even when they're clearly contradicted by evidence. These insights suggest that our skill at deceiving others—combined with our vulnerability[11] to being deceived—is especially consequential in the age of social media. Research has shown, for example, that we are especially prone to accepting lies that affirm our worldview. False news stories thrive on the internet and in social media because of this vulnerability, and disproving them does not tend to **lessen** their power. This is because people assess the evidence presented to them through a framework of preexisting beliefs and prejudices, says George Lakoff, a cognitive linguist at the University of California, Berkeley. "If a fact comes in that doesn't fit into your frame, you'll either not notice it, or ignore it, or ridicule it, or be puzzled by it—or attack it if it's threatening."

P What then might be the best way to **impede** the rapid advance of untruths into our collective lives? The answer isn't clear. Technology has opened up a new frontier for deceit, adding a 21st-century **twist** to the age-old conflict between our lying and trusting selves.

Adapted from "Why We Lie," by Yudhijit Bhattacharjee: National Geographic Magazine, June 2017

Yudhijit Bhattacharjee is an award-winning writer whose features and essays on science, espionage, cybercrime, and medicine have appeared in *The New Yorker, The New York Times Magazine, National Geographic, Wired,* and other publications.

▲ ***Lying for fun:*** **Jacob Hall's tall tales have won him numerous awards, including West Virginia's "Biggest Liar" award. According to Hall, "My stories would be pretty boring without deception."**

---

[11] To have a **vulnerability** is to be open to harm in a certain way.

UNDERSTANDING THE READING

A **UNDERSTAND MAIN IDEAS** Check (✓) the four topics that the writer covers in the reading passage.

- ☐ 1. the reasons that people lie
- ☐ 2. how often people lie
- ☐ 3. why people believe lies
- ☐ 4. cross-cultural differences in lying
- ☐ 5. the emotional effects of lying and being deceptive
- ☐ 6. the relationship between lying and cognitive development

B **UNDERSTAND DETAILS** Read paragraphs L–O of the reading passage and complete the summary. Use no more than two words from the reading passage for each answer.

We can't function in life without trust because a lot of the [1]__________________ we need comes from other people. We therefore generally trust people because the benefits of doing so significantly outweigh the harm of occasionally being tricked or lied to. However, this tendency to trust does leave people [2]__________________. According to Frank Abagnale, Jr., this is why scams work. Psychologist Robert Feldman refers to this as the [3]__________________. People do not usually expect or look for lies. Furthermore, they are often happy to hear them—especially lies that comfort, praise, or promise high returns on investments. These lies are even more believable when told by people with wealth, power, and status. Today, in the age of social media, people are more likely to believe lies, especially ones that support their [4]__________________. These lies flourish online, and [5]__________________ them does not reduce their effectiveness. This is because we interpret [6]__________________ based on our beliefs and biases. If a fact does not match what we believe, we simply dismiss, ridicule, or attack it.

Critical Thinking

C **INFER MEANING** Find and underline the following words and phrases in the reading passage. Use the context to identify their meanings. Then match each word or phrase to its definition.

unjust (paragraph A)	**impostor** (paragraph A)	**transgression** (paragraph C)
milestone (paragraph F)	**on track** (paragraph F)	**get duped** (paragraph L)

1. __________________ an action that is wrong or immoral
2. __________________ a person who pretends to be someone else
3. __________________ an important event in the development of something
4. __________________ not fair
5. __________________ following a course likely to result in success
6. __________________ to be tricked into believing something that is not true

D **INTERPRET** Look back at the quote from George Lakoff in the final sentence of paragraph O. What does he mean by "doesn't fit into your frame"? Discuss with a partner.

Critical Thinking

____

____

CRITICAL THINKING Evaluating Research

Writers sometimes refer to scientific research and studies to support their main ideas. When you read information about an experiment or study, it is important to ask yourself questions to evaluate the quality of the research. For example:

- How did the researchers choose or gather their subjects?
- Were the subjects representative of the population studied (in terms of age, gender, etc.)?
- Were the results reliable? Were they interpreted correctly?
- Were there flaws in the way the research was done?

E **EVALUATE RESEARCH** Think about DePaulo's research studies in paragraph C of the reading passage. Note answers to the questions below. Then discuss with a partner.

Critical Thinking

1. How truthful or complete would the participants' answers have been? Why?

____

____

2. Which kind of untruths do you think the participants were more likely to record?

____

____

3. How would you motivate the test subjects to record their lies truthfully and completely?

____

____

F **INTERPRET VISUAL DATA** Look at the infographic on lying frequency in the reading passage. Choose the correct words to complete the sentences.

Critical Thinking

1. Six- to eight-year-olds lie **more than** / **less than** nine- to twelve-year-olds.
2. People between the ages of **13–17** / **18–44** tell the most lies.
3. People start telling **more** / **fewer** lies after the age of 17.

Review this Critical Thinking Skill in Unit 8

G **APPLY** Think about your own experiences growing up. Discuss with a partner.

Critical Thinking

1. Read the statements in Exercise F. What are some possible explanations for each fact?
2. Are there any other inferences you can make from the information in the chart? What are they?
3. The reading passage talks about false news stories that thrive online in the age of social media. Why do you think social media has made stories like these more effective?

Review this Critical Thinking Skill in Unit 3

DEVELOPING READING SKILLS

READING SKILL Understanding a Research Summary

When writers refer to studies, they often summarize the main points of the research.

These points usually include:

- The **purpose** (why the study was done)
- The **method** (how the study was done)
- The **results** (data from the study)
- The **conclusion** (the significance of the results)

When reading a research summary, it is useful to highlight these points and label them in the margins.

A **UNDERSTAND A RESEARCH SUMMARY** The sentences below summarize a piece of research known as "The Matrix Experiments." What does each sentence describe? Write *purpose*, *method*, *results*, or *conclusion*.

1. ________________ In the experiment, over 40,000 volunteers were given a test with 20 simple math problems. Because they were given only five minutes to complete the test, no one was able to answer all 20 questions. They were then asked how many questions they had answered correctly.
2. ________________ The Matrix Experiments were a series of studies designed to measure dishonesty in adults.
3. ________________ The results suggested that while lying is common, there are very few people who tell big lies.
4. ________________ Most answered only four questions. However, about 70% of the participants lied about their test results, adding an average of two to the number of questions they answered correctly. 20 out of the 40,000 participants claimed to have solved all 20 problems.

B **UNDERSTAND A RESEARCH SUMMARY** Reread paragraphs G–J of the reading passage. Label the parts that explain the purpose, method, and results of Kang Lee's study.

C **UNDERSTAND A RESEARCH SUMMARY** Read the conclusion of Kang Lee's study in paragraph K. In your own words, summarize this conclusion.

____

____

____

VOCABULARY EXTENSION

WORD FORMS *-ence* and *-ance*

The suffixes *-ence* and *-ance* are often used to turn adjectives ending in *-ent* or *-ant* into nouns (e.g., *innocent—innocence, instant—instance*). In addition, *-ance* (and sometimes *-ence*) can be added to some verbs to create nouns (e.g., *resist—resistance, emerge—emergence*).

A Complete the chart by writing the adjective and noun forms of the words.

Verb form	Adjective form	Noun form (with *-ence* or *-ance*)
–	intelligent	
–	prominent	
–	brilliant	
ignore		
differ		
persist		

WORD WEB *deceit* and *deception*

While the words *deceit* and *deception* are often thought to be synonymous, there are subtle differences. *Deceit* refers to dishonesty and generally has negative connotations (e.g., lying for personal gain). *Deception*, however, refers to a trick or scheme intended to mislead. It too can have negative connotations, but it can also be more neutral (e.g., the use of camouflage to hide from predators). The words have several commonly used forms:

deceit (n) *deceive (v)* *deceiver (n)* *deceitful (adj)*
deceitfully (adv) *deception (n)* *deceptive (adj)* *deceptively (adv)*

B Complete the passage by choosing the correct form of *deceit* or *deception*.

Frank Abagnale, Jr. was famous for being [1] **deceiver** / **deceptive**. He pulled off many scams in his life, but perhaps his most elaborate trick was pretending to be an airline pilot. By using a fake employee ID, Abagnale [2] **deceit** / **deceived** an airline operator into thinking he was a qualified pilot. He flew over 1.5 million kilometers using this fake ID.

Abagnale later became an attorney through another convincing act of [3] **deceptive** / **deception**. This time, he faked a degree from Harvard Law School. After his eventual capture and arrest, Abagnale left his life of [4] **deceit** / **deceptive** behind and became a security consultant. Abagnale believes that he got away with so much largely because people are trusting and do not generally expect others to behave [5] **deceitfully / deceptive**.

Participants in one of Kang Lee's studies

In Kang Lee's development lab, researchers conduct deception studies to better understand the nature of lying. Children are put through a range of playful scenarios designed to elicit cheating and dishonesty.

Critical Thinking

A **PREVIEW** What have you learned so far about lying? Discuss the questions with a partner.

1. What are some reasons people lie, and how often do people lie on average?
2. What is lying a sign of in children, and how do children get better at lying as they grow?

B **MAIN IDEAS** Watch the video. Choose the correct option to complete each sentence.

1. The first experiment tests if children can **detect lies** / **lie to be polite**.
2. The second experiment tests the ability to lie to **cover up something** / **help someone**.

C **DETAILS** Watch the video again. Complete the notes below.

Test one: The researcher gives a child ______________________________.

The child is asked if she ______________________________.

Test two: The researcher promises a child a prize if she can guess something without looking.

The researcher then ______________________________.

The researcher asks the child if ______________________________.

Critical Thinking

D **APPLY** Kang Lee sees the ability to lie as a positive development in children. How do you think parents should react if their child lies to them? Discuss with a partner.

Writing

EXPLORING WRITTEN ENGLISH

LANGUAGE FOR WRITING Introducing Results and Describing Data

When introducing the results of a study, both the active and the passive voices can be used. Here are some words and expressions you can use to introduce results:

Active: Researchers *found / discovered / saw / observed / noticed that …*
Passive: It was *found / discovered / observed / noticed that …*

When describing data, words and phrases are often easier to understand than numbers and percentages. They also make your writing more interesting and less repetitive. You can express percentages and numerical data using words and phrases like these:

1 in 10	*a quarter*	*a third*	*two-fifths*
half	*the majority (of)*	*three-quarters*	*all (of)*

You can add modifiers such as *only, fewer/less than, more than, approximately, nearly, almost, exactly, precisely,* and *just over.*

More than a quarter *of those who took part in the study were children.*
Approximately a third *of those aged 13–17 told no lies over the 24-hour period.*

Modifiers can be used to suggest that a number is big or small.

More than *a third of the people selected preferred option b.*
Nearly half *the participants got the answers wrong.*
Less than *a quarter of the group thought it was a good idea.*

More than and *nearly* both imply that the number of people described is large. *Less than* implies that the number of people described is small.

See the Grammar Reference on page 250

A **NOTICE** Read the sentences. How else could the quantities in bold be expressed? Discuss with a partner. Then check how they were expressed in paragraph H of the reading passage.

1. Among two-year-olds who peek, **approximately 30 percent** lie about it.
2. Among three-year-olds, **50 percent** lie.
3. And by age eight, **about four-fifths** claim they didn't peek.

B **APPLY** Look at the chart on lying frequency in the reading passage. Then replace the percentages in the sentences below with words and phrases for describing numerical data. Use modifiers when appropriate to imply whether the numbers are big or small.

1. Researchers found that **34%** of people aged 60–77 told one to five lies over a 24-hour period. ____________________
2. **50%** of people aged 45–59 told no lies. ____________________
3. **57%** of children aged 9–12 told at least one lie in 24 hours. ____________________
4. **29%** of children aged 6–8 told one to five lies. ____________________

C **APPLY** Read the sentences and consider their purposes. Then replace the **bold** numbers and words to better achieve that purpose. Discuss with a partner.

1. The results are amazing. **71%** of the people surveyed love it.
2. The turnout was worse than expected. **29%** of the seats in the hall were filled.
3. If you sign up for our internet plan, you'll save **$19** a month.
4. Our drinks are healthier. They contain **4 milligrams** of sugar per serving.

D **REFLECT** Look at the infographic in the Explore the Theme section again. Write three sentences describing some of the numbers that stand out to you. Use words and phrases for describing numerical data, as well as modifiers when appropriate.

1. ____________________
____
____

2. ____________________
____
____

3. ____________________
____
____

Review Writing a Summary in Unit 5

WRITING SKILL Summarizing a Research Study

A research summary covers briefly the main points of a study. When writing a research summary, paraphrase and list only the most important points.

Part 1: Purpose

This part of the research summary includes background information on the issue. It also states the question or questions the researchers want to answer.

Part 2: Method

This section explains how the researchers set up the study, what they did, and what they had their research participants/subjects do. There is no need for a topic sentence in your paragraph describing the method. Simply describe the steps in order.

Part 3: Results

This part uses numerical data to describe what the researchers observed, how the participants behaved, or what happened. Again, there is no need for a topic sentence when describing the results. Just list the findings that are relevant in order of importance.

Part 4: Conclusion

This final section explains the implications of the results, as well as how the results answered the questions the researchers wanted answered at the beginning of the study. If there are flaws in the experiment, they can be mentioned here, too. Explain whether these flaws nullify the experiment, or if the results are still useful. Finally, if possible, express how the findings of the research can be of use in the real world.

E Read the notes for a research summary. Match each point (a–g) with the part of the research summary it belongs to.

Outline

Purpose: _____ Results: _____ _____ _____

Method: _____ _____ Conclusion: _____

The Stanford Marshmallow Experiment

a. The aim was to find out if children could delay gratification, and how the ability to delay gratification affects people's lives.

b. About 33 percent of children were able to delay gratification long enough to eat both marshmallows.

c. Researchers took children into a room with a chair, a small desk, two marshmallows, and a bell.

d. About 33 percent of subjects rang the bell and ate one marshmallow immediately after the researchers left. The final third tried hard not to ring the bell, but gave up before the 15 minutes were up.

e. While the results seem to suggest a clear link between the ability to delay gratification at a young age and future success in life, this conclusion is flawed. It was discovered many years later that the original experiment did not account for participants' different socio-economic backgrounds. Subsequent tests that did showed no clear link between the ability to delay gratification as a child and success later in life.

f. Several years after the experiment, researchers observed that the participants who had delayed gratification earned higher SAT scores and were better able to deal with stress.

g. The researchers left the room and presented the children with a dilemma: they could ring the bell and eat only one of the marshmallows right away, or they could wait until the researchers came back and eat both marshmallows.The researchers then left the children alone for about 15 minutes.

F **VOCABULARY FOR WRITING** The following verbs can be useful for writing about the different parts of research studies. Choose the correct word to complete each sentence below.

Purpose	Method	Results	Conclusion
determine	measure	discovered	prove
ascertain	gauge	observed	confirm
uncover	evaluate	noticed	disprove
investigate	test	revealed	contradict

1. It was **observed** / **measured** that over two-thirds of people refused to take the money.
2. The researchers showed them images and **gauged** / **ascertained** their responses.
3. The purpose of the study was to **prove** / **determine** at what age children start lying.
4. These results **uncover** / **disprove** the ideas put forth by the other team of researchers.

WRITING TASK

GOAL You are going to write a research summary on the following topic:
Write a research summary of a famous study.

Review this Writing Skill in Unit 7

A **RESEARCH** Look up some of the experiments below. Decide which one you will summarize. Then find two or more articles that give details about the experiment you have chosen.

- The Invisible Gorilla Experiment; conducted by Daniel Simons and Christopher Chabris
- The Good Samaritan Experiment; conducted by John Darley and Daniel Batson
- The Blue Eyes/Brown Eyes Experiment; conducted by Jane Elliott
- Ross's False Consensus Effect Study; conducted by Lee Ross
- Car Crash Experiment; conducted by Elizabeth Loftus and John Palmer
- The Chameleon Effect; conducted by Tanya Chartrand and John Bargh

Review Paraphrasing in Unit 5

B **TAKE NOTES** Read the articles once to understand the main points of the experiment. Then take notes in your own words in the chart below.

Purpose	
Method	
Results	

C **WRITE A CONCLUSION** Look at the results above and think about their implications or significance. In one or two sentences, write down your conclusion.

____

____

____

D **PLAN** Use your information in Exercises B–C to complete an outline for your research summary.

OUTLINE

Body paragraph 1: purpose

Background on topic: ______________________________

____

____

Purpose of study: ______________________________

____

____

Body paragraph 2: method

____

____

____

Body paragraph 3: results

____

____

____

Body paragraph 4: conclusion

____

____

____

____

____

E **FIRST DRAFT** Use the information in your outline to write a first draft of your research summary. Remember to use words and phrases instead of numbers to describe numerical data when appropriate.

F **REVISING PRACTICE** The research summary on the next page is similar to the one you are writing. Follow the steps to create a better second draft.

1. Add the sentences (a–c) in the most suitable spaces.
   a. If they couldn't wait until the researchers returned, the children could ring the bell and eat one of the marshmallows, but not both.
   b. They also found that in adulthood, the participants who had been able to wait long enough to get both marshmallows had fewer unhealthy addictions, more stable marriages, and better physical health.
   c. Mischel's experiment eventually evolved into a longitudinal study (one conducted over several years) to find out to what extent the ability to delay gratification affects people's levels of success in life.

2. Now fix the following problems (a–b) with the research summary.
   a. Replace a percentage with a word or phrase for expressing numerical data at the start of the Results section.
   b. Replace an incorrect word for introducing results in the Results section.

The Stanford Marshmallow Experiment

Purpose

In the 1960s and 1970s, Stanford psychologist Walter Mischel conducted a series of experiments relating to the ability to forego smaller short-term gains for larger long-term rewards. Initially, Mischel's studies—which involved 653 preschool students aged three to five—were designed to determine the age at which children develop the ability to resist their impulses. ____

Method

In the study, researchers placed individual children in a room with nothing but a chair and a small desk. On the desk were two marshmallows and a bell. The researchers then told each child that they would be leaving them alone with the marshmallows for a few minutes. They also told them that if they waited until the researchers came back, they would be allowed to eat both marshmallows. ____ The researchers then left the children alone with the marshmallows for about 15 minutes and observed whether the children were able to resist ringing the bell.

Results

The researchers found that about 33% of the children were able to delay gratification long enough to get both marshmallows. Another third of the subjects rang the bell and ate one marshmallow immediately after the researchers left. And the final third tried hard to wait but eventually gave in before the researchers returned to the room. The researchers continued to monitor the participants' lives for many more years after the test. They tested that as teenagers, participants who had been able to delay gratification ended up with higher SAT scores, better self-esteem, and the ability to tolerate higher stress levels than participants who had not been able to delay gratification. ____

Conclusion

While Mischel's longitudinal study seems to suggest that the ability to delay gratification as a child is a key predictor of success later in life, this conclusion is flawed. It was discovered many years later that the original experiment did not account for participants' different socio-economic backgrounds. Subsequent tests that did showed no clear link between the ability to delay gratification as a child and success later in life. Nonetheless, despite its flaws, Mischel's study does raise interesting questions about the importance of impulse control and long-term planning in our adult lives.

G REVISED DRAFT Now use the questions below to revise your research summary.

- ☐ Do you explain the purpose of the study clearly?
- ☐ Do you describe the method using enough detail?
- ☐ Are the results of the study presented using data and numerical findings?
- ☐ Does your conclusion state the implications and practical applications of the results?
- ☐ Do you correctly use phrases for introducing results?
- ☐ Do you use a variety of words and phrases to express numerical data?

H EDITING PRACTICE Read the information below. Then find and correct one mistake with words and phrases for describing data in each of the sentences (1–4).

In sentences with words and phrases that describe data, remember:

- The verb usually agrees with the main noun. For example:
  Two-thirds of the country's drinking water ***is*** *imported from abroad.*
  A third of all the customers in the survey ***were*** *unhappy with the service they received.*
- Include *of* before a noun, after phrases such as *a third*, *three-quarters*, and *the majority*.
- Use *fewer than* with plural countable nouns and *less than* with uncountable nouns.

1. A third of the participants was able to delay gratification.
2. The majority of the research were carried out in South America.
3. Around two-thirds the participants were not convinced by the story.
4. Less than 100 children took part in the study.

I FINAL DRAFT Follow these steps to write a final draft.

1. Check your revised draft for mistakes with words and phrases for referring to results and numerical data.
2. Now use the checklist on page 248 to write a final draft. Make any other necessary changes.
3. Work in pairs and read your partner's final research summary. Give feedback on each other's writing.

In the Stanford marshmallow experiment, about one-third of children were able to resist the temptation to eat the marshmallow.

Review

SELF-ASSESS **Consider the language and skills you learned in this unit.**

How well can you . . . ?	Very well	Pretty well	I need improvement
use the key vocabulary from this unit	☐	☐	☐
evaluate research	☐	☐	☐
understand a research summary	☐	☐	☐
introduce results and describe data	☐	☐	☐
summarize a research study	☐	☐	☐

A **VOCABULARY** Do you remember the meanings of these words and phrases? Look back at the unit and review the ones you don't know.

cover up	deceptive	foundation AW	fundamental AW	impede
implicit AW	lessen	prominent AW	prone to	reassuring
speculate	systematically	tendency	twist	universally

B **VOCABULARY EXTENSION** Complete these tasks with a partner.

1. Write the noun forms of these words with *-ence* or *-ance*.

ignore ____________ intelligent ____________ persist ____________

2. Write the verb, adjective, and adverb forms of the word *deceit*.

verb: ____________ adjective: ____________ adverb: ____________

C **READING SKILL** Which parts of a research study do the following describe?

1. how the study was conducted
2. the reason for the study
3. what the results signify
4. findings and data from the study

D **LANGUAGE FOR WRITING** Write two sentences about the infographic from the Unit 4 Explore the Theme section. Use words and phrases to describe the data instead of numbers.

SELF-ASSESS **Look back at the chart above. Did you assess your skills correctly? What skills or language do you still need help with?**

CHANGING THE PLANET 10

Sand dunes in Grand Canaria, Spain

IN THIS UNIT, YOU WILL:

- Read an article about how humans impact the planet
- Watch a video about rainforests and deforestation
- Write about an organization that protects the environment

THINK AND DISCUSS:

1. The photo above shows a lush neighborhood next to dry sand dunes in Grand Canaria, Spain. Why do you think the two areas are so different?
2. How much do you think your everyday actions reshape the world?

EXPLORE THE THEME

Look at the information on these pages and answer the questions.

1. In what ways do humans impact the environment?
2. How could underwater farming benefit the environment?
3. What could you do to lessen your impact on the environment?

The Human Impact

Termites build nests up to 10 meters tall, and beavers build dams visible from space. But no other species on Earth has the ability to reshape the planet quite like we do.

Human ingenuity has allowed us to mine the planet's resources in ways that are unmatched. This has led to important milestones, like the development of agriculture and the rise of industrialization. But it has also had unintended consequences.

Humans release air and water pollutants by the ton. We lay waste to forests to extract resources and create land for farming. Industries create toxic waste, farmers release pesticides, and vehicles spew smoky fumes into the atmosphere.

Human ingenuity has reshaped the planet in ways that are destructive and long-lasting. The question remains: Can human ingenuity help us repair the damage we've done?

Underwater farms like this could help reduce the environmental impact of agriculture. Underwater farming would require no pesticides, nor would it require the clearing of forests to make space for farmland.

Reading

PREPARING TO READ

A **BUILD VOCABULARY** The words in **blue** are used in the reading passage. Read the text below. Then write the correct form of each word next to its definition.

In December 2015, representatives from almost every country got together in Paris, France, and agreed on one thing: that humanity's role in accelerating climate change had gotten out of hand, and that something **profound** needed to be done about it. In a rare moment of solidarity, these countries signed what the world refers to today as the Paris Agreement.

By doing so, each nation made a commitment to radically reduce or **eliminate** greenhouse gas emissions by **shifting** toward renewable energy. The goal was to collectively limit global temperature rise by 1.5 degrees Celsius by the end of the century. The agreement included several other terms: Participating nations had to create a transparent framework to ensure accountability and to allow clear targets and **criteria** to be set. In addition, larger nations had to support developing nations, which in general contribute much less to the problem.

While much progress has been made since the signing of the Paris Agreement, more needs to be done to ensure we don't experience the worst effects of climate change. The problem, though, is a challenging one: The same fuels that heat up our atmosphere power our economies and sustain our way of life. Nonetheless, if left unchecked, climate change will lead to extreme weather, widespread destruction, and perhaps even our **extinction**. Most experts **conclude** that drastic steps need to be taken now to ensure the **preservation** of our species.

1. ____________________ (n) standards by which something is assessed
2. ____________________ (n) the act of keeping something in its current state
3. ____________________ (adj) extreme, or deeply felt
4. ____________________ (v) to get rid of
5. ____________________ (n) the loss of an entire species
6. ____________________ (v) to arrive at an opinion
7. ____________________ (v) to move or change gradually

World leaders celebrate after the signing of the Paris Agreement.

B **BUILD VOCABULARY** Complete the sentences below with the correct form of the words in blue. Use a dictionary to help you.

erosion (n)	**geology** (n)	**grasp** (v)	**intriguing** (adj)
irony (n)	**merit** (n)	**perspective** (n)	**subtle** (adj)

1. The evidence he presented wasn't strong, so the committee didn't see much ______________ in his argument.
2. It's a complex issue, and different people tend to have different ______________ on it.
3. The two materials may seem the same at first glance, but if you study them carefully, you'll notice ______________ differences in their texture.
4. Some people thought her idea was silly, but I found it ______________.
5. The disaster was entirely their fault. The ______________ is that they were brought in to prevent it.
6. Planting trees is a great way to reduce soil ______________ caused by rain.
7. The concept is rather abstract and hard to ______________.
8. She wants to study ______________ because she's interested in the natural structures and materials that make up our planet.

C **USE VOCABULARY** Discuss these questions with a partner.

1. Do you think it's important to consider the **perspectives** of people who disagree with you? How does doing so benefit us?
2. Have you ever held a strong opinion, but **shifted** your position over time? What was the opinion, and why did it shift?
3. Have any of the ideas covered in this book had a **profound** impact on you? Which were they, and why did they affect you?
4. Can you think of examples that illustrate the concept of **irony**?

D **PREDICT** Look at the title of the reading passage and the chart on page 224. What do you think the Anthropocene refers to?

Critical Thinking

____

____

E **BRAINSTORM** Discuss the questions with a partner.

Critical Thinking

1. What do you think Earth was like before humans existed?
2. Which of the changes that have happened since then are because of humans?
3. What evidence or geological footprints will the humans of today leave behind for future humans?

Check your answers as you read the passage.

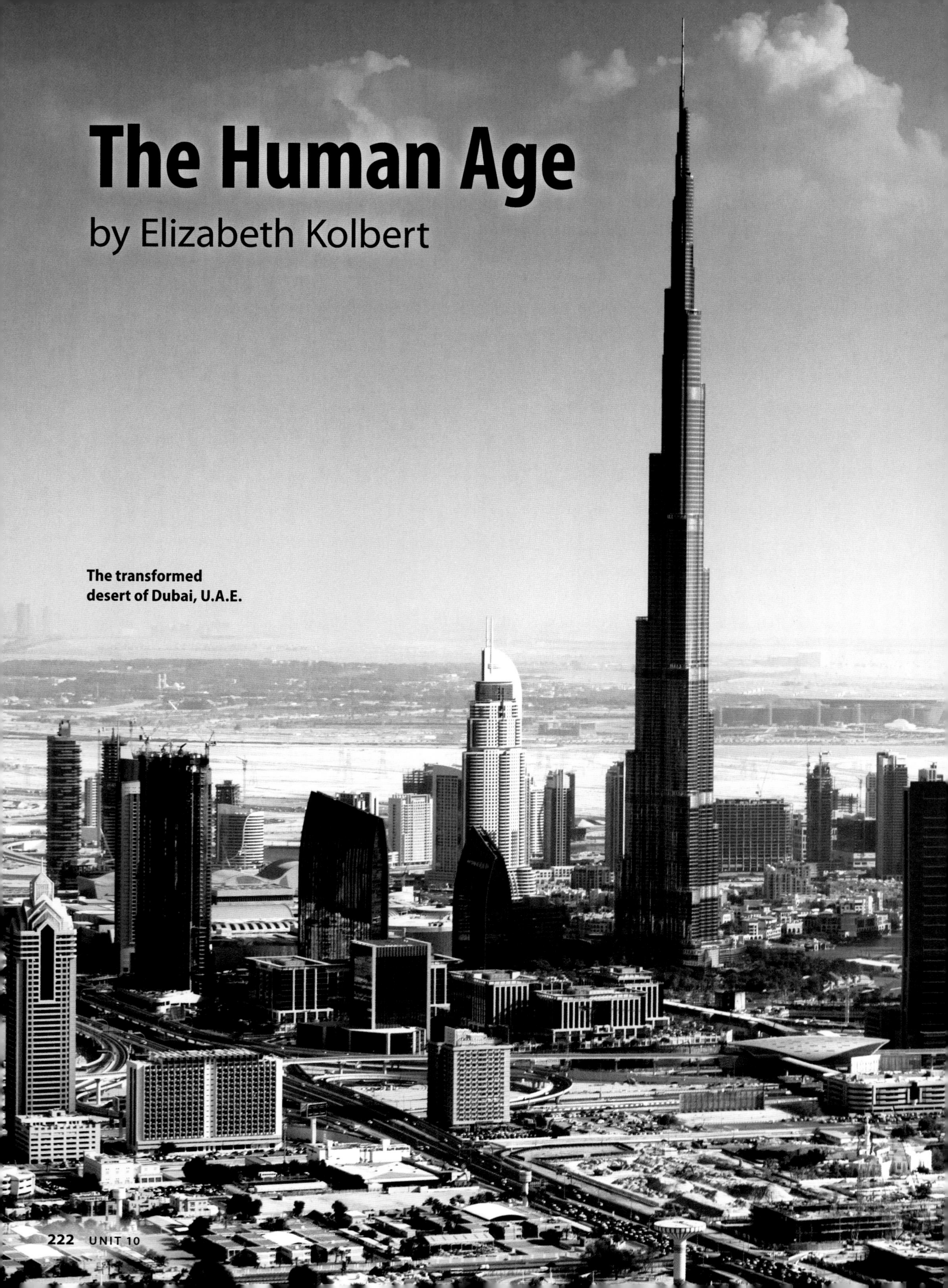

The Human Age

by Elizabeth Kolbert

The transformed desert of Dubai, U.A.E.

Human beings have altered the planet so much in just the past century or two that we are now in a new epoch: the Anthropocene.

A The word Anthropocene was coined by Dutch chemist Paul Crutzen in 2002. Crutzen, who shared a Nobel Prize for discovering the effects of ozone-depleting compounds, was sitting at a scientific conference one day. The conference chairman kept referring to the Holocene, the epoch that began 11,500 years ago, at the end of the last ice age, and that—officially, at least—continues to this day.

B "Let's stop it," Crutzen recalls blurting out. "We are no longer in the Holocene. We are in the Anthropocene." It was quiet in the room for a while. When the group took a coffee break, the Anthropocene was the main topic of conversation.

C Way back in the 1870s, an Italian geologist named Antonio Stoppani proposed that people had introduced a new era, which he labeled the Anthropozoic. Stoppani's proposal was ignored; other scientists found it unscientific. The Anthropocene, by contrast, struck a chord. The human impact on the world had become a lot more obvious since Stoppani's day, in part because the size of the population had roughly quadrupled,[1] to nearly seven billion.

D When Crutzen wrote up the Anthropocene idea in the journal *Nature*, the concept was immediately picked up by researchers working in a wide range of disciplines. Soon, it began to appear regularly in the scientific press. At first, most of the scientists using the new geologic term were not geologists. Jan Zalasiewicz, a British geologist, found the discussions **intriguing**. "I noticed that Crutzen's term was appearing in the serious literature, without quotation marks and without a sense of **irony**," he says.

E In 2007, Zalasiewicz was serving as chairman of the Geological Society of London's Stratigraphy[2] Commission. At a meeting, he decided to ask his fellow stratigraphers what they thought of the Anthropocene. Twenty-one of twenty-two thought the concept had **merit**. The group agreed to look at it as a formal problem in **geology**. Would the Anthropocene satisfy the **criteria** used for naming a new epoch?

F The rock record of the present doesn't exist yet, of course. So the question was: When it does, will human impacts show up as "stratigraphically significant"? The answer, Zalasiewicz's group decided, is yes—though not necessarily for the reasons you would expect.

G Probably the most obvious way humans are altering the planet is by building cities, which are essentially vast stretches of man-made materials—steel, glass, concrete, and brick. But it turns out most cities are not good candidates for long-term **preservation**: they're built on land, and on land the forces of erosion tend to win out over those of sedimentation. From a geologic **perspective**, the most plainly visible human effects on the landscape today "may in some ways be the most transient,[3]" Zalasiewicz observes.

---

[1] If something **quadruples**, it increases by a factor of four.
[2] **Stratigraphy** is a branch of geology concerned with the study of rock layers.
[3] **Transient** describes a situation that lasts only a short time or is constantly changing.

Earth's Geological Timeline

Start of the Anthropocene

Era	Period		Epoch	Millions of Years Ago
Cenozoic	Quaternary		Holocene	
			Pleistocene	1.5
	Neogene		Pliocene	
			Miocene	2.3
	Paleogene		Oligocene	
			Eocene	
			Paleocene	65
Mesozoic	Cretaceous			
	Jurassic			
	Triassic			250
Paleozoic	Permian			
	Carboniferous	Pennsylvanian		
		Mississippian		
	Devonian			
	Silurian			
	Ordovician			
	Cambrian			540
Precambrian	Proterozoic			2500
	Archean			3800
	Hadean			4600

In geology, *epochs* are relatively short time spans, though they can extend for tens of millions of years. *Periods*, such as the Ordovician and the Cretaceous, last much longer, and *eras*, like the Mesozoic, longer still. The boundaries between epochs are defined by changes preserved in sedimentary rocks[4] —for example, the emergence of one type of commonly fossilized organism, or the disappearance of another.

H Humans have also transformed the world through farming; more than half of the planet's habitable land is now devoted to agriculture. Here again, some of the effects that seem most significant today—runoff from the use of fertilizers on fields, for example—will leave behind only subtle traces at best. Future geologists are most likely to grasp the scale of 21st-century industrial agriculture from the pollen[5] record—from the monochrome[6] stretches of corn, wheat, and soy pollen that will have replaced the varied record left behind by rainforests or prairies.

I The leveling of the world's forests will send at least two coded signals to future stratigraphers, though deciphering the first may be tricky. Massive soil erosion is causing increasing sedimentation[7] in

[4] **Sedimentary rocks** are formed from sediment—solid material that settles at the bottom of a liquid.
[5] **Pollen** is a powder produced by flowers that fertilizes other flowers of the same species.
[6] If something is **monochrome**, it has just one color.
[7] **Sedimentation** is the process by which solid material—especially earth and pieces of rock—settles at the bottom of a liquid.

some parts of the world—but at the same time, the dams we've built on most of the world's major rivers are holding back sediment that would otherwise be washed to sea. The second signal of deforestation should come through clearer. Loss of forest habitat is a major cause of **extinctions**, which are now happening at a rate hundreds or even thousands of times higher than during most of the past half billion years. If current trends continue, the rate may soon be tens of thousands of times higher.

J Probably the most significant change, from a geologic perspective, is one that's invisible to us—the change in the composition of the atmosphere. Carbon dioxide emissions are colorless, odorless, and—in an immediate sense—harmless. But their warming effects could easily push global temperatures to levels that have not been seen for millions of years. Some plants and animals are already **shifting** their ranges toward the Poles, and those shifts will leave traces in the fossil record. Some species will not survive the warming at all. Meanwhile, rising temperatures could eventually raise sea levels 20 feet (6 meters) or more.

K Long after our cars, cities, and factories have turned to dust, the consequences of burning billions of tons' worth of coal and oil are likely to be clearly discernible. As carbon dioxide warms the planet, it also seeps into the oceans and acidifies them. Sometime this century, they may become acidified to the point that corals can no longer construct reefs, which would register in the geologic record as a "reef gap." Reef gaps have marked each of the past five major mass extinctions. The most recent one—which is believed to have been caused by the impact of an asteroid—took place 65 million years ago, at the end of the Cretaceous period; it **eliminated** not just

Aerial photography at the Colorado River Delta in Mexico illustrates the scale of the impact humans have had on the landscape.

the dinosaurs but also the plesiosaurs, pterosaurs, and ammonites.[8] Since then, there has been nothing to match the scale of the changes that we are now seeing in our oceans. To future geologists, Zalasiewicz says, our impact may look as sudden and **profound** as that of an asteroid.

L If we have indeed entered a new epoch, then when exactly did it begin? When did human impacts rise to the level of geologic significance?

M William Ruddiman, a paleoclimatologist at the University of Virginia, proposed that the invention of agriculture some 8,000 years ago—and the deforestation that resulted—led to an increase in atmospheric CO_2 just large enough to stave off what otherwise would have been the start of a new ice age. In his view, humans have been the dominant force on the planet practically since the start of the Holocene. Crutzen suggested that the Anthropocene began

[8] **Plesiosaurs, pterosaurs,** and **ammonites** are extinct prehistoric animal species.

Rocks structures like these in Isle of Skye, Scotland, contain records of millions of years of history.

in the late 18th century, when, ice cores show, carbon dioxide levels began what has since proved to be an uninterrupted rise. Other scientists put the beginning of the new epoch in the middle of the 20th century, when the rates of both population growth and consumption accelerated rapidly.

N To answer the question definitively, a working group of the International Commission on Stratigraphy (ICS) was assembled. Initially headed by Zalasiewicz, the group was tasked with officially determining whether the Anthropocene deserves to be incorporated into the geologic timescale. As expected, the investigation dragged on for many years. However, the decision did become easier over time as the impact of humans on the planet grew and became even more stratigraphically significant. In 2016, a decision was finally reached. The working group agreed that the Anthropocene is indeed a distinct epoch, separate from the Holocene. They also **concluded** that the human age began in the year 1950, when the Great Acceleration—a dramatic increase in the rate of population growth and human activity affecting the planet—took off.

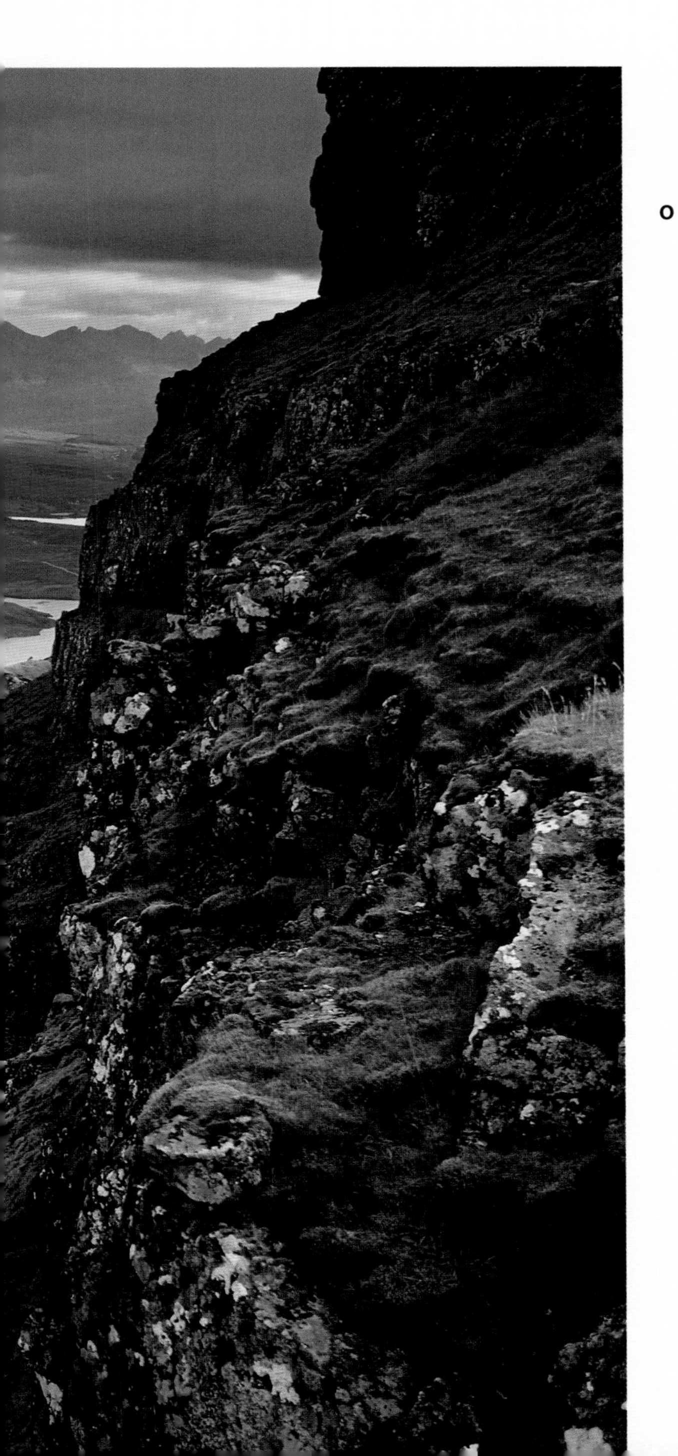

O For Crutzen, who started the debate, the real value of recognizing the Anthropocene doesn't lie in the revisions that have to be made to geology textbooks. His purpose is broader: He wants to focus our attention on the consequences of our collective action—and on how we might still avert the worst. "What I hope," he says, "is that the term Anthropocene will be a warning to the world."

Adapted from "The Age of Man," by Elizabeth Kolbert: National Geographic Magazine, March 2011

Elizabeth Kolbert is an award-winning writer who has written extensively about environmental issues for *National Geographic Magazine*, *The New Yorker*, and other publications. Her book *The Sixth Extinction* won the 2015 Pulitzer Prize for general nonfiction.

UNDERSTANDING THE READING

A **UNDERSTAND THE MAIN IDEA** What does "Anthropocene" mean? Explain it in your own words.

____

____

B **UNDERSTAND MAIN IDEAS** Skim paragraphs G–K. What are the four main areas of human impact the author covers?

1. *cities*
2. ______________
3. ______________
4. ______________

Critical Thinking

C **SUMMARIZE** Complete the chart summarizing the human impact on our planet.

Four areas of human impact	How it will change the planet	Details
1. *cities*		
2.		
3.		
4.		

Critical Thinking

D **INTERPRET VISUAL DATA** Look at the timeline on page 224 and note answers to the questions below. Then discuss your ideas with a partner.

Review this Critical Thinking Skill in Unit 8

1. What era, period, and epoch are we currently living in?

   Era: ______________ Period: ______________

   Epoch: ______________

2. When did the current era begin? ______________
3. How do scientists decide when one epoch ends and another one begins?

   ____

   ____

E **INFER MEANING** Find and underline the following words and phrases in the reading passage. Use the context to identify their meanings. Then write the correct form of each word or phrase next to its definition.

Critical Thinking

coined (paragraph A)	**struck a chord** (paragraph C)	**deciphering** (paragraph I)
discernible (paragraph K)	**stave off** (paragraph M)	**dragged on** (paragraph N)

1. ____________________ to sound logical, meaningful, or relevant to someone
2. ____________________ able to be identified or detected
3. ____________________ to prevent from happening
4. ____________________ to come up with a phrase or the name of something
5. ____________________ to go on for a long time
6. ____________________ to figure out the meaning of something

CRITICAL THINKING Synthesizing Information

Synthesizing means creating something by combining different things. As a critical thinking skill, it means considering information from different sources to form new ideas. For example, information from this unit's reading passage and Unit 4's Explore the Theme section could be synthesized to consider how a shift to electric vehicles might affect Earth's geologic record.

F **SYNTHESIZE INFORMATION** Work with a partner. You are going use the ideas in the reading passage to think about the short- and long-term impacts of two human actions previously mentioned in the Student's Book.

Critical Thinking

1. Look at the chart below. Note the environmental effects of the two actions.
2. Next, note how these environmental effects might impact Earth's long-term geologic record (i.e., rock, fossil, coral, and pollen records).

Human action	Environmental effects	Impact on long-term geologic record
1. Switching to electric vehicles		
2. Switching to underwater farming		

DEVELOPING READING SKILLS

READING SKILL Understanding Rhetorical Purpose

Rhetorical purpose can refer to an author's reason for writing an entire essay or article, or their reason for including a specific sentence, paragraph, or section in a text.

Overall purpose of a text

When considering the overall purpose, ask yourself:

- Who is the text meant for?
- What would the author like readers to take away from the text?

Purpose of a sentence, paragraph, or section

Often the purpose of a sentence or section is self-evident, but sometimes, its significance isn't immediately obvious. Readers have to infer or look beyond what's written on the page.

When you encounter a sentence or section of text like this:

- Visualize the situation being described.
- Ask yourself, "What is the author really saying?"

A **IDENTIFY THE TARGET AUDIENCE** Who do you think was the main target audience of the reading passage? Consider the article's original source, and its likely readership.

a. professors b. the general public c. government officials

B **UNDERSTAND RHETORICAL PURPOSE** What do you think the author wanted readers to take away from the passage?

____

____

C **UNDERSTAND RHETORICAL PURPOSE** Find the sentences below in the reading passage. Write down why you think the author included them in the text.

1. Paragraph B: When the group took a coffee break, the Anthropocene was the main topic of conversation.

   ____

   ____

2. Paragraph D: "I noticed that Crutzen's term was appearing in the serious literature, without quotation marks and without a sense of irony," he says.

   ____

   ____

3. Paragraph K: Reef gaps have marked each of the past five major mass extinctions. The most recent one … took place 65 million years ago, at the end of the Cretaceous period; it eliminated not just the dinosaurs but also the plesiosaurs, pterosaurs, and ammonites.

   ____

   ____

VOCABULARY EXTENSION

WORD LINK *-logy*

The suffix *-logy* is sometimes used at the end of words that represent fields of study. For example, *geology* refers to the study of *geo*, which is the Greek word for earth. Whenever you see a word with the suffix *-logy*, look at the first part of the word to help you guess its meaning. Think of other words that start with the same root word: for example, the common school subject *geography*. These other words can provide you with useful clues.

A Match the fields of study to their definitions. Use a dictionary to help you.

1. ____ psychology	a. the study of how and why people break the law
2. ____ biology	b. the study of how groups of people organize and behave
3. ____ anthropology	c. the study of ancient artifacts
4. ____ sociology	d. the study of the human mind
5. ____ archeology	e. the study of diseases and how they spread
6. ____ epidemiology	f. the study of the origins and development of the human race
7. ____ criminology	g. the study of the natural processes of living things

WORD PARTNERS *dramatic* + Noun

The adjective *dramatic* is often used to intensify nouns, like *increase* in paragraph N of the reading passage. Here are some common collocations with the word *dramatic:*

dramatic change	*dramatic decline*
dramatic reversal	*dramatic improvement*
dramatic effect	*dramatic action*
dramatic moment	*dramatic difference*

B Choose the better option to complete each sentence.

1. The world's governments need to take dramatic **action** / **change** to halt climate change.
2. The most dramatic **difference** / **moment** came toward the end of the movie.
3. Unfortunately, the past year has seen a dramatic **decline** / **increase** in company profits.
4. Studying philosophy has had a dramatic **change** / **effect** on the way I think about life.
5. There is a dramatic **difference** / **improvement** between the lives of the richest and poorest people on Earth.
6. He doesn't go out anymore. I'm not sure what caused this dramatic **change** / **impact**.
7. In a dramatic **change** / **reversal**, the governor announced that he would not be running for re-election as he had previously planned.
8. The dramatic **effect** / **improvement** in the quality of his work is largely due to his new manager.

Video

Trees of Life

Our forests provide us with valuable resources, but are we exploiting them unsustainably? Forests are home to thousands of animal species, and they are a crucial part of Earth's ecology. How much more deforestation can our planet take before it is too late?

Critical Thinking

A **PREVIEW** What is deforestation, and how does it affect our planet and the people and animals that live on it? Discuss with a partner.

B **MAIN IDEAS** Watch the video. Choose **T** for true or **F** for false.

1. Transportation produces more greenhouse gases than forestry and agriculture. **T** **F**
2. Forests are home to more than 80% of the plants and animals that live on land. **T** **F**
3. Increases in the size of urban areas are the primary cause of deforestation. **T** **F**

C **UNDERSTAND CAUSES AND EFFECTS** Watch the video again. Complete the chart about deforestation. Use no more than three words from the video for each answer.

CAUSES	EFFECTS
Biggest driver: • 1 ____________	• More 4 ____________ in the atmosphere
Other causes: • 2 ____________ for paper and wood	• Four to six thousand rainforest species 5 ____________ each year
• 3 ____________ sprawl: development of land for dwellings	• Affects people who rely on forests for 6 ____________

Critical Thinking

D **REFLECT** Do you think we can prevent our forests from disappearing in a hundred years? What are some solutions to the problem? Discuss with a partner.

EXPLORING WRITTEN ENGLISH

LANGUAGE FOR WRITING Using a Variety of Sentence Types

One way to make your writing more interesting is by including a variety of sentence types.

Simple sentences consist of one independent clause. They can have:

A subject and a verb:	*Crutzen is a scientist.*
More than one subject, and a verb:	*Crutzen and Zalasiewicz are scientists.*
More than one subject and verb:	*Animals and corals could die or go extinct.*

Compound sentences consist of two or more independent clauses joined by coordinating conjunctions (*for, and, or, but, so, nor, yet*).

Some plants and animals are already shifting their ranges toward the Poles, and those shifts will leave traces in the fossil record.

Note that each clause of a compound sentence has its own subject.

Complex sentences consist of at least one independent clause and one or more dependent clauses—clauses that begin with either relative pronouns (e.g., *that, who,* or *which*) or subordinating conjunctions (e.g., *because, although, before, after, while,* or *when*).

But their warming effects could easily push global temperatures to levels that have not been seen for millions of years.

It is possible for dependent clauses to be at the beginning of sentences:

When the group took a coffee break, the Anthropocene was the main topic of conversation.

Remember: too many simple sentences can make your writing sound awkward. Combine your simple sentences to make your writing smoother.

The conference chairman kept referring to the Holocene. The epoch began 11,500 years ago. That was at the end of the last ice age. The epoch—officially, at least— continues to this day.

↓

The conference chairman kept referring to the Holocene, the epoch that began 11,500 years ago, at the end of the last ice age, and that—officially, at least— continues to this day.

A NOTICE Read the excerpts from the reading passage (a–c) and answer the questions (1–3). Then decide if the sentences are simple, compound, or complex.

1. _____ Which sentence has one independent clause and no dependent clause?
2. _____ Which sentence has two independent clauses and no dependent clause?
3. _____ Which sentence has one independent clause and one dependent clause?

a. Crutzen, who shared a Nobel Prize for discovering the effects of ozone-depleting compounds, was sitting at a scientific conference one day.
b. They're built on land, and on land the forces of erosion tend to win out . . . .
c. Reef gaps have marked each of the past five major mass extinctions.

B **IDENTIFY** The sentences below form a short story about a pilot in distress. Read the sentences and identify the sentence types. Write **S** for simple, **CD** for compound, or **CX** for complex.

1. _____ The airplane's autopilot stopped working.
2. _____ Sufian was afraid because he'd never been in a situation like this before.
3. _____ He held on to the controls tightly and radioed the control tower.
4. _____ A voice told him to relax and remember his training, which calmed him down.
5. _____ The landing was a little rough, but Sufian made it down safely.
6. _____ Sufian thanked the reassuring voice at the other end of the line, and he got off the plane.

C **APPLY** Combine the following simple sentences to form compound or complex sentences.

1. The sea rose. The islanders had to flee.

   ____

2. They sailed to the mainland. The people there welcomed them.

   ____

3. They shared stories from their culture. The stories were passed down by their parents.

   ____

4. The stories were recorded by historians. They didn't want the stories to be lost.

   ____

D **APPLY** The following paragraph contains only simple sentences. Rewrite it using compound and complex sentences where suitable. Then discuss in pairs. Compare your revised paragraph with the original. Is your revised version an improvement?

The rain poured nonstop. The water rose quickly. Their house would soon be flooded. They had to pack their things fast. The boat would arrive soon. It would take them to the school. They would be safe there. Sara took her brother's hand. They walked together to the second floor. They waited by the window. Sami held on tight to his favorite toy. The boat arrived. Sara told Sami to leave the toy behind. It broke her heart.

____

____

____

____

____

____

____

____

____

WRITING SKILL Reviewing Essay Writing

Essays are short pieces of writing that include an introduction, a body, and a conclusion. You usually write an essay in response to a prompt. When responding to a prompt, think about:

- your position on the topic.
- ways to support or explain your position.

Introduction: The introductory paragraph presents general information on the topic. Grab the reader's attention by starting your introduction with a hook: a surprising statement, an interesting question, a quotation, or a brief anecdote related to the topic.

The introduction also includes a thesis statement. A good thesis statement:

- presents your position on the topic.
- lists the reasons for your position on the topic.
- only expresses ideas that you explain in your body paragraphs.

Body paragraphs: These flesh out the ideas in your thesis by providing facts, details, explanations, and other information.

- Each body paragraph should start with a topic sentence.
- Each topic sentence describes a key point mentioned in your thesis.
- The order of your body paragraphs should match the order of ideas in your thesis.

Use transition words between body paragraphs to help readers follow along easily.

Conclusion: The concluding paragraph gives the reader a sense of completeness. Conclusions usually include:

- a restatement of the thesis.
- a summary of the main supporting points.
- a final thought on the topic in the form of a provocative statement or question.

E Read the essay prompt below and research the topic. Then write a thesis statement. Include two reasons or conditions to support your position.

Essay prompt: Can we reverse deforestation?

____

____

F Write topic sentences based on the information in your thesis in Exercise E.

Body paragraph 1: ____

____

Body paragraph 2: ____

____

G Write a final thought on the topic that you could include in your concluding paragraph.

____

____

WRITING TASK

GOAL You are going to write an essay on the following topic:

Describe how the activities of a charity or a nonprofit organization are having a positive impact on the environment.

Review this Writing Skill in Unit 7

A RESEARCH Search online for organizations that are having a positive impact on the environment. Make brief notes about three organizations whose work stands out to you.

Organization	Environmental impact
1. ________	________
	________
2. ________	________
	________
3. ________	________
	________

Review Supporting a Thesis in Unit 3

B GIVE DETAILS Choose the organization that interests you most, or that you have the most to write about. Then complete the chart below. Note down three of its ongoing activities or past accomplishments, and the impacts these have had on the environment.

Charity/Nonprofit: ________

Activities/Accomplishments	Environmental Impact

Review this Writing Skill in Unit 1

C WRITE A THESIS STATEMENT Use your information in Exercise B to draft a thesis statement for your essay.

____

____

____

D **PLAN** Use your information in Exercises B–C to complete an outline for your essay. Write down your thesis statement, topic sentences, and details. Then think of an interesting way to start your essay, and a final thought to include in your conclusion.

Review Writing Introductions and Conclusions in Unit 6

OUTLINE

Introduction:

____

____

____

Thesis statement: ________________________________

____

____

Body paragraph 1:

Topic sentence: ________________________________

____

Details: ____________________________________

____

Body Paragraph 2:

Topic sentence: ________________________________

____

Details: ____________________________________

____

Body paragraph 3:

Topic sentence: ________________________________

____

Details: ____________________________________

____

Conclusion:

____

____

____

E **FIRST DRAFT** Use the information in your outline to write a first draft of your essay. Remember to use a variety of sentence types to make your writing more interesting.

F **REVISING PRACTICE** The essay below is similar to the one you are writing. Follow the steps to create a better second draft.

1. Add the sentences (a–c) in the most suitable spaces.
   a. The WWF is a strong advocate of renewable energy—energy generated from natural sources such as the sun or wind.
   b. This is because habitat loss is the biggest cause of animal extinction today.
   c. The WWF actively works to preserve the environment by protecting natural habitats and promoting the transition to greener, renewable sources of energy.

2. Now fix the following problems (a–b) with the essay.
   a. Combine the underlined sentences in paragraph C to form a complex sentence.
   b. Combine the underlined sentences in paragraph D to form a compound sentence.

A For most of human history, the rate of extinction of animal species has been about 1 to 5 a year. Today, we are losing several species to extinction every day. The reason for this is us. Human activity is killing wildlife and eradicating natural habitats at rapid rates. Fortunately, there are organizations working to address the issue. One such organization is the World Wildlife Fund (WWF). However, while the WWF's mission was originally focused on animal conservation, its purpose today is broader. _____

B One of the WWF's main goals is to preserve natural habitats. _____ As humans chop down forests and release industrial by-products into rivers and the sea, the amount of space left for animals to live in and feed lessens. However, it isn't just animals that are impacted. These natural habitats help regulate Earth's climate and natural water cycles—both of which are crucial to humans. The work that the WWF does protects these. By working closely with communities to protect oceans, forests, and freshwater sources, the organization not only protects the animals that rely on them—it helps ensure that the planet remains habitable to humans as well.

C A secondary goal of the WWF is to promote the transition away from fossil fuels. _____ The purpose of this is to combat climate change. Climate change not only threatens humans but wildlife everywhere. As the planet gets warmer, forests get destroyed by wildfires, ocean temperatures rise, and freshwater reserves lessen. All of these changes mean widespread habitat loss for animals both on land and in our rivers and seas. The WWF combats climate change by helping communities, businesses, and governments to swap fossil fuels—which are responsible for the bulk of the greenhouse gases in our atmosphere—for greener methods of energy production.

D In its efforts to preserve wildlife, the WWF helps protect the environment by preserving natural habitats and promoting a transition away from fossil fuels. These actions protect animals. People benefit from them, too. This is clearly a major theme in the organization's messaging. For the WWF, the best way to protect wildlife is to come up with environmental solutions that are people-centered.

G **REVISED DRAFT** Now use the questions below to revise your essay.

- ☐ Does your introduction contain an interesting hook?
- ☐ Does your thesis state the main points of the essay?
- ☐ Do your body paragraphs include topic sentences and enough details?
- ☐ Do you use a mix of simple, compound, and complex sentences?
- ☐ Do all your sentences relate to the main idea?
- ☐ Does your concluding paragraph have a summary statement and a final thought?

H **EDITING PRACTICE** Read the information below. Then find and correct one mistake with compound and complex sentences in each sentence (1–4).

When using compound sentences, remember to:

- use an appropriate coordinating conjunction (*for, and, or, but, so, nor, yet*).
- use a comma before a coordinating conjunction that joins two independent clauses.

When using complex sentences, remember to:

- use an appropriate relative pronoun (*e.g., who, whom, which, what, that*).
- use an appropriate subordinating conjunction (e.g., *because, although, before, after, when*).
- place a comma after the dependent clause if it comes before the independent clause.

1. When it was formed in the early 1970s Greenpeace's mission was to protest nuclear testing off the coast of Amchitka Island near western Alaska.
2. Amchitka was home to several endangered animal species and other wildlife so it was important that its ecosystem was protected.
3. The nuclear test Greenpeace was attempting to stop went ahead, and their protests were heard.
4. Nuclear testing at Amchitka ended, yet the island was later declared a bird sanctuary.

I **FINAL DRAFT** Follow these steps to write a final draft.

1. Check your revised draft for sentence variety.
2. Now use the checklist on page 248 to write a final draft. Make any other necessary changes.
3. Work in pairs and read your partner's final essay. Give feedback on each other's writing.

The coast of Amchitka Island

Review

SELF-ASSESS **Consider the language and skills you learned in this unit.**

How well can you . . . ?	Very well	Pretty well	I need improvement
use the key vocabulary from this unit	☐	☐	☐
synthesize information	☐	☐	☐
understand rhetorical purpose	☐	☐	☐
use a variety of sentence types	☐	☐	☐
write an essay	☐	☐	☐

A **VOCABULARY** Do you remember the meanings of these words? Look back at the unit and review the ones you don't know.

conclude AW	criteria AW	eliminate AW	erosion AW	extinction
geology	grasp AW	intriguing	irony	merit
perspective AW	preservation	profound AW	shift AW	subtle AW

B **VOCABULARY EXTENSION** Complete these tasks with a partner.

1. Which fields of study would be interested in:

   a. germs and viruses ______________________

   b. human behavior ______________________

2. Write two sentences containing collocations with the word *dramatic.*

   a. ______________________

   b. ______________________

C **READING SKILL** Work with a partner. Choose three sentences from the essay you wrote, and have your partner infer the purpose of each sentence. Then summarize the overall purpose of each other's essays.

D **LANGUAGE FOR WRITING** Write two or three related simple sentences. Then work with a partner. Combine your partner's simple sentences to form complex or compound sentences.

SELF-ASSESS **Look back at the chart above. Did you assess your skills correctly? What skills or language do you still need help with?**

Anshun Bridge in Chengdu, China

TIPS FOR READING FLUENTLY

Reading slowly, one word at a time, makes it difficult to get an overall sense of the meaning of a text. As a result, reading becomes more challenging and less interesting. In general, it is a good idea to first skim a text for the gist, and then read it again more closely so that you can focus on the most relevant details. Use these strategies to improve your reading speed:

- Read groups of words rather than individual words.
- Keep your eyes moving forward. Read through to the end of each sentence or paragraph instead of going back to reread words or phrases.
- Skip functional words (articles, prepositions, etc.) and focus on words and phrases carrying meaning—the content words.
- Use clues in the text—such as **bold** words and words in *italics*—to help you know which parts might be important and worth focusing on.
- Use section headings, as well as the first and last lines of paragraphs, to help you understand how the text is organized.
- Use context clues, affixes, and parts of speech—instead of a dictionary—to guess the meanings of unfamiliar words and phrases.

TIPS FOR READING CRITICALLY

As you read, ask yourself questions about what the writer is saying, and how and why the writer is presenting the information at hand.

Important critical thinking skills for academic reading and writing:

- **Analyzing:** Examining a text in close detail in order to identify key points, similarities, and differences.
- **Applying:** Deciding how ideas or information might be relevant in a different context, e.g., applying possible solutions to problems.
- **Evaluating:** Using evidence to decide how relevant, important, or useful something is. This often involves looking at reasons for and against something.
- **Inferring:** "Reading between the lines"; in other words, identifying what a writer is saying indirectly, or *implicitly,* rather than directly, or *explicitly.*
- **Synthesizing:** Gathering appropriate information and ideas from more than one source and making a judgment, summary, or conclusion based on the evidence.
- **Reflecting:** Relating ideas and information in a text to your own personal experience and viewpoints.

TIPS FOR NOTE-TAKING

Taking notes will help you better understand the overall meaning and organization of a text. Note-taking also enables you to record the most important information for future uses—such as when you are preparing for an exam or completing a writing assignment. Use these techniques to make your note-taking more effective:

- As you read, underline or highlight important information such as dates, names, and places.
- Take notes in the margin. Note the main idea and supporting details next to each paragraph. Also note your own ideas or questions about the paragraph.
- On a separate piece of paper, write notes about the key points of the text in your own words. Include short headings, key words, page numbers, and quotations.
- Use a graphic organizer to summarize a text, particularly if it follows a pattern such as cause-effect, comparison-contrast, or chronological sequence. See page 64 for an example.
- Keep your notes brief by using these abbreviations and symbols. Don't write full sentences.

approx.	approximately	→	leads to / causes
e.g./ex.	example	↑	increases / increased
i.e.	that is / in other words	↓	decreases / decreased
etc.	and others / and the rest	& or +	and
Ch.	Chapter	*b/c*	because
p. (pp.)	page (pages)	*w/*	with
re:	regarding, concerning	*w/o*	without
incl.	including	=	is the same as
excl.	excluding	>	is more than
info	information	<	is less than
yrs.	years	~	is approximately / about
para.	paragraph	∴	therefore

TIPS FOR LEARNING VOCABULARY

You often need to use a word or phrase several times before it enters your long-term memory. Here are some strategies for successfully learning vocabulary:

- Use flash cards to test your knowledge of new vocabulary. Write the word you want to learn on one side of an index card. Write the definition and/or an example sentence that uses the word on the other side.
- Use a vocabulary notebook to note down a new word or phrase. Write a short definition of the word in English and the sentence where you found it. Write another sentence of your own that uses the word. Include any common collocations (see *Word Partners* in the Vocabulary Extensions).
- Use memory aids, or mnemonics, to remember a word or phrase. For example, if you want to learn the idiom *keep an eye on someone*, which means "to watch someone carefully," you might picture yourself putting your eyeball on someone's shoulder so that you can watch the person carefully. The stranger the picture is, the more likely you will remember it!
- Make word webs or word maps. See the example below.

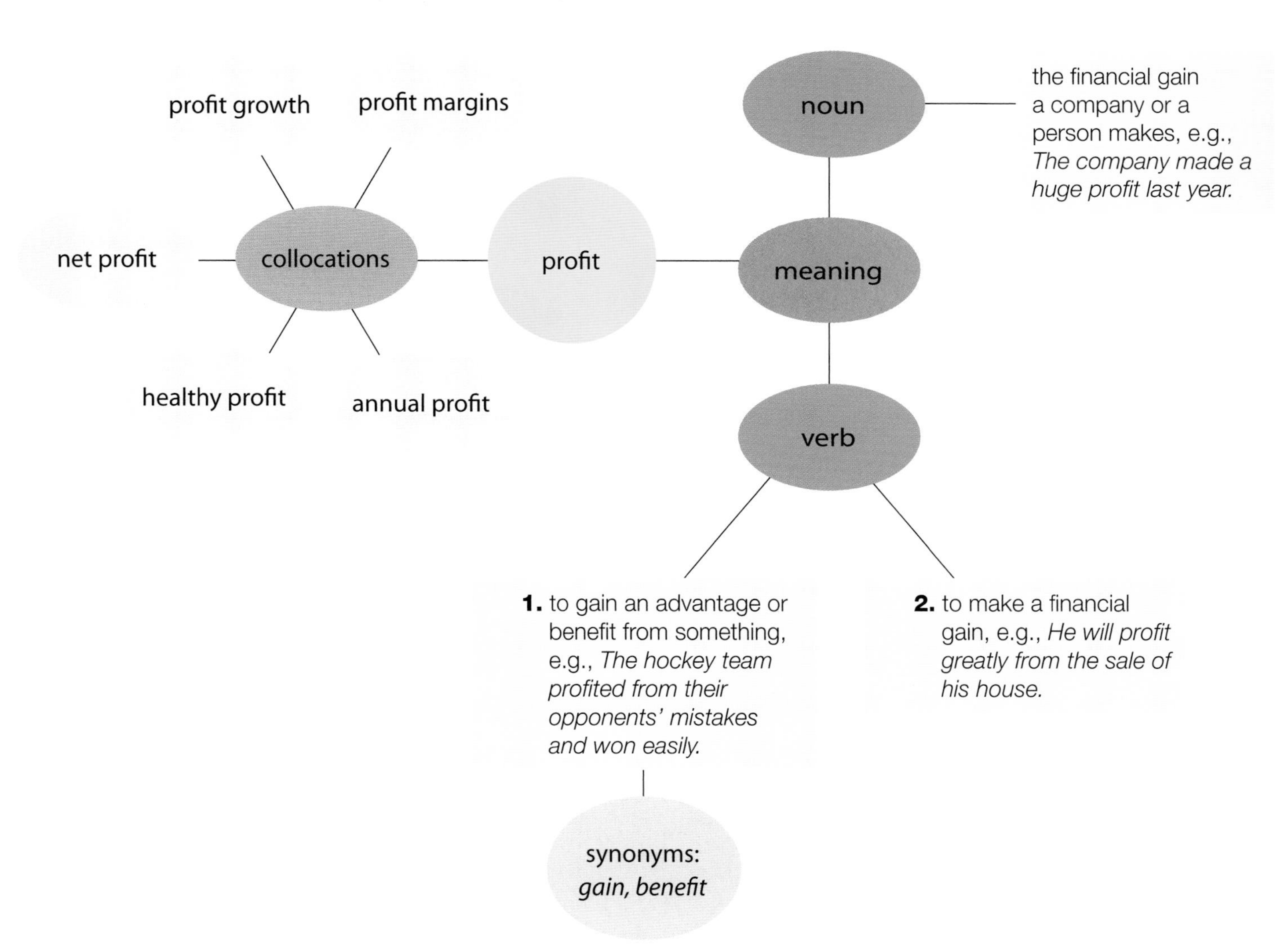

Common Affixes

Some words contain an affix at the start of the word (*prefix*) and/or at the end (*suffix*). These affixes can be useful for guessing the meaning of unfamiliar words and for expanding your vocabulary. In general, a prefix affects the meaning of a word, whereas a suffix affects its part of speech. See the examples below.

Prefix	Meaning	Example
com-	with	compile
con-	together, with	constitute
em- / en-	making, putting	empower, endanger
ex-	away, from, out	explode
im- / in-	not	imperfect, independent
inter-	between	interact
mis-	wrongly	mislead
mono-	one, only	monotonous
pre-	before	preview
pro-	forward, outward	prominent
re-	back, again	restore
trans-	across	transfer
un-	not	unclear
vid- / vis-	seeing	video, vision

Suffix	Part of Speech	Example
-able / -ible	adjective	affordable, feasible
-al	adjective	traditional
-ary	adjective	evolutionary
-ate	verb	generate
-ed	adjective	dedicated
-ent / -ant	adjective	confident, significant
-er	noun	researcher
-ful	adjective	harmful
-ic	adjective	nostalgic
-ical	adjective	hypothetical
-ism	noun	mechanism
-ity	noun	minority
-ive	adjective	inventive
-ize	verb	criticize
-ly	adverb	definitely
-ment	noun	replacement
-tion	noun	determination

TIPS FOR ACADEMIC WRITING

There are many types of academic writing (descriptive, argumentative/persuasive, narrative, etc.), but most types share similar characteristics. Generally, in academic writing, you should:

- write in full sentences.
- use formal English. (Avoid slang or conversational expressions such as *kind of.*)
- be clear and coherent—keep to your main point; avoid technical words that the reader may not know.
- use signal words or phrases and conjunctions to connect your ideas. (See examples below.)
- have a clear point (main idea) for each paragraph.
- use a neutral point of view—avoid overuse of personal pronouns (*I, we, you*) and subjective language such as *nice* or *terrible*.
- use facts, examples, and expert opinions to support your argument.
- avoid using abbreviations or language used in texting. (Use *that is* rather than *i.e.,* and *in my opinion,* not *IMO.*)
- avoid using contractions. (Use *is not* rather than *isn't.*)

Signal Words and Phrases

Use signal words and phrases to connect ideas and to make your writing more academic.

Giving personal opinions	Giving details and examples	Linking ideas
In my opinion, ...	*An example of this is ...*	*Furthermore, ...*
I (generally) agree that ...	*Specifically, ...*	*Moreover, ...*
I think/feel (that) ...	*For instance, ...*	*In addition, ...*
I believe (that) ...		*Additionally, ...*
		For one thing, ...
Presenting similar ideas	**Presenting contrasting views**	**Giving reasons**
Similarly, ...	*On the other hand, ...*	*This is because (of) ...*
Both ... and ...	*In contrast, ...*	*This is due to ...*
Like ..., ...	*While it may be true that ...*	*One reason (for this) is ...*
Likewise, ...	*Despite the fact that ...*	
	Even though ...	
Describing causes and effects	**Describing a process**	**Concluding**
Therefore, ...	*First (of all), ...*	*In conclusion, ...*
As a result, ...	*Then / Next / After that, ...*	*In summary, ...*
Because of this, ...	*As soon as ...*	*To conclude, ...*
If ..., then ...	*Once ...*	*To summarize, ...*
	Finally, ...	

WRITING CITATIONS

Below are some examples of how to cite print sources according to the American Psychological Association Style.

Guidelines	Reference entry	In-text citation
For an **article**, include the author's name, year and month of publication, article title, the name of the magazine/journal, and page references.	White, M. (2011, June). Brimming pools. *National Geographic*, 100–115.	(White, 2011) White (2011) says ...
For a **book**, include the author's name, year of publication, title of the book, and the name of the publisher.	Hawking, S. (1988). *A brief history of time*. Bantam.	(Hawking, 1988) Hawking (1988) says ...
If there are **two authors**, use & to list their names.	Sherman, D., & Salisbury, J. (2008). *The west in the world: Renaissance to present*. McGraw-Hill.	(Sherman & Salisbury, 2008) Sherman and Salisbury (2008) say ...
For a **book that is not the first edition**, include the edition number after the title.	Turnbull, C. M. (2009). *A history of modern Singapore, 1819–2005*, (3rd ed.). NUS Press.	(Turnbull, 2009) According to Turnbull (2009), ...

TIPS FOR EDITING

Capitalization

Remember to capitalize:

- the first letter of the word at the beginning of every sentence.
- proper nouns such as names of people, geographical names, company names, and names of organizations.
- days, months, and holidays.
- the word *I*.
- the first letter of a title such as the title of a movie or a book.
- the words in titles that have meaning (content words). Don't capitalize *a, an, the, and*, or prepositions such as *to, for, of, from, at, in,* and *on*, unless they are the first word of a title (e.g., *The Power of Creativity*).

Punctuation

- Use a period (.) at the end of any sentence that is not a question. Use a question mark (?) at the end of every question.
- Exclamation marks (!), which indicate strong feelings such as surprise or joy, are generally not used in academic writing.
- Use commas (,) to separate a list of three or more things. (*She speaks German, English, and Spanish.*)
- Use a comma after an introductory word or phrase. (*However, William didn't let that stop him.*)
- Use a comma before a combining word—*and, but, so, or*—that joins two sentences. (*Black widow spider bites are not usually deadly for adults, but they can be deadly for children.*)
- Use an apostrophe (') for showing possession. (*James's idea came from social networking websites.*)
- Use quotation marks (" ") to indicate the exact words used by someone else. (*"Our pleasures are really ancient," says psychologist Nancy Etcoff.*)

Other Proofreading Tips

- Print out your draft and read it out loud.
- Use a colored pen to make corrections on your draft so you can see them easily when you write your next draft.
- Have someone else read your draft and give you comments or ask you questions.
- Don't depend on a computer's spell-check. When the spell-check suggests a correction, make sure you agree with it before you accept the change.
- Check the spelling and accuracy of proper nouns, numbers, and dates.
- Keep a list of spelling and grammar mistakes that you commonly make so that you can be aware of them as you edit your draft.
- Check for frequently confused words:
  - *there, their,* and *they're*
  - *its* and *it's*
  - *your* and *you're*
  - *then* and *than*
  - *to, too,* and *two*
  - *whose* and *who's*
  - *where, wear, we're,* and *were*
  - *affect* and *effect*

Editing Checklist

Use the checklist to find errors in the second draft of your writing task for each unit.

	Unit				
	1	2	3	4	5
1. Did you use capitalization correctly? (e.g., for the first word of sentences, for proper nouns)					
2. Do your subjects and verbs agree?					
3. Did you use commas and other punctuation marks correctly?					
4. Have you used an appropriate level of formality?					
5. Is the spelling of places, people, and other proper nouns correct?					
6. Did you check for frequently confused words? (see examples in the *Tips for Editing* section)					
7. Did you use appropriate signal words and phrases to introduce and connect ideas? (see examples in the *Tips for Academic Writing* section)					
8. For essays that require research and the use of information from external sources, did you cite all sources properly? (see examples in the *Writing Citations* section)					

	Unit				
	6	7	8	9	10
1. Did you use capitalization correctly? (e.g., for the first word of sentences, for proper nouns)					
2. Do your subjects and verbs agree?					
3. Did you use commas and other punctuation marks correctly?					
4. Have you used an appropriate level of formality?					
5. Is the spelling of places, people, and other proper nouns correct?					
6. Did you check for frequently confused words? (see examples in the *Tips for Editing* section)					
7. Did you use appropriate signal words and phrases to introduce and connect ideas? (see examples in the *Tips for Academic Writing* section)					
8. For essays that require research and the use of information from external sources, did you cite all sources properly? (see examples in the *Writing Citations* section)					

Grammar Reference

Unit 3

Restrictive and Nonrestrictive Relative Clauses	
There are two types of relative clauses. One type gives essential information about the noun. These are called restrictive relative clauses. Do not use commas with restrictive relative clauses.	I saw a photograph that illustrated all of Griffiths's aesthetic principles. I read the essay on photography that Annie Griffiths wrote.
The other type of relative clause gives extra, or nonessential, information about the noun. These are called nonrestrictive relative clauses. Commas always set off nonrestrictive relative clauses.	Photography, which is a relatively recent invention, influenced our notions of beauty. Susan Sontag, who was a noted essayist, wrote a book on photography. Japonaiserie, which is also referred to as Japonism, is an artistic movement from the mid-1800s. Vincent van Gogh, who/whom many people consider one of the greatest Impressionists, was influenced by Japanese woodblock prints.

Unit 4

Initial Phrases	
You can use initial phrases (prepositional, time, and verbal phrases) to avoid short, choppy sentences. Using initial phrases is also a way to vary your sentence style and to show the relationship between ideas.	
Prepositional phrases	In Africa, Nigeria is the most populous country. At a distance of 4.3 light-years, Alpha Centauri is the nearest star outside our Solar System. Just opposite this building, you can find a really good restaurant.
Time phrases	Since I was a young child, I've had a keen interest in science. When she first started the business, there were many problems to deal with. Once I met her, I realized why she'd been so successful in life.
Verbal phrases	Starting in Peru, the Amazon River runs through seven separate countries. Concerned about the increasing workload, he decided to look for a new job. Painted by Leonardo da Vinci, the Mona Lisa is one of the most valuable paintings in the world.

Unit 5

Paraphrasing

When you want to report what someone else wrote but don't want to quote the person directly, you can paraphrase. Paraphrasing is using your own words to express another person's idea. Paraphrasing is different from summarizing. When you summarize a paragraph, you restate just the main points of the paragraph. When you paraphrase a paragraph, you restate all of the ideas of the paragraph. Follow these steps to help you paraphrase successfully:

1. Read the original passage that you want to paraphrase several times to make sure that you understand its meaning. Look up any words that you don't understand.
2. Without looking at the original passage, write notes about it on a piece of paper. Don't write complete sentences.
3. Use your notes to write a paraphrased version of the passage. Don't look at the original.
4. Compare your paraphrased passage with the original and make sure it expresses the same meaning as the original. If they are too similar, change your sentence structures and word choices. Use more synonyms for content words (e.g., nouns and verbs) in the original.

Here's an example of paraphrasing:

Original:

Between 1960 and 2000, Seoul's population increased from fewer than three million to almost ten million people. In the same period, South Korea went from being one of the world's poorest countries, with a per capita GDP of less than $100, to being richer than some countries in Europe.

Paraphrased:

The population of Seoul grew a lot between 1960 and 2000. In 1960, there were fewer than three million people living in Seoul. By 2000, just under 10 million people were living there. In 1960, the per capita GDP of South Korea was less than $100, and the country was one of the poorest in the world. However, by 2000, South Korea was wealthier than some European countries.

Unit 9

Describing Data: Fractions

In most cases, fractions that are spelled out should always be hyphenated.
For example:

Fractions used as adjectives	He won the election by a **four-fifths** majority.
Fractions used as adverbs	The money is **three-quarters** gone!
Fractions used as nouns	**Two-thirds** of the people lied in the experiment.

Do not hyphenate fractions when one of the numbers in the fraction is already hyphenated.
For example:

37/100	The sprinter won the race by **thirty-seven hundredths** of a second.
1/29	On average, the group lied **one twenty-ninth** of the time.

Also, do not hyphenate when you are using the article *a* to refer to a fraction.
For example:

1/4	He answered incorrectly **a quarter** of the time.
1/3	**A third** of the people involved were unable to spot the error.

Vocabulary Index

Word	Unit	CEFR Level	Example sentence / definition
abstract*	6	B2	
accelerate*	1	C1	
accomplish	5	C1	
adaptation*	7	C1	
advocate*	4	C2	
alongside	4	C1	
ambiguous*	3	C2	
analytical*	3	C1	
anonymous	5	C2	
arise	7	C1	
assembly*	1	C2	
associate	7	C1	
automation*	1	-	
aviation	4	-	
boundary	2	C1	
burden	7	C1	
campaign	4	C1	
capability*	5	C1	
capacity*	4	B2	
catch on	4	C1	
coherent*	6	C2	
committee	4	B2	
competitive	4	B2	
complexity*	5	C2	
component*	8	C1	

Word	Unit	CEFR Level	Example sentence / definition
conceive*	6	C2	
conclude*	10	C1	
conservation*	3	B2	
consistently*	2	C2	
constraint*	2	C2	
contradictory*	8	C2	
conversion*	4	C2	
coordinate*	5	-	
corruption*	7	C1	
counterpart	2	C1	
cover up	9	C1	
criteria*	10	C1	
deceptive	9	C2	
detect*	5	C1	
dilemma*	4	B2	
dismiss	8	C1	
disruption	4	C1	
distinct*	7	C1	
dominant*	7	C1	
dread	6	C2	
eliminate*	10	C1	
elite*	4	C1	
embrace	2	C1	
envision	3	C1	
equivalent*	6	C1	

Word	Unit	CEFR Level	Example sentence / definition
eradicate	2	C2	
erosion*	10	C1	
excessive	4	C1	
executive	1	C1	
exhibit*	3	C1	
exquisite	3	C2	
extinction	10	C1	
fake	3	C1	
foremost	3	C1	
foundation*	9	C1	
founder*	1	C2	
fundamental*	9	C2	
genetic*	8	C1	
geology	10	C1	
glimpse	6	C1	
grasp*	10	C1	
habitat*	2	C1	
historically*	8	C1	
horizon*	6	C1	
hospitality	6	C1	
hypothesis*	2	C2	
imaginary	1	C1	
imitate	5	C1	
impede	9	-	
implication*	8	C1	

Word	Unit	CEFR Level	Example sentence / definition
implicit*	9	C2	
imply*	3	C2	
impression	3	B2	
incentive	1	C2	
inevitable*	1	C1	
influence	1	B2	
interpretation*	3	C2	
intimate	3	C2	
intriguing	10	C2	
irony	10	C2	
lessen	9	C1	
life span	8	C2	
limitation	6	C1	
longevity	8	C2	
master	1	B2	
maximize*	1	C2	
mechanism*	8	C1	
merit	10	C1	
minimize*	2	C1	
mining	7	C1	
misfortune	7	C1	
ongoing*	3	C2	
outcome*	8	C1	
outnumber	8	C1	
paradigm*	6	C2	

Word	Unit	CEFR Level	Example sentence / definition
peer	6	C1	
perceive*	2	C1	
perspective*	10	C1	
phenomenon*	5	C1	
predator*	2	C1	
preservation	10	C1	
profound*	10	C2	
prominent*	9	C1	
prone to	9	C2	
radically*	7	C1	
random*	6	C1	
ratio*	8	C1	
realistically	5	C1	
reassuring	9	C1	
reconstruct*	8	C1	
relate to	1	C1	
reliance*	2	C2	
repetitive	1	C1	
resemble*	7	C1	
restriction*	8	C1	
reversal*	2	C2	
scrutiny	6	C2	
shift*	10	C1	
shrewd	5	C2	
simulation*	5	C1	

Word	Unit	CEFR Level	Example sentence / definition
sole*	7	C1	
solitary	5	C2	
speculate	9	C2	
spur	1	C2	
stem from	2	C1	
stereotype*	6	C1	
subtle*	10	C2	
swap*	4	C1	
swarm	5	-	
synchronized	5	-	
synonymous	2	C2	
systematically	9	C2	
tendency	9	C1	
texture	6	C1	
theoretically*	3	C2	
thrive	7	C1	
trigger*	3	C1	
troublesome	1	C2	
twist	9	C1	
ultimately*	8	C1	
uncertainty	5	C1	
undergo	7	C1	
universally	9	C1	
urge	4	C1	
workforce	7	C1	

* These words are academic words—the most frequent word families in academic texts.

Index of Exam Skills and Tasks

The activities in *Pathways Reading, Writing, and Critical Thinking* develop key reading skills needed for success on standardized tests such as TOEFL® and IELTS. In addition, many of the activities provide useful exam practice because they are similar to common question types in these tests.

Key Reading Skills	IELTS	TOEFL®	Page(s)
Recognizing vocabulary from context	✓	✓	4, 13, 19, 28, 37, 52, 63, 78, 87, 102, 109, 126, 132, 157, 163, 172, 181, 196, 204, 220, 229
Identifying main ideas	✓	✓	12, 36, 62, 86, 109, 132, 156, 180, 204, 228
Identifying supporting ideas	✓	✓	12, 36, 62, 110, 157, 181, 228
Scanning for details	✓	✓	12, 36, 62, 86, 110, 132, 157, 180, 204, 228
Making inferences	✓	✓	133, 158, 174, 182, 205, 230
Recognizing pronoun references	✓	✓	14, 17
Understanding charts and infographics	✓		64, 76, 110, 147, 170, 179, 194, 200, 234

Common Question Types	IELTS	TOEFL®	Page(s)
Multiple choice	✓	✓	12, 16, 36, 40, 62, 66, 87, 90, 114, 136, 160, 180, 182, 184, 204, 230
Completion (notes, diagram, chart)	✓		36, 64, 88, 110, 156, 181, 228, 229
Completion (summary)	✓		157, 204
Short answer	✓		12, 14, 37, 62, 86, 88, 90, 109, 111, 112, 114, 133, 134, 156, 157, 158, 180, 182, 184, 205, 208, 228, 230, 232
Matching headings / information	✓	✓	12, 86, 109, 132, 156
Categorizing (matching features)	✓		62, 66, 69, 160
True / False / Not given	✓		12, 16, 36, 40, 62, 132, 136, 232
Prose summary		✓	116, 117, 118, 210, 212
Rhetorical purpose		✓	103, 109, 230

Level 4 of *Pathways Reading, Writing, and Critical Thinking* also develops **key writing skills** needed for exam success.

Key Writing Skills	Unit(s)
Writing a strong introduction and conclusion	1, 2, 3, 6, 10
Expressing and justifying opinions	2, 3, 6, 7, 8, 10
Giving reasons and examples	2, 3, 4, 7, 8, 10
Paraphrasing / Summarizing	5
Making comparisons	4
Describing problems and solutions	2
Explaining a process	9
Expressing agreement and disagreement	3, 8
Describing a graph or chart	9

Pathways	CEFR	IELTS Band	TOEFL® Score
Level 4	**C1**	**7.0–8.0**	**94–110**
Level 3	B2	5.5–6.5	46–79
Level 2	B1–B2	4.5–6.0	32–60
Level 1	A2–B1	0–5.5	0–46
Foundations	A1–A2		

ACKNOWLEDGMENTS

The Authors and Publisher would like to acknowledge the educators around the world who participated in the development of the third edition of *Pathways Reading, Writing, and Critical Thinking.*

A special thanks to our Advisory Board for their valuable input during development.

Advisory Board

Baher F. AlDabba, Amideast Gaza; **Hossein Askari**, Houston Community College; **Dilara Ataman Akalin**, TOBB University; **Andrew Boon**, Toyo Gakuen University; **Fatih Bozoğlu**, Antalya Bilim University; **Cath Brown**, University of Sheffield; **Julie Cote**, Houston Community College; **Kristen Cox**, Global Launch at ASU; **Patricia Fiene**, Midwestern Career College; **Ronnie Hill**, Royal Melbourne Institute of Technology; **Greg Holloway**, University of Kitakyushu; **Ragette Jawad**, Lawrence Technological University; **Michael King**, Community College of Qatar; **Maureen Lanseur**, Henry Ford College; **Elizabeth Macdonald**, Sacred Heart University; **Daniel Paller**, Kinjo Gakuin University; **Kes Poupaert**, INTO Manchester; **Juan Quintana**, Instituto Cultural Peruano Norteamericano; **Anouchka Rachelson**, Miami Dade College; **David Ruzicka**, Shinshu University; **Naoki Senrui**, Fukushima College; **Gabrielle Smallbone**, Kingston University; **Debra Wainscott**, Baylor University

Global Reviewers

Asia

John Paul Abellera, San Beda College-Alabang; **Andrew Acosta**, Udonpittayanukoon School; **Jherwin Adora**, Department of Education Philippines; **Mubarak Ali**, Unilever; **Joan Arado**, TESDA PTS-Misamis Occidental; **Frederick Bacala**, Yokohama City University; **Katherine Bauer**, Clark Memorial International High School; **Richard Bent**, Kwassui Women's University; **Teresa Bolen**, Ryukoku University; **Johnny Burns**, Kansai Daigaku; **Darine Chehwan**, Rest-art Studio; **Simon Cornelius**, Kansai University; **Aurelio Da Costa**, UNICEF/Senai Language Centre; **Carlos Daley**, London Institute; **Maria del Vecchio**, Nihon University; **Ria De Ocera**, Udomsuksa School; **Michael Donzella**, Kaichi International University; **David Groff**, Meiji University; **Akiko Hagiwara**, Tokyo University of Pharmacy and Life Sciences; **Sisilia Halimi**, Humanities Universitas Indonesia; **Jane Harland**, Fukuoka University; **Makoto Hayashi**, Nagoya University; **Patrizia Hayashi**, Meikai University; **Andrea Noemie Hilomen**, Private teacher; **Ha Hoang**, Au Chau Language School; **Ana Sofia Hofmeyr**, Kansai University; **Stephen Hofstee**, Kanto Gakuin University; **Stephen Howes**, Tokyo Seitoku University Fukaya Junior High School; **Yuko Igarashi**, Ritsumeikan University; **Mari Inoue**, Tokyo University of Science; **David Johnson**, Kyushu Sangyo University; **Sarita Joyaka**, Nongkipittayakhom; **Chong Jui Jong**, Universiti Sains Malaysia; **Yuko Kawae**, Kindai University; **Megumi Kobayashi**, Seikei University; **Mutsumi Kondo**, Kyoto University of Foreign Studies; **Gomer Jay Legaspi**, Caraga State University; **Indah Ludij**, Academic Writing Center, Universitas Indonesia; **Kelly MacDonald**, Fukuoka University; **Anh Mai**, Van Lang University; **Tiina Matikainen**, Tamagawa University; **Eiko Matsubara**, Rissho University; **Jason May**, Den-en Chofu Gakuen; **Sean Collin Mehmet**, Matsumoto University; **Mabell Mingoy**, Teach for the Philippines; **Mari Miyao**, Kyoto University of Foreign Studies; **Wah Mon**, Private teacher; **Masaki Mori**, Aoyama-Gakuinn University; **Gerald Muirhead**, Tohoku Gakuin University; **Charlotte Murakami**, Kurume University; **Duong Nguyen**, APU; **Ly Huyền Nguyễn**, FPT High School; **Vinh Nguyen**, Hanoi University; **Ngan Nguyễn**; **Thảo Nguyễn**, Gia Việt English Center; **MaiKhoi NguyenThi**, Danang Architecture University; **Takeshi Nozawa**, Ritsumeikan University; **Naomi Ogasawara**, Gunma Prefectural Women's University; **Mari Ogawa**, Meiji University; **Megumi Okano**, Keio University; **Hisako Osuga**, Meiji University; **Gellian Ostrea**, Manolo Fortich National High School; **Tina Ottman**, Doshisha University, Bukkyo University; **Ardy Paembonan**, SMA El-Shaddai Jayapura; **Anthony Paxton**, Ibaraki Prefectural Takezono High School; **Hong Pham**, Brendon Primary School; **Huong Pham**, Foreign Languages Specialised School, University of Languages and International Studies; **John Plagens** Lutheran College; **Javeria Rana**, The City School; **Rebecca Reyes**, Captain Albert Aguilar National High School; **Florencio Salmasan**, School of the Holy Spirit; **Sherri Scanlan**, Toyama Prefectural University; **Naoki Senrui**, Komazawa University; **Nanik Shobikah**, IAIN Pontianak; **Coleman South**, Saga National University; **Yukiko Sugiyama**, Keio University; **Pavloska Susanna**, Doshisha University; **Eri Tamura**, Ishikawa Prefectural University; **Yuko Tokisato**, Kansai University; **Saeko Toyoshima**, Tsuru University; **Janssen Undag**, Darunapolytechnic Technological College; **Carl Vollmer**, Ritsumeikan Uji Junior and Senior High School; **Isra Wongsarnpigoon**, Kanda University of International Studies

Europe

Ana Maria Andrei, Liceul Teoretic de Informatica; **Regina Bacanskiene**, Kaunas School; **Janice Bain**, Glasgow International College; **Oana Banu**, LPS; **Daniela Berntzen**; **Sarah Bishopp**, Kaplan International College London; **Anna Broumerioti**; **Cath Brown**, The University of Sheffield; **Laura Cannella**, Kaplan International College London; **Barbara Cavicchiolli**, INTO Manchester; **Ioana Mirela Cojocaru**, Liceul Tehnologic Anghel Saligny; **Viorica Condrat**, USARB; **Astrid D'Andrea**, I.I.S. Croce-Aleramo; **Liesl Daries**, English with Liesl; **Kurtis De Souza-Snares**, Kaplan International Pathways; **Elona Dhepa**, 7 Marsi; **Maral Dosmagambetova**, Lingua College; **Camelia-Adriana Dulau**, Simion Bărnuțiu; **Ruthanna Farragher**, Kaplan; **Olesia Fesenko**, Vyshhorod Lyceum "Suziria"; **Cristina Foltmann**, ITCS Abba Ballini; **Laura Gheorghita**, Scoala Gimnaziala Grigore Geamanu Turcinesti; **Marian Gonzalez**, Liceo de Idiomas Modernos; **Paulina Holesz**, Private teacher; **Lindsey Hollywood**, University of Liverpool International College; **Sarah Hopwood**, University of Nottingham International College; **Barbara Howarth**, Glasgow International College; **Jana Jilkova**, ICV & Pedagogical Faculty; **Alina Loata**, Colegiul National Dimitrie Cantemir;

Ia Manjgaladze, Access Program Teacher; **Christiana Mili**, Private teacher; **Laura Morrison**, Glasgow International College; **Robert Pinkham-Smith**, University of Essex International College; **Yuliya Pokroyeva**, Private teacher; **Eva Rodaki**, Private teacher; **Alina Rotaru**, Twinkle Star; **Carme RR**, CEIP Joan Mas Pollença; **Tatiana Silvesan**, Centrul Scolar de Educatie Incluziva; **Bianca Somesan**, Palatul Copiilor Targu Mures; **Elena Strugaru**, Britanica Learning Centre; **Mina Vermot**, Miduca; **Matthew Wilson**, Brunel University London; **Emily Wright**, Arden University

Latin America and the Caribbean

Maria Aguilar, Universidad Nacional de La Rioja; **Karina Aldana**, Colegio la Asuncion; **Mariela Amarante**, Sunshine Academy; **Auricéa Bacelar**, Top Seven Idiomas; **Verónica Bonilla**, Universidad Anáhuac de Puebla; **Lucila Caballero**, MEDUCA; **Milagros Calderón Miró**, Colegio San Antonio IHM; **Maria Carrizo**, Nores; **Erika Ceballos**, Escuela Nacional Preparatoria; **Johana Coronel**, Private teacher; **Marcelo D'Elia**, Centro Britanico Idiomas; **Sophia De Carvalho**, Inglês Express; **Corina Diaz**, CCSA; **Isabela Dias**, Inglês Express; **Joseph Duque**, Unidad Educativa Leibnitz; **Esperanza Espejo**, Iteso; **Susana Espinosa**, ICPNA; **Carolina Ferreira**, Private teacher; **Matheus Figueiredo**, Private teacher; **Andrea Garcia Hernandez**, Bilingual School; **Alessandra Gotardo**, IYEnglish - Language & Culture; **Santo Guzmán**, JFK Institute of Languages, Inc.; **Cecibel Juliao**, Meduca / Udelas; **Letícia Kayano**, Private teacher; **Sandra Landi**, Private teacher; **Patricia Lanners**, Universidad de las Americas Puebla; **Arenas Laura**, ITESO; **Diana Lopez**, ITSE; **Mario López Ayala**, Universidad Autónoma de Sinaloa; **Rosa Awilda Lopez Fernandez**, Universidad Acción Pro-Educación y Culturalic Dominicana; **Fabricio Romeo Mejia Lopez**, Academia Europea; **Silvia Luna**, Universidad Evangélica; **Manuel Malhaber Diaz**, Colegio Nacional San Juan De Chota; **Daniel Martins Aragão**, Private teacher; **Victor Hugo Medina Soares**, Cultura Inglesa Belo Horizonte; **Angélica Parada**, CBA; **Adela Perez del Viso**, Fundación E.S.Y.C.; **Byron Quinde**, Unidad Educativa Particular de la Asunción; **Maria Alejandra Quirch**, Instituto San Roman; **Joselyn Ramos Cuba**, UNMSM; **Jorge Reategui**, Universidad Continental; **Jazmin Reyes**, La Dolorosa; **Iliana Rivas**, ITESO; **Sheirys Hidalgo Ruiz**, Ministerio de Educacion Publica; **Adelina Ruiz Guerrero**, Instituto Tecnológico y de Estudios Superiores de Occidente; **Maribel Santiago**, Colegio de Bachilleres; **Margaret Simons**, English Center; **Sheily Sosa García**, ICPNA; **Jane Stories**, Private teacher; **María Trigos**, ITSX; **Henrique Ucci**, Liverpool English Institute; **Ana Carolina Vargas Arreola**, Colegio Vizcaya; **Laura Zurutuza**, ITESO

Middle East and Africa

Merve Akyiğit, Adana Doğa Schools; **Yousef Albozom**, America-Mideast Educational and Training Services; **Rehab Alzeiny**, IPS; **Rais Attamimi**, UTAS-Salalah; **Ezgi Avar**, Tuzla Doğa Lisesi; **Pınar Çakır**, Doğa Koleji; **Burçe Çimeli**, Doğa Koleji; **Christelle Gernique Djoukouo Talla**, Government Bilingual High School Ekangte; **Canan Dülger**, Doğa Koleji; **Manal ElMazbouh**, American University of the Middle East; **Fatma el-zahraa El-sayed zaki nassef**, Damietta Official Language schools; **Necmi Ersungur**, İtü Eta Vakfı Doğa Koleji; **Mary Goveas**, University of Bahrain; **Farhad Hama**, Sulaimani University; **Michael King**, Community College of Qatar; **Georgios Kormpas**, Al Yamamah University; **Volga Kurbanzade**, Okan University; **Eni Ermawati Lasito**, Lusail University; **Gonca Mavuk**, Atasehir ITU Doga College; **Amina Moubtassim**, ALC; **Doaa Najjar**, PISOD; **Mohammad Esmaeel Nasrabadi**, Private teacher; **Naki Erhan Ozer**, Doga Schools; **Rehab Raouf**, Al Safwa School; **Nurhayat Şenman**, Özlüce Doğa Koleji Lise; **Choukri Serhane**, CHSS; **Hussam Tannera**, America-Mideast Educational and Training Services; **Pedro Vemba**, Liceu do Soyo; **Cüneyt Yüce**, Istanbul Okan University

USA and Canada

Galyna Arabadzhy, St. Cloud State University; **Elizabeth Armstrong**, Midwestern Career College; **Judy Bagg**, Pierce; **Karin Bates**, Intercambio Uniting Communities; **Mandie Bauer**, ASC English; **Elisabeth Bowman**, Schoolcraft College; **Teresa Cheung**, North Shore Community College; **Colleen Comidy**, Seattle Central College; **Jacquelin Cunningham**, Harold Washington College; **Jean Danic**, Hillsborough Community College; **Rosalia dela Cruz**, NorQuest College; **Christine Dick**, Arizona State University; **Yvonne Dunham Slobodenko**, University of Tennessee at Chattanooga; **Karen Eichhorn**, International English Center; **Thomas Fox**, Dallas College; **Diana Garcia**, Union County College; **Bertha George**, Union County College; **Thomas Germain**, University of Colorado Boulder; **Debra Gibes**, Mott Community College; **John Glover**, Old Saybrook High School; **Christine Guro**, University of Hawaii at Manoa; **Carrie Hein-Paredes**, MATC; **Deanna Henderson**, Language Consultants International; **Tom Justice**, North Shore Community College; **Evan Kendall**, Los Angeles City College; **Michael Kelley**, Hillsborough Community College; **Karen E. Kyle**, Aims Community College; **Laura Lamour**, Florida International University; **Maureen Lanseur**, Henry Ford College; **Heidi Lieb**, Bergen Community College; **Layla Malander**, PLACE/Colorado State University; **Tim Mathews**, Nashville State Community College; **Richard McDorman**, Language On; **Susan McElwain**, Mohawk College of Applied Arts and Technology; **Jason McKenzie**, Apex Language and Career College; **William Miller Jr.**, H.EN; **Lilia Myers Van Pelt**, Colorado State University Pueblo; **Sandra Navarro**, Glendale Community College; **Linda Neuman**, Anne Arundel Community College; **Susan Niemeyer**, Los Angeles City College; **Mariah Nix**, Lumos Language School; **Cheryl Pakos**, Union County College; **Jim Papple**, York University; **Cora Perrone**, Southern CT State University; **Deborah Pfeifer**, Fort Hays State University; **Loretta Quan**, Schoolcraft College; **Thomas Riedmiller**, University of Northern Iowa; **Lisa Rivoallon**, Gavilan College; **Noele Simmons**, George Mason University; **Pamela Smart-Smith**, Virginia Tech; **Kelly Smith**, English Language Institute, UCSD Extension; **Brandt Snook**, University of Louisiana – Lafayette; **Shoshanna Starzynski**, Global Launch, Arizona State University; **Kirsten Stauffer**, Immigrant and Refugee Center of Northern Colorado; **JoAnn Stehly**, North Orange County Community College District; **Karen Vallejo**, University of California, Irvine; **Sharifeh Van Court**, Dallas College; **Melissa Vervinck**, ESL Institute at Oakland University; **Christy Williams**, INTO USF; **Paula Yerman**, Los Angeles City College

CREDITS

Photos

Cover © Lance Gerber © Rasheed AlShashai, **iii** © Reuben Wu, **iv** (from top to bottom) Rick Madonik/Toronto Star/Getty Images, Pyrosky/iStock Unreleased/Getty Images, © Reuben Wu, Majonit/Shutterstock.com, © Ami Vitale/National Geographic Image Collection, **vi** (from top to bottom) Horst Friedrichs/Anzenberger/Redux, Anna Boeva/500px/Getty Images, Mint/Hindustan Times/Getty Images, David Fleetham/Nature Picture Library, Marco Bottigelli/Moment/Getty Images, **viii** (tl1) KTSDesign/Science Photo Library/Getty Images, (tl2) © Ryan Morris/National Geographic Image Collection, (tl3) Taylor Hill/FilmMagic/Getty Images, (tl4) IanDagnall Computing/Alamy Stock Photo, (cl) © Brian Yen, (c) Prisma by Dukas Presseagentur GmbH/Alamy Stock Photo, **x** © Brian Yen, **1** Rick Madonik/Toronto Star/Getty Images, **2–3** (spread) H. Armstrong Roberts/ClassicStock/Archive Photos/Getty Images, **4** PA Images/Alamy Stock Photo, **6** © Spencer Lowell/Great Bowery Inc. dba Trunk Archive, **8–10** © Spencer Lowell/Great Bowery Inc. dba Trunk Archive, **16** © National Geographic Television/National Geographic Image Collection, **23** Tim Hazael/Science Photo Library/Science Source, **25** Pyrosky/iStock Unreleased/Getty Images, **26–27** (spread) Dhwee/Moment/Getty Images, **28** Tim Robberts/Stone/Getty Images, **30–33** © Corey Arnold/National Geographic Image Collection, **34–35** (spread) © Corey Arnold/National Geographic Image Collection, **40** National Geographic, **41** Dethan Punalur/Stockbyte/Getty Images, **47** Paul Carstairs/Alamy Stock Photo, **49** © Reuben Wu, **50–51** © Reuben Wu, **53** © Nina Chen/Berndnaut Smilde Nimbus Visual, 2013/Ronchini, **54** © Sophie Green Fine Art, **56** © Contemporary artist & conservationist/Environmentalist/Sophie Green, **57** © Stephan Gladieu/National Geographic Image Collection, **58** © Stephan Gladieu/Institute Artist, **59–61** © Craig Cutler/National Geographic Image Collection, **66** © Brian Yen, **69** CNMages/Alamy Stock Photo, **73** Strauss/Curtis/The Image Bank/Getty Images, **75** Majonit/Shutterstock.com, **78** Drazen Zigic/Shutterstock.com, **80** © Davide Monteleone/National Geographic Image Collection, **82** © Davide Monteleone/National Geographic Image Collection, **83** SeongJoon Cho/Bloomberg/Getty Images, **85** Darryl Dyck/Bloomberg/Getty Images, **90** Viennaslide/Alamy Stock Photo, **97** (bl) Lex Rayton/Alamy Stock Photo, (br) JLBvdWOLF/Alamy Stock Photo, **99** © Ami Vitale/National Geographic Image Collection, **100–101** (spread) David Ramos/Getty Images News/Getty Images, **102** Xinhua/Alamy Stock Photo, **104** David Williams/Minden Pictures, **106** © Mark Thiessen/National Geographic Image Collection, **107** Design Pics Inc/Alamy Stock Photo, **114** Rio Woy/500px/Getty Images, **123** Horst Friedrichs/Anzenberger/Redux, **124–125** (spread) Klaus Vedfelt/DigitalVision/Getty Images, **126** Davidf/E+/Getty Images, **128** Prisma by Dukas Presseagentur GmbH/Alamy Stock Photo, **130** FG Trade/E+/Getty Images, **131** Bob Daemmrich/Alamy Stock Photo, **136** © Jeremy Fahringer/Living Tongues Institue/National Geographic Image Collection, **143** FotoVoyager/E+/Getty Images, **145** Anna Boeva/500px/Getty Images, **146–147** (spread) Chalermkiat Seedokmai/Moment/Getty Images, **150** © Kees Veenenbos/National Geographic Image Collection, **152** Nikada/E+/Getty Images, **153** Natphotos/DigitalVision/Getty Images, **154–155** (spread) © Pascal Maitre/National Geographic Image Collection, **160** Anadolu Agency/Getty Images, **169** Mint/Hindustan Times/Getty Images, **170** (tl) Oliver Thompson-Holmes/Alamy Stock Photo, (tc) Khalil Ahmed/Shutterstock.com, (tr) Zocha_K/E+/Getty Images, (c) Fon Duangkamon/Shutterstock.com, **171** (tl) Cyrille Gibot/Moment/Getty Images, (tc) David De Lossy/Photodisc/Getty Images, (tr) Ivan Vdovin/Alamy Stock Photo, (cr1) Marc Guitard/Moment/Getty Images, (cr2) Adamkaz/E+/Getty Images, (bl) Shanshan0312/Shutterstock.com, (bc) Nature Picture Library/Alamy Stock Photo, (br) PhotoAlto/Frederic Cirou/Getty Images, **173** Oliver Bolch/Anzenberger/Redux, **175–180** © Gianluca Colla/National Geographic Image Collection, **184** View Stock/Alamy Stock Photo, **186** Imaginechina Limited/Alamy Stock Photo, **193** David Fleetham/Nature Picture Library, **194–195** (spread) KTSDesign/Science Photo Library/Getty Images, **195** (bl1) Taylor Hill/FilmMagic/Getty Images, (bl2) IanDagnall Computing/Alamy Stock Photo, **197** Picture Alliance/Getty Images, **198** © National Geographic Image Collection, **201–203** © Dan Winters Photography, **208** © National Geographic Image Collection, **215** © University of Rochester, **217** Marco Bottigelli/Moment/Getty Images, **218–219** (spread) Alexis Rosenfeld/Getty Images News/Getty Images, **220** Jonathan Raa/Pacific Press/LightRocket/Getty Images, **222** Franckreporter/E+/Getty Images, **225** © Edward Burtynsky, **226–227** (spread) © Jim Richardson/National Geographic Image Collection, **232** Angelo Cavalli/Stone/Getty Images, **239** Wirestock, Inc./Alamy Stock Photo, **241** Dmitry Rukhlenko - Travel Photos/Alamy Stock Photos

Text Sources

6–11 Adapted from "The Robots Are Here" by David Berreby: NGM Sep 2020, **30–35** Adapted from "Why Cities Are Going Wild" by Christine Dell'Amore: NGM Jul 2022, **41** Adapted from "In India, a city takes its beach back from the sea" by Neha Bhatt: NGC Mar 2022, **52** Adapted from "Conjuring Clouds" by Daniel Stone: NGM Mar 2019, **54–56** Adapted from "This artist's animal paintings bridge a gap between photography and reality" by Simon Ingram: NGC Oct 2022, **57–58** Adapted from "Transforming Trash into Protest Art" by Ayodeji Rotinwa: NGM Jun 2022, **58–61** Adapted from "The Future Is Folded" by Maya Wei-Haas: NGM Feb 2023, **80–85** Adapted from "How Green, How Soon?" by Sam Howe Verhovek: NGM Oct 2021, **104–108** Adapted from "Swarm Theory" by Peter Miller: NGM Jul 2007, **128–131** Adapted from "Is Joy the Same in Every Language?" by Jen Rose Smith: NGM Jan 2021, **150–155** Adapted from "The Shape of Africa," by Jared Diamond: NGM Sep 2005, **175–179** Adapted from "On Beyond 100," by Stephen S. Hall: NGM May 2013, **198–203** Adapted from "Why We Lie," by Yudhijit Bhattacharjee: NGM Jun 2017, **222–227** Adapted from "The Age of Man," by Elizabeth Kolbert: NGM Mar 2011

NGM = National Geographic Magazine, NGC = nationalgeographic.com

Infographics

26–27 © Cengage; source: worldsbestcities.com, **76–77** © Jason Treat/National Geographic Image Collection, **147** © Cengage; source: ourworldindata.org, **179** © Cengage, **195** © Ryan Morris/National Geographic Image Collection, **200** © Ryan Morris/National Geographic Image Collection, **224** © Cengage